Praise for
simple compassion

Keri's journey of compassion is truly reflective of a woman who wants to impact her community and her world. Throughout these devotionals, Keri tells the story of many courageous people who have made bold choices to live a lifestyle of compassion and justice. I think these stories will stir others to do the same.

> —HEATHER LARSON, Director of Compassion and Justice Ministries, Willow Creek Community Church

In an age that wrongly separates devotion to God (Mary) from serving others (Martha), here are thought-provoking, weekly digestible morsels to cultivate the compassion of Jesus in your heart and move it into your hands.

> —JAN JOHNSON, author, *Growing Compassionate Kids* and *Invitation to the Jesus Life*

True devotionals are not just books filled with fluffy stories and neat anecdotes, but also are books that should stir us to devote our lives to something bigger than ourselves. Here is a devotional that will not just warm your heart but will actually break your heart with the things that break God's. *Simple Compassion* is a weekly reminder that things are not right in the world and that this matters to God, and, perhaps strangest of all, that God doesn't want to change the world without us.

> —SHANE CLAIBORNE, author, activist, and recovering sinner

Other Books by Keri Wyatt Kent

Rest: Living in Sabbath Simplicity

Oxygen: Deep Breathing for the Soul

Listen: Finding God in the Story of Your Life

Breathe: Creating Space for God in a Hectic Life

simple compassion

Devotions to Make a
Difference in Your Neighborhood
and Your World

keri wyatt kent

ZONDERVAN.com/
AUTHORTRACKER
follow your favorite authors

ZONDERVAN

Simple Compassion
Copyright © 2009 by Keri Wyatt Kent

This title is also available as a Zondervan ebook.
Visit www.zondervan.com/ebooks.

This title is also available in a Zondervan audio edition.
Visit www.zondervan.fm.

Requests for information should be addressed to:
Zondervan, *Grand Rapids, Michigan 49530*

Library of Congress Cataloging-in-Publication Data

Kent, Keri Wyatt, 1963 –
    Simple compassion : devotions to make a difference in your neighborhood and your
    world / Keri Wyatt Kent.
        p.   cm.
    ISBN 978-0-310-29077-3 (softcover)
    1. Christian women – Prayers and devotions. 2. Compassion – Religious aspects –
    Christianity – Prayers and devotions. I. Title.
    BV4844.K47   2009
    242'.643 – dc22   2009021682

Interior design by Michelle Espinoza

Printed in the United States of America

09 10 11 12 13 14 15 • 24 23 22 21 20 19 18 17 16 15 14 13 12 11 10 9 8 7 6 5 4 3 2 1

contents

Part 3: Compassion Extends beyond Our Comfort Zones

Part 4: Compassion Offers God's Love to the World

hunger

What does it mean to walk with God? I mean, where do you go on this walk? What happens along the way?

Growing up evangelical, I came to understand that my "walk with God," which well-meaning people asked me about all the time, was measured by the benchmarks of whether I had a "quiet time," which consisted of careful Bible study and prayer, and how skillfully I sidestepped certain sins. While study and prayer are admirable disciplines, and sin avoidance is certainly preferable to going looking for trouble, I still have to ask, Did these practices form me into the image of Christ? Did they satisfy my hunger for God?

I remember, even as a teen, deeply desiring to grow spiritually. I wondered if I was making progress and, if so, how I would know.

The practices of my youth — study, memorization, prayer — launched my spiritual journey well. These simple tools formed me, and continue to do so. Still, eventually, I found myself hungry for more.

That hunger showed up as a rather basic question: what is the point of spiritual growth? Where was my "walk with God" taking me? What did God want? Did he just want me to obey him, like a child? You could make a case for that, I suppose, but I kept thinking there had to be more to faith than just obeying the rules.

Long ago other people asked that same question. What matters? What should our lives be about if we are following God? God answered through the prophet Micah, "He has shown all you people what is good. And what does the LORD require of you? To act justly and to love mercy and to walk humbly with your God" (Mic. 6:8).

When I first heard this verse, I was in my early twenties, coming back into the church after a few years of staying away, wrapped up in myself and my doubts. Even with all my childhood years of memorizing and studying the Bible, I didn't remember hearing Micah's words. As I read the verse this time, the simplicity stirred me. It invited me away from legalism and guilt into a simple compassion.

Even so, I wasn't sure how to live it out. It sounded so simple, yet almost too difficult at the same time. I was still trying to make space in my life for God. I found it immensely challenging to do the just "walk humbly" part, since for several years my life had been almost entirely focused on myself. "Stumble proudly" was accurate of me.

So I needed church, and it needed me. As I became reacquainted with the God who had never really left me, I found myself drawn to contemplative practices of the Christian faith—solitude, silence, meditation on Scripture. I wanted to go deeper with God; I wanted to supplement my intellectual understanding of facts *about* God with a deeper experience *of* God. I was hungry for deeper relationship. I began reading a wide variety of authors, venturing beyond the works of C. S. Lewis, Philip Yancey, and A. W. Tozer, which had informed my high school and college years. I read Dallas Willard, Richard Foster, Henri Nouwen, and David Benner. A few years later I was mentored and taught by some incredible teachers, including Ruth Barton and John Ortberg. I was on a fascinating inner journey. I meditated on Scripture; it spoke to me in a new and fresh way. I fell deeper in love with Jesus, spent time in solitude and prayer. I even tried fasting. I found ancient spiritual practices to be a way to revive my faith.

After years of doubt and cynicism, I was excited to be reconnected with God in a fresh way. Still, it felt incomplete. I knew that God wants me to live a life that matters not just to myself but also to others, to the world. This verse in Micah calls us to put faith into action; not just by "witnessing," as I called it growing up—talking about Jesus, with the intent of getting people to believe. I began to ask myself questions. What if the witnessing I did with my actions was just as important as the witnessing I did with my mouth? What if feeding someone physically was equally as important as feeding them spiritually? After all, Jesus declared loving God and loving your neighbor his "top two" commandments. Loving your neighbor does not just mean sitting at home thinking warm and fuzzy thoughts about the people next door. It means taking action to serve others.

In the last few years, I've become aware that my focus on spiritual formation had a purpose larger than myself, and in fact even larger than my individual relationship with Jesus. As I got to know Jesus more intimately, I noticed how deeply concerned he seemed to be for the poor. It began to dawn on me that following him, really walking with him, would require more than just an intellectual or emotional exercise. It would demand action. As I searched the Old Testament, I became increasingly aware that every book included something about God's concern for the poor and for justice—not only justice that God metes out to sinners but also justice that fights against the systemic injustices of our world.

The deeper connection provided by spiritual practices such as solitude and prayer began to push me toward a desire to share with others the love I experienced. Beyond that, I realized that if I was being spiritually transformed, my actions and attitudes would be changed as well. Jesus was compassionate—in a confront-the-social-order, care-about-justice-for-the-poor-and-marginalized way. If the goal of Christian spiritual formation is to become more Christlike, then I should be more compassionate, more concerned for fighting against injustice.

My hunger for God would include a hunger for justice. If I were walking humbly with him, I would begin to love mercy and to act justly. These three strands intertwine into a single cord.

Spiritual growth leads us to understand our own spiritual poverty, our own need for grace, and God's amazing love. So this book will offer a thoughtful, unhurried approach that will allow you to rest in God's love and then inspire you to move from being filled with God's Spirit to pouring out God's love.

To read just one short chapter of this book a week is to offer God a year to mess with you, to equip and strengthen you, to live the adventure of following him. It is to let go of being too busy and bored all at the same time, to start living your faith. I'm inviting you to embark on an adventure in which God may change your thinking, may change your life.

This book is a guide toward becoming a more compassionate person, a person who doesn't just talk about faith or social justice but is trying to live it out. Compassion flows from those who are so full of God's love that it simply sloshes onto everyone around them. When we act justly and love mercy, it strengthens our walk with God. When we walk with God, it leads us to love mercy (because we have been shown mercy) and to act justly (because we are becoming more like Jesus).

To become more merciful and just, we first must get a glimpse of how much we each matter, and of the fact that we can make a difference. If we think we can't do anything, our hunger for justice will soon diminish.

The first quarter of the book will focus on understanding our own worth (as deeply loved children of God) as a starting point for understanding the worth of others. In the second quarter, we'll look at simple ways to show compassion to those closest to us: our family and our neighbors. From there, the ripples continue to extend; in the third quarter of the book, we'll consider how to bring God's kingdom to a wider geographic area: the poor in our cities and towns. Finally, the last quarter of the book will offer steps of compassion on a global scale. As we go along, I hope that you'll begin to see that every person on the planet—whether she lives in a suburban mansion or a housing project, in Los Angeles or Sierra Leone—is deeply loved by God. Each person matters to God. Because that's true, we ought to matter to each other.

Over the next year, you'll get some practical guidance on how to love your neighbors, both those next door and those around the world. You'll see that a life of compassion consists, as Mother Teresa said, of small things done with great love. When we realize the worth of every person, we will move toward compassion and justice; we will wrestle with how to actually live it.

We'll look at what the Bible says about how we are to respond to poverty and suffering, and consider small steps we can take to grow in compassion for the poor and the marginalized. We'll listen to the stories of a variety of fellow travelers who have taken steps to grow in compassion and courage. These small steps of compassion *matter*. They make a difference in the world, and our faithful actions transform our hearts. They feed our souls so that they can grow.

Using this book is easy. Here's what I suggest: each week, read a chapter. They're stories about my life and about the lives of people I've met through my work as a journalist and a writer. Some are stories about women from history, including women in the Bible. Each story has Scripture woven in. Don't skip over the Bible verses (which is something I tend to do when using a devotional). Read them. Look them up in your Bible and read the context. During the week, reflect on what you've read. Maybe write the verses or quotes from the chapter in a journal or on note cards that you can carry around with you. Read over those notes once or twice during the week. Pray about what you've read.

If you are the type of person who likes a more structured approach, the group leader's guide in the back of the book will be helpful. There you'll find an outline of the book, a list of Scripture references, and some suggestions for group structure. While I recommend reading this book with others, you can use the leader's guide even if you are reading on your own.

Each chapter ends with two action steps. The first is an individual compassion step, a question to get you thinking or something you can do to make a difference, to shine a light in the darkness of your neighborhood, your city, your world. During each week, engage with God via the questions or challenges in the compassion step. Listen to his voice and respond. Don't just think; take action as God leads.

The second is a community step. The Christian life is meant to be lived in community, and I hope that you are a part of a group of people who know, pray for, and care for each other. The community step will provide ways for groups to interact with this book, to discuss it, and to live out what they are learning. Of course, if you don't have a group, you can modify the community steps to do them on your own, but they work better with a group. Again, the leader's guide in the back will help you to use the community steps more effectively.

Don't skip those steps at the end, please. If this book is going to help you grow, you've got to take some action. Pray each week that God will provide you opportunities and that you will respond courageously to them. Just reading the book won't do much besides maybe entertain you or fill you with the longing to take action. Respond to that longing— take action!

This book is an invitation to make your life more interesting. Full disclosure also would require me to say that "interesting" might include "messy" or "complex." It could also mean "focused" and "meaningful." I want to help us to find a life that overflows with joy, a life that shines the light of Christ everywhere.

I'd love to have you visit me online (www.keriwyattkent.com) as you're reading and let me know how those action steps are going. My hope is that as you read, you will be infused with confidence and strength to change the world, one life at a time. Starting with your own.

part I

compassion
begins with you

position

as I write this, the first American woman to run for president has just ended her campaign, a campaign which, although it did not lead to the Oval Office, people took seriously, and in which she gathered the support of eighteen million Americans. Another woman has received the vice presidential nomination.

This feels historic, yet other countries have had women presidents or prime ministers (the United Kingdom, for example, during Margaret Thatcher's time in office), and certainly throughout history both kings and queens have wielded great influence. Just a century ago, women in America did not have the right even to vote, let alone run for office. Prior to 1917, no women served in Congress. Today, sixteen of the one hundred U.S. senators are women, as are seventy-four U.S. representatives. In 2007 Nancy Pelosi became the highest-ranking elected woman in American history by becoming the first woman Speaker of the House of Representatives.

Beyond politics, how do we make a difference in the world? Some women exert influence in the corporate world, and many have risen to the rank of CEO, although members of that upper echelon are still predominantly male.

Women should never give up their quest to hold positions of power or influence in politics, business, or the church, if that is where God is calling them (which he sometimes does, because God calls all believers, without any gender bias).

While we are not all called to such aspirations, we are called to show Christ's compassion to the people around us. We are called to be difference makers. How can we do this from whatever position we find ourselves in?

The Bible says that when we begin to mature spiritually, we become steadfast, not "blown here and there.... Instead, speaking the truth in love, we will in all things grow up into him who is the Head, that is, Christ" (Eph. 4:14–15).

One of the great heroines of the Bible, Esther, made a difference by speaking truth. A corrupt king chose her to be one of his concubines, against her will. She went from a reluctant, scared teenager to a woman who risked her life to speak the truth. Her willingness to risk telling the truth saved a nation. We can learn a lot about how to make a difference by looking at her life.

Read the story for yourself, in the book of Esther in the Old Testament.[1] Here's the Cliff's Notes version of just part of the story:

King Xerxes falls in love with Esther and makes her his queen. Unfortunately, the king is led astray by his evil sidekick, Haman. He is tricked into ordering the genocide of the Jews, who he does not realize are Esther's people. Esther's uncle challenges her to ask the king to repeal his edict, though such a request could result in her death. He says to her, "Do not think that because you are in the king's house you alone of all the Jews will escape. For if you remain silent at this time, relief and deliverance for the Jews will arise from another place, but you and your father's family will perish. And who knows but that you have come to royal position for such a time as this?" (Est. 4:13–14).

Esther is afraid but agrees that she must act to save her people and herself. How? Consider her strategy: she does not rush in and demand anything. First, she goes to the source of all truth. She begins her quest to speak the truth with prayer and fasting, asking God for wisdom. She courageously tells her uncle, "Go, gather together all the Jews who are in Susa, and fast for me. Do not eat or drink for three days, night or day. I and my attendants will fast as you do. When this is done, I will go to the king, even though it is against the law. And if I perish, I perish" (Est. 4:16).

So often I want to speak the truth first and pray later (which means that my prayers end up focused on damage control necessitated by my rashness). Wise women know that God is in control and that his wisdom is the key to their success. The first step of making a difference by speaking the truth is prayer—heartfelt, focused prayer. The first step in speaking wisely is realizing that your own wisdom is not enough; you need God's wisdom. You need the light of his truth to flow through you. Prayer is what gave Esther both courage and an amazing plan for winning the king's favor. Read the story for yourself—Esther's strategy, combined with God's amazing provision, is brilliant. She is a perfect illustration of what James wrote five centuries later: "If any of you lacks wisdom, you should ask God, who gives generously to all without finding fault, and it will be given to you" (James 1:5).

Notice how God gives wisdom: not just to a few, not just to the perfect, not just to the powerful, but to anyone. To *all*. He gives that wisdom unconditionally, liberally, "without finding fault," without nitpicking or bias. As *The Message* translation puts it, "If you don't know what you're doing, pray to the Father. He loves to help. You'll get his help, and won't be condescended to when you ask for it. Ask boldly, believingly, without a second thought."

While you may not have been chosen to be queen, you do have power and influence in your neighborhood, in your workplace, in your family, in your church. And who knows? Perhaps you've been given whatever influence you have for such a time as this.

Esther's decree "If I perish, I perish" is a huge turning point for her. Prior to that she had seemed rather passive, basing all of her actions on her uncle's directions. She mostly seemed to let things happen to her, rather than making things happen. Then her uncle's challenge, "Who knows but that you have come to royal position for such a time as this?" brings something forth in Esther. At that moment, she shifts from follower to leader. From shy girl to decisive woman, a woman who, by telling the truth, saves her people from destruction. The first truth she tells is this: before we act, we must fast and pray.

Every woman matters — including you. Things need to be done in your own heart and home, in your neighborhood, in your city, in this world. God has equipped you to do them. He's not going to force you. If you pay attention, you'll notice that his invitations to change the world are all around you. You matter and can make a difference. Believe it, and have the courage to act on that belief.

You can make a difference by simply being who you are, by bringing your whole and best self to the table. Developing your gifts and using them will transform not only you but also the people around you.

This book is about making a difference. Do you think you cannot change the world? Is there some situation you are facing that you've convinced yourself you can't do anything about? Look to Esther's example: begin by fasting and praying. Ask God for wisdom.

Then pray you'll be both winsome and wise, and ask God for opportunities to speak the truth where it needs to be spoken. You may not think you are in "royal position," but you are! You are a child of the King. You have a position from which you can wield influence. You have more power than you realize, because if you have accepted God's invitation of adoption, you are fully his child and filled with his Spirit. You are filled with his light and love, and that light wants to shine through you. And if you don't let that light of truth shine, it will come from some other place, some other person who is willing to speak truth. Why not let it shine through you?

Compassion Step

Are you facing a situation you don't know how to handle? Are others looking to you to step up in a circumstance in which you feel inadequate? Have you prayed about it? Not just talked to God about it but listened to his guidance? Read Esther's story in the Bible. Then spend some time in prayer. You may even want to fast as you pray. As this chapter noted, "The first step of making a difference by speaking the truth is prayer — heartfelt, focused prayer."

Community Step

Have group members read the book of Esther in the Bible before you meet. For your meeting, rent the video of the Veggie Tales version of this story, called *Esther: The Girl Who Became Queen*. Believe it or not, this is a funny, well-crafted video that appeals to all ages. Watch it together. Discuss the story. What can you learn from Esther? What do you have in common with her? What situation do you need to fast and pray about and then speak truth in?

woman

One of my favorite biblical characters is a woman named Priscilla. I discovered her in college, when I was having a small faith crisis, wondering if I could be a feminist and a Christian at the same time. I didn't buy the whole feminist agenda; neither could I fully endorse the particularly conservative stripe of Christianity that many people around me seemed to condone. Thankfully, one of my college professors, Dr. Gilbert Bilezikian, was a leading New Testament scholar and also an egalitarian. Prior to meeting him, I didn't even know what an egalitarian was. He pointed me to resources that essentially saved my faith.

Priscilla was a woman who made a difference, who impacted her community. She lived in a society in which Jewish men prayed daily, "Thank you, God, for not making me a slave, a Gentile, or a woman." So it would have been perfectly reasonable for her to doubt herself, to figure she was "just a woman" and therefore not able to make a difference. Blessed with a bright mind and a heart dedicated to Jesus, she was part of a culture which did not value the spiritual and intellectual contributions of women. That didn't stop her.

Acts 18 describes the apostle Paul's travels. Priscilla and her husband, Aquila, are traveling with him. It's interesting that the Bible, in a jarring break from social convention, frequently mentions Priscilla's name before her husband's (see Acts 18:18, Rom. 16:3, and 2 Tim. 4:19). Putting Priscilla's name first in the text is like sending a formal invitation addressed to Mrs. and Mr. Mary Jones, rather than Mr. and Mrs. John Jones—only it was even more shocking in ancient culture.

The couple worked as tentmakers, just as Paul did. They worked in the same trade and also in ministry. So Priscilla, like many of her contemporaries, was a working woman.

Acts 18 tells us that the trio eventually reached Ephesus, which was an important commercial center, in part because it was also the site of the pagan Temple of Artemis, one of the seven wonders of the ancient world. Artemis was a goddess of hunting and wildlife, among other things.

In this large city, where pagan religion strongly influenced the culture, Paul, Priscilla, and Aquila all visited the synagogue, where they tried to teach the Jews about Jesus. Eventually Paul sailed on, leaving Priscilla and Aquila behind, apparently to continue his work there. Then the text says, "Meanwhile a Jew named Apollos, a native of Alexandria, came to Ephesus. He was a learned man, with a thorough knowledge of the Scriptures. He had been instructed in the way of the Lord, and he spoke with great fervor and taught about Jesus accurately, though he knew only the baptism of John. He began to speak boldly in the synagogue. When Priscilla and Aquila heard him, they invited him to their home and explained to him the way of God more adequately" (Acts 18:24–26).

Notice that the text does not say or imply that Aquila instructed Apollos while Priscilla made tea. They both explained the way of God to him, helping him go deeper in his understanding, explaining to him the role of the Holy Spirit, and so forth. They taught him together. We learn from other references to this couple that they co-led a church, which met in their home. (See 1 Cor. 16:19.) Priscilla's influence on Apollos, who was a gifted teacher as well, strengthened him to go out to other locations to preach. Acts 18 continues, "When Apollos wanted to go to Achaia, the believers encouraged him and wrote to the disciples there to welcome him. When he arrived, he was a great help to those who by grace had believed. For he vigorously refuted the Jews in public debate, proving from the Scriptures that Jesus was the Messiah" (Acts 18:27–28).

Dr. Bilezikian notes, "Under the instruction of Priscilla and Aquila, Apollos became an able pastor to whom Paul could entrust one of the most critical church situations at the time. For all practical purposes, Priscilla and Aquila acted as seminar faculty for a promising male pastoral student. They taught him those redemptive events in the life of Christ about which he had been left uninformed along with their theological significance, and they gave him an overview of Christian doctrine that is suggested by the expression 'the way of God' (Acts 18:26)."[2]

In the index of his book, Bilezikian argues that Priscilla very possibly may be the writer of the book of Hebrews.[3] Some scholars believe Apollos to be the author, which means that Priscilla, as his teacher, had a strong influence on its contents.

Priscilla was one of several women leaders in the early church; Paul's letters mention many other women who led, had churches that met in their homes, and so on. She didn't say to herself, as I might be tempted to do, "Well, Apollos has it mostly right. I know he's a little off track, but I wouldn't want to make waves or make him feel badly." Rather, with grace and kindness, she explained where his theology needed some tweaking. She made a difference by believing in herself enough to speak the truth. This would be a bold move today; back then, it was even more so.

If this story is true, why is it that for centuries the church so limited women's freedom to contribute to its work, except in behind-the-scenes roles? Why is it that so many churches still refuse to let women teach or lead when Priscilla, who is mentioned repeatedly in the New Testament, did just that? Why does the Bible tell the story of a woman teaching a man in such favorable terms if that is not what God wants? How come, growing up in a Bible-believing church, I didn't hear Priscilla's story?

My purpose with this book is not to argue theology but to ask you, as a reader, to consider how the restrictions placed on women throughout the Christian tradition affect your view of yourself. So many women I talk to think that they can't make a difference, that their contribution doesn't matter. They either fall into the "little old me" syndrome or give up on their faith. Many women who are gifted leaders have left the church because the workplace values their contributions more than the church does, and the church is bereft as a result. We've missed out on all the things that women could have brought to the table. We've boxed up and refused to use half the gifts God has given, because he gave them to women. By rejecting women's contribution, we have, in a way, rejected God.

When you look at living a life of justice and compassion, how often do you find yourself thinking, "What can I do? I'm just not that important"? Such thinking does not reflect the truth of God's Word. Jesus, when he walked this earth, treated all of his followers, men and women, with equal respect. He valued women. Women were the first witnesses to several major events in his ministry: the annunciation and the resurrection, for example. There were greater numbers of female disciples than male ones at the crucifixion.

I'm not looking to pick a fight with conservatives. Well, okay—maybe I am. My point is this: if you are a woman, you are just as capable of making a difference as a man is. But to do it, you will have to believe that you can. Our society (and unfortunately, the church) is structured in a way that sometimes makes this more difficult. Just because it is sometimes harder doesn't mean you can just give up on it. In God's eyes, you are highly valued. You can make a difference, even if you reach only one person.

Priscilla co-led a church in her home, so it's likely that she influenced others besides Apollos. Even if she did not, her influence on that one person was significant, because he went on to teach other people what Priscilla had taught him. He spread the news of Jesus, which Priscilla and her husband had helped him to understand. So her teaching had a ripple effect in her city, then all over Asia Minor, and, eventually, throughout the world.

Compassion Step

Journal about the following questions: If you grew up in a church, how did your religious tradition see women? Did women lead and teach (beyond children's Sunday school)? Were they prohibited, formally or informally, from certain roles or positions? What messages (perhaps not so subtle) were communicated to you with regard to gender in your church, family, or school? Do you ever find yourself falling into "little old me" thinking? How might your childhood experiences have influenced that? This chapter asserts that "Jesus valued women." Do you agree or disagree?

Community Step

Share some of the things you discovered in your journaling this week. As a group, discuss the following: if Priscilla had been a member of the church you grew up in, would she have been allowed to do what the Bible says she did in the early church? Talk about how speaking the truth is a way to make a difference in the world. Brainstorm ways that you as a group can become truth tellers. What can you learn from Priscilla about how to make a difference?

shine

O ne of my favorite films is *Akeelah and the Bee*, a story about a work-ing-class African-American girl who qualifies, against all odds, for the Scripps National Spelling Bee. Akeelah Anderson's father was killed when she was six, leaving her hardworking single mom (played spectacu-larly by Angela Bassett) to raise Akeelah and her older brother alone in south Los Angeles.

Akeelah tries to hide her intelligence from the mean girls at her school, who call her a "brain-iac." Her teachers know she's never missed a single word on her spelling tests and encourage her to participate in the school spelling bee. She agrees to do so only when the principal offers to excuse her from detention (which she's been assigned for missing classes) in return.

The movie is, like any good coming-of-age film, about transforma-tion. Akeelah's love of words had previously been a way for her to con-nect with the memory of her father. Eventually, it becomes a way to connect with her mother, brother, and even the community around her. As she prepares with the help of Dr. Larabee, a college professor on sab-batical who volunteers to coach her, Akeelah discovers who she is and becomes willing to lean into her strengths. Along the way, she makes some new friends, struggles to understand and embrace her giftedness, and transforms her community — not by helping them but by letting them help her. She takes on the challenge of being herself and reaching for her dreams; she realizes that she cannot do this without the help of the "teachers" all around her.

When Akeelah's doubts and fear threaten to undo her efforts, Dr. Larabee asks her to read the following quote out loud:

> Our deepest fear is not that we are inadequate. Our deepest
> fear is that we are powerful beyond measure. It is our light, not
> our darkness, that most frightens us. We ask ourselves, Who am
> I to be brilliant, gorgeous, talented, fabulous? Actually, who are
> you not to be?

You are a child of God. Your playing small does not serve the world. There is nothing enlightened about shrinking so that other people won't feel insecure around you. We are all meant to shine, as children do. We were born to make manifest the glory of God that is within us.

It is not just in some of us; it is in everyone. And as we let our own light shine, we unconsciously give other people permission to do the same. As we are liberated from our own fear, our presence automatically liberates others.[4]

I have this quote, printed out in bright colors, on my wall. Once in a while I read it, out loud. To remind myself not to "play small." To remind myself that Jesus told us to let our light shine—and that it is his love that fills me up and shines through me. I remind myself that, as with Akeelah, my love for words has potential to transform my life, and others' as well. I remember that sometimes shining God's light means letting others help me, as well as helping others.

One day I was riding in a car with the women on my tennis team. These women, like me, are middle-aged moms. They got on this discussion of how much they hate their bodies. It made me sad. Each one talked about what part of their body (thighs, stomach, etc.) they just could not stand. These are women who are attractive and quite fit. They don't look like twenty-year-old fashion models. Who does? They are athletic enough to play on a tennis team, for crying out loud.

I know that these women are not the exception but the unfortunate norm. I'd like to say that women who follow Jesus have been transformed in such a way that they don't wrestle with body-image issues. I know it's not true because I've been there too, unhappy with the way I look.

Unfortunately, Christianity doesn't seem to affect our ability to love ourselves. Oddly, there is a gap between our intellectual assertion that God loves all people and our capacity to apply this truth to ourselves fully enough that we believe ourselves to be lovable. All people are created in the image of God; it is our relationship with God that ought to transform us. Why is it so hard to shine? Why do we notice our imperfections rather than our gifts?

In a passage about the love and respect between a husband and wife, the apostle Paul wrote that "people have never hated their own bodies, but they feed and care for them, just as Christ does the church" (Eph.

5:29). Do we care for our bodies? I know a lot of women who cannot truthfully say, "I've never hated my own body." In fact, most women would say that at one point or another they had a love-hate thing going with their bodies, or at least had a lot of complaints about them. Did women in Paul's day ask their husbands, "Does this toga make me look fat?" Or is the whole compulsion about body image part of our culture? Either way, I still wonder: if we have trouble loving ourselves, won't it be difficult to love others?

As women, we are sometimes afflicted by what I call the "little old me" syndrome. We describe ourselves with self-deprecating phrases that always start "I'm just ..." When someone asks, "What do you do?" we say, "I just stay home with the kids." When talking about our involvement at school or church, we say, "I'm just a volunteer." Are we being humble, or do we see those roles as less worthy somehow?

Have you ever met a woman who is essentially a partner in her husband's business? And yet if you ask what she does, she'll say, "Oh, I *just* help my husband with his company. I *just* keep the books." No offense to men, but if you asked a man who was doing that same job what he does, he would most likely reply, "I'm the chief financial officer of a privately held company." As well he should. Most men, even if they struggle with self-esteem, have been conditioned to present bravado. They rarely say, "Oh, I just ..." anything. Learn from your brothers. Your playing small does not serve the world.

While humility is a virtue, we sometimes quash our potential by thinking humility means avoiding accomplishments. Humility is not *avoiding* accomplishments. Rather humility is not thinking too highly of yourself, even though you have accomplished much. It's using those accomplishments to bless others and glorify God rather than self, and calling forth the best in others.

Ruth Barton, whom I mentioned earlier, is a woman who has accomplished much and yet remains humble. When she was my small group leader, I was just starting my speaking career. I'd often ask her for advice. She would gently refuse to tell me what to do, instead exhorting me to listen to God and to trust the gifts he'd given me. She'd say things like, "Everything you need is already within you." I learned a lot by watching her teach, by spending time praying with her, by watching how she listened to me and to others. Ruth has followed God's calling with enthusiasm and commitment, in a way that blesses and inspires others.

I love reading the Gospels, which tell the story of Jesus' life on earth. After a brief mention of his birth and childhood, they focus on the last three years of his life, when he traveled around, teaching and preaching, just living life with a band of followers. Everything, from bread to bushes, provided object lessons as he tried to tell them about the kingdom of God. Which, he said, was not a someday, pie-in-the-sky promise but a here-and-now reality. The kingdom of God is among you, he said. It's within you.

Jesus leaned into his calling, which, according to Luke 4:18 – 19, was to "preach the good news to the poor ... proclaim freedom for the prisoners and recovery of sight for the blind, release the oppressed, and to proclaim the year of the Lord's favor." As he did what God had called him to do, the people around him changed. They were, in many ways, reborn. Not by saying a certain prayer but by simply engaging in relationship with him. Their priorities shifted, and nothing was the same. It was as if they were all new people. In part because he taught and helped them, but also — and this is the amazing thing about love — because of their role in helping him as well.

Luke's account of Jesus' life reflects the meticulous attention to detail that you'd expect from a physician (Luke's profession). He provides more detail about Jesus' disciples than do the other Gospels. In addition to the twelve followers which Jesus had designated as apostles — those who could pass his teachings along to others — Jesus also had a larger group of disciples, people who followed him, who participated in his ministry, who believed or at least hoped he was the Messiah.

In Luke 6:12 – 16, we read that Jesus "called his disciples to him and chose twelve of them, whom he also designated apostles." Clearly the group of people called "disciples" was bigger than twelve. Acts 1 also talks about the disciples, after Jesus' death, choosing a replacement for Judas from among those disciples who had "been with us the whole time" (v. 21).

That larger group included both men and women. All of them tried to live as their rabbi did. They didn't just agree with him theologically or philosophically; they dedicated themselves to doing what he did. They wanted to be like him. They literally *followed* him. Luke 8:1 – 3 notes, "After this, Jesus traveled about from one town and village to another, proclaiming the good news of the kingdom of God. The Twelve were with him, and also some women who had been cured of evil spirits and diseases: Mary (called Magdalene) from whom seven demons had come out; Joanna the wife of Chuza, the manager of Herod's household; Susanna; and many others. These women were helping to support them out of their own means."

Jesus quit his day job, carpentry, to go into full-time ministry. He was poor to begin with, even as a working guy; when he started just being a rabbi, he didn't have any income. Some verses indicate that he was homeless, or at least that he depended on the hospitality of strangers and friends when he traveled about. He didn't come to preach to the wealthy, although certainly some people of means believed in him, followed him, even supported him. He came to preach to everyone, and he did not exclude the poor.

Among his followers were some women. Jesus *needed* them. He chose to depend on others, which is an amazing style of leadership. What's more empowering to a *follower* than being needed? Did you ever consider that just as Jesus needed these women to support his cause, he needs you too? I'm not saying this to load on the guilt. I want to give you a glimpse of what an important part you play as one of his disciples. You were meant to shine.

It's funny that some churches don't allow women to serve on their board of directors when Jesus' "board of directors" was predominately female. The women were not perfect. The text says Jesus had healed some of them, from disease, from "evil spirits"—afflictions of their emotional and spiritual health—which perhaps manifested themselves in what we would label depression, or worse. Jesus gave them new life. He invited them not just to follow him but also to minister to him. To care for him, provide for him. These women weren't just *told* that they matter; they knew it experientially. They quit worrying about what others would think because they had become a part of something more important.

It's interesting *where* in his narrative Luke decides to include this information about these women. Notice that the chapter begins, "After this ..." After what? The previous passage describes Jesus being anointed by a sinful woman. She comes to him in repentance, and he offers her forgiveness and acceptance. The juxtaposition is not accidental. Luke is pointing out that all women matter, whether they are prostitutes or wives of political leaders.

Take a look at Luke 24:10. These same women are the very first people to encounter the risen Christ.

If you have trouble believing that you can make a difference, think of those women who kept Jesus' ministry going. Before encountering Jesus, many of them suffered from mental illness. I'm guessing they didn't have much self-esteem. Their society perhaps didn't value them. Yet Jesus invited them to make a difference. They mattered to him. They helped change the world.

While we don't want to be narcissistic, it's hard to change the world if you go to the opposite extreme of not seeing your value at all. How can you love your neighbor as yourself if you don't love yourself? You are meant to shine. We all are. You are powerful. Just embracing that power will begin to change the world—starting with you.

Compassion Step

Read the Marianne Williamson quote ("Our deepest fear . . .") again, out loud. In what ways do you play small? In what ways have you not let the light and gifts within you shine? How can you live humbly yet still make a difference? How does your view of yourself affect your ability to help others? Do you agree or disagree with Williamson's assertions? In what ways might your decision to shine help other people?

Community Step

Read the story referenced above in Luke 7:36–50. What do you notice about Jesus in his encounter with the sinful woman and the Pharisee? How does he respond to the humility of this woman and the pride of the Pharisee?[5] Now read Luke 8:1–3. Does it surprise you to know that Jesus' larger group of followers, or disciples, included women? Based on the role he gave them in his ministry, how did Jesus' view of women differ from that of the culture around him?

week 4

rest

If we want to shine, if we want to be women who make a difference, we must adopt a long-term perspective. The Bible says this about love: "It always protects, always trusts, always hopes, always perseveres" (1 Cor. 13:7). How can we persevere? Do we just keep pushing ourselves, meeting every need we see? No. The secret to perseverance is to know when to rest. Taking regular rest will allow us to continue on the journey. When we live according to God's rhythm, we receive his power. Resting with God, Sabbathing with God, allows him to strengthen and sustain us. His power, not our own, keeps us going.

We are mindful that our hope is in God, not in ourselves. We don't save people; Jesus does. Our job is to love people. When we admit our neediness, are humble enough to notice that we are not so different from the suffering, the poor, or the disadvantaged, we realize that we cannot save them.

Sometimes, though, we need a rest. There's no shame in that. In fact, God commanded that we rest, that every seven days, we take a day off to renew our strength. Jesus invited us, "Come to me, all you who are weary and burdened, and I will give you rest" (Matt. 11:28).

The theme of God's sufficiency permeates the Bible, shining from its pages. God rescues his people, frees them from slavery, allows them to win battles that they logically could never win, feeds them with manna and quail. He is Jehovah-Jirah, the all-sufficient provider.

Our culture, on the other hand, values self-sufficiency. While the Bible exhorts us to be responsible and hardworking, absolute autonomy and self-sufficiency rob us of community and limit our ability to trust God. Rather than seeing all we have as evidence of his provision, we see it as the fruit of our own labor. We think of God as our divine assistant and say, "God helps those who help themselves," which many people believe is in the Bible but is actually a quote from Benjamin Franklin.

Psalm 46:10 says, "Be still, and know that I am God." The New American Standard Bible translates the phrase, "Cease striving ..."

Our can-do culture looks at this verse as a to-do list: (1) be still; (2) know that God is God. We work hard at both, ironically. However, it's not a to-do list. It's a statement of spiritual truth. When we are still, we will experience the presence of God. If we can cease striving (which is not something you *do* but the absence of doing), then we will know who God is and trust his sufficiency.

If you read the context of this often-quoted verse, you'll see a picture of chaos. It's a poem about the world's turmoil. In the midst of that turmoil, God calls us to be still, to rest, to trust. While we are called to action, we are also called to live in a rhythm of work and rest, action and reflection. God invites us to be still, to allow him to refill us and know him intimately. The Sabbath calls us to community and intimacy with him.

Sabbath rest offers a picture of God's economic policies, which are vastly different from capitalism, communism, or any other -ism in the world. God told his people to work hard for six days, then rest for one day. Rest doesn't just mean chill out; it means cease your labor. To understand why God wants us to stop, or to cease, from our work, we have to think, Why do we work? We work to provide for ourselves and our families. Sometimes we overwork. Why? Because we want more, we are striving after something, we want to climb the ladder. If we rest, then, we affirm that it is ultimately God who provides for us. We rest because we have enough. We cease striving, to experience the presence of God. In resting, we affirm God's sufficiency and the truth that we serve him, not money.

Sabbath is not just a day off. It is a spiritual practice that is part of what I call a Sabbath Simplicity lifestyle: a sanely paced, God-focused life. It is a life in which we live simply, because we trust in God's sufficiency and so that we can be generous. The call to rest one day is also a call to full engagement in our work the other six days of the week.

The Sabbath commands of the Old Testament are connected to an economic worldview of social justice. Theologian Ched Meyers writes, "Sabbath observation means to remember every week this economy's two principles: the goal of 'enough' for everyone, and the prohibition on accumulation."[6]

So if you are weary, rest. Affirm that you do not need to keep grasping, earning, striving, collecting, accumulating. Even if you don't feel weary, rest anyway. Open the gift of Sabbath. Affirm the sufficiency of God. Take a day to experience God's goodness, to affirm that you are not just a consumer; you are a child of God. Sabbath cultivates generosity in our hearts, because in it we experience the generosity of God. We are renewed to again go into the world to make a difference, to do the work he's given us to do.

God told his people, "Six days you shall labor and do all your work, but the seventh day is a sabbath to the LORD your God. On it you shall not do any work, neither you, nor your son or daughter, nor your male or female servant, nor your ox, your donkey or any of your animals, nor any foreigner residing in your towns, so that your male and female servants may rest, as you do" (Deut. 5:13 14).

In my previous book, *Rest*, I wrote,

> To observe Sabbath is to flatten social hierarchy. The Deuteronomy and Exodus commands have this in common: they both include a radically inclusive list of who is to be allowed rest on Sabbath: everyone. Men and women, children, servants, aliens (strangers, that is, non-Jews), even animals. The Deuteronomy account goes so far as to list a few specific animals for good measure....
>
> It's as if God expected us to look for loopholes, and wanted to make sure to close those off. It's not just men who get a day off, but women too. It's not just free people, but even slaves should have a day to rest. And don't delegate your work to someone else, even your ox or your donkey.[7]

God's economic policies are vastly different from those that govern our society. He told his people that they did not own the land, that he did, and they were merely stewards of it.

The tie between Sabbath and social justice becomes more obvious when we read Leviticus 25, where God's people are told to allow the land to rest every seven years, and then, after doing that seven times, have a huge celebration of the Jubilee on the fiftieth year (seven times seven).

Jubilee was a celebration in which God's people were told to return parcels of land to their original owners and set slaves free. It was also a time to very tangibly pay attention to the sufficient provision of God.

> Consecrate the fiftieth year and proclaim liberty through-
> out the land to all its inhabitants. It shall be a jubilee for you;
> each of you is to return to your family property and to your own
> clan. The fiftieth year shall be a jubilee for you; do not sow and
> do not reap what grows of itself or harvest the untended vines.
> For it is a jubilee and is to be holy for you; eat only what is taken
> directly from the fields.
>
> Leviticus 25:10–12

It's a strange command—to stop working for a year and trust that
what springs up in the fields will be enough. Don't hoard, give freely, set
free the slaves. Why did God tell his people to practice this celebration?
The text goes on with very detailed instructions:

> If anyone among you becomes poor and sells some of their
> property, their nearest relative is to come and redeem what they
> have sold. If, however, there is no one to redeem it for them but
> later on they prosper and acquire sufficient means to redeem it
> themselves, they are to determine the value for the years since
> they sold it and refund the balance to the one to whom they sold
> it; they can then go back to their own property. But if they do not
> acquire the means to repay, what was sold will remain in the pos-
> session of the buyer until the Year of Jubilee. It will be returned in
> the Jubilee, and they can then go back to their property.
>
> Leviticus 25:25–28

Jesus told us to forgive "seventy times seven" (Matt. 18:22). I wonder
if he was calling us not just to be extravagant with our forgiveness but
also to embrace a Jubilee mindset in all our relationships, to release those
held captive by our grudges.

Our society is not a theocracy, and our private-property laws actually
prohibit the practice of Jubilee. So how can we live out the Jubilee that
Jesus declares and in fact calls us to?

Rather than get caught up in the "rules" for the Jubilee, consider the
theology that supports it. The whole idea turns social stratification on its
head. God urged his people to let go of land, slaves, and debts. Scholar
Donald Kraybill notes, "The use and distribution of these resources—
natural, human, and financial—tilts the balance of justice in any soci-

ety. In the modern world, technology has become a fourth variable in the equation. By controlling these resources, some people become wealthy as others slide into poverty."[8]

When Jesus began his earthly ministry, he announced that he had come to "proclaim the year of the Lord's favor" — the Jubilee. (Some scholars believe that Jesus' proclamation in Luke 4:18 – 19 happened in a sabbatical year, possibly even a Jubilee year.)[9]

Jesus was preaching in Nazareth, where many of his neighbors were poor or slaves. All of them lived under the tyranny of Rome. I'm guessing they did not spiritualize his words and say he was speaking about people who were spiritually blind or needed their souls to be set free. They took him literally, believing that his words had political and economic consequences.

The question then becomes, Do we take Jesus literally, or do we take those words that make us uncomfortable and decide that they are meant only symbolically? Kraybill challenges us to see the true consequences of God's Sabbath and Jubilee commands: "Just as the Hebrew response to God's liberation had real consequences, so must ours. It's not enough to sit and ponder the Jubilee's theological beauty. We must act. The biblical model calls us to start forgiving not only interpersonal insults but financial ones as well. We lower rents and raise salaries. In the words of the Lord's Prayer, 'forgive us our debts, as we also have forgiven our debtors' (Matt. 6:12)."[10]

How do we live this? It's counterintuitive, but the spiritual practice of Sabbath-keeping transforms us. It teaches us contentment and trust; it invites us to live simply so we can be generous. It's a practice of obedience. It also allows us to fully rest so we can fully engage during the rest of the week. Just as a good night's sleep gives us energy for the next day, consistent Sabbath-keeping empowers us to know and then do God's will.

Sabbath is the foundation of Jubilee, which is a Sabbath of Sabbaths. The best place to start acting on Jubilee is to begin to practice Sabbath-keeping. If you do this consistently, it will be transformational in ways you don't expect.

Compassion Step

Take some time to assess your energy level. Are you weary? Are you experiencing compassion fatigue or some other form of fatigue? Do you take time to rest? Refuse to beat yourself up for not getting more done. Instead, be kind to yourself. What specific things can you do this week to treat your body and soul with kindness? What steps could you take to give yourself one day a week to rest and to spend time with God?

Community Step

Begin by reading all of Leviticus 25 out loud. As a group, talk about what you think it means to live out Jubilee in our day. Discuss the following: In what ways is the Jubilee command a foreshadowing of Jesus' ministry? How are Sabbath and Jubilee connected? Do you take a day of rest each week? What does that look like?

expectations

am I good enough? I've made a career of being an overachiever, and yet — is it enough? I'm sometimes so aware of shortcomings, confusion, doubts, and the propensity to sin that lies beneath my carefully groomed exterior. Now, I can say with great bravado that God loves me unconditionally. The question is, Do I live as if that is true? As if I know that I am deeply loved by the creator of the universe? Or am I worried that I've somehow disappointed God and everyone else? Have I somehow fallen short?

What does God expect, anyway? What does he want from us? The world is full of problems, and it seems like people have a lot of different ideas about what it means to follow God, about what he wants us to do. They focus on rules, sometimes. By keeping the rules, can you make God love you?

God answered this question through the Old Testament prophet Micah: "He has shown all you people what is good. And what does the LORD require of you? To act justly and to love mercy and to walk humbly with your God" (Mic. 6:8). The footnote to this verse in the TNIV says that the word *humbly* can also be translated "prudently" — to walk wisely with your God.

While the purpose of this book is to unpack in great detail what it means to act justly and love mercy, I want to start with that last phrase — to walk humbly with your God. Not to exclude the other two; just to begin there.

We sometimes think of humility as being self-deprecating or overly modest. Consider that phrase: to walk humbly with your God. If you walk with someone, beside them, you share a certain intimacy. To walk with God implies an ongoing relationship, a certain familiar constancy, a daily dwelling with rather than an occasional encounter. It also implies action. You aren't just thinking about God; you're going and doing with him. You'd expect us to have a certain sense of self-worth from the privilege of that intimacy, that relationship.

As women, we walk a tightrope. How can we be assertive without being considered pushy? How can we have healthy self-esteem without being self-absorbed or overly self-important?

If we live humbly, by the Bible's definition, we will have a right-sized view of ourselves. We'll be neither grandiose nor trapped in the "little old me" syndrome. How do we live in that balance? The Bible offers this advice: "Brothers and sisters, if someone is caught in a sin, you who live by the Spirit should restore that person gently. But watch yourselves, or you also may be tempted. Carry each other's burdens, and in this way you will fulfill the law of Christ. If any of you think you are something when you are nothing, you deceive yourselves. Each of you should test your own actions. Then you can take pride in yourself, without comparing yourself to somebody else, for each of you should carry your own load" (Gal. 6:1–5).

This verse tells us that if others are making mistakes, we need to restore them, not just criticize them. As we correct others, we need to be careful that we don't fall into sin ourselves. The Bible doesn't say we are worthless; far from it. It says we need to be accurate in our self-assessment. When that happens, we can take pride in ourselves. Our worth is not based on comparison to others, or only on our own accomplishments. Our value lies in what God has given us the ability to do and in God's love for us. First John 3:1 reminds us, "How great is the love that the Father has lavished upon us, that we should be called children of God! And that is what we are!" (NIV). I love the exclamation points, which are so rarely found in Scripture. We are daughters of God! He's *lavished* his love upon us!

We're deeply loved daughters of God. Sometimes when I look in the mirror, it's hard to remember that. Our culture creates crazy-making pressure to have a perfect external appearance. I've talked to women who get up every morning and spend the first few minutes of their day standing in front of the mirror trashing themselves. They don't see themselves as daughters of God, as women deeply loved. If they have to go out in public—especially, for some reason, if they have to go to *church*—they find themselves full of self-loathing: worrying about how they look, that they are too fat, that their hair or face is too plain, that people will be looking at them critically. This is not humility. It's crippling self-absorption. We're so intent on comparing and on telling ourselves how many ways we fall short that we miss the opportunity to help others. We don't live by the Spirit when we do this; we live by the flesh.

If you are standing in front of the mirror worrying about how those pants make your butt look, it's hard to listen to the voice of truth, which says, "You are the beloved."

When we have the courage to accept God's love for us, we're better able to love others. In fact, what if the first step to loving others, to making a difference in their lives, is to embrace the fact that God loves us, that we are lovable? What if we lived in that reality enough to believe that God feels this way about everyone? That would give us confidence and also humility. We would carry our own load, be responsible for our own emotional and spiritual health, and yet we would be helping others. As the quote from two weeks ago said, "As we let our own light shine, we unconsciously give other people permission to do the same." We bear others' burdens. What if carrying our own load didn't mean, necessarily, keeping our problems and struggles to ourselves but rather meant letting God love us, meant embracing and receiving the fact that we are deeply loved?

It's always been harder for me to accept my strengths than to accept my flaws. I'm okay with my imperfections; I accept that they are just a part of who I am. I may have critically compared myself with models in magazines when I was a teenager, but I have since, as the Bible tells us, put away childish things. I know now that they look that way because of Photoshop or eating disorders or cocaine or youth or all of these. Even as I accept my imperfections, I often find myself focused on them. I forget to think about my strengths.

To embrace my strengths, to accept that God gave me certain abilities and wants me to use them to point others toward him — that's a tougher thing, because it means I have to do something, not just think something.

Henri Nouwen writes, "The greatest gift my friendship can give to you is the gift of your Belovedness. I can give that gift only insofar as I have claimed it for myself."[11] He goes on to observe that we are tempted not by power and success but by self-rejection. He continues, "Maybe you think that you are more tempted by arrogance than by self-rejection. But isn't arrogance, in fact, the other side of self-rejection? Isn't arrogance putting yourself on a pedestal to avoid being seen as you see yourself? ... Both self-rejection and arrogance pull us out of the common reality of existence and make a gentle community of people extremely difficult, if not impossible, to attain.... Self-rejection is the greatest enemy of the spiritual life because it contradicts the sacred voice that calls us the 'Beloved.'"[12]

True humility flows out of confidence. Think about it—the person who is always talking about herself or bragging is often doing so because she wants to shore up her failing self-esteem. The humble person is not rejecting herself or her accomplishments; rather she cultivates an inner confidence. She knows that God loves her, and that empowers her to accomplish things; it frees her from the trap of arrogance. The Bible says, "Who is wise and understanding among you? Let them show it by their good life, by deeds done in the humility that comes from wisdom" (James 3:13).

To make a difference in the world, to share God's love with others, we have to trust that we actually can do that. We need the self-confidence that comes from knowing that *God* has enough confidence in us to entrust us with his calling. And he does! If you have trouble believing that, ask God to give you that confidence. Ask him to help you see yourself as he sees you—beloved.

We may not ever get this totally figured out. That's why the Bible says we walk humbly with God. Walking along, one step at a time, one day at a time. The journey is what transforms us, and the process is ongoing. God knows where we're going, so we can humbly walk along with him, trusting that his guidance is good, his grace is sufficient.

Compassion Step

An essential first step to becoming a more compassionate person is learning to be compassionate with yourself. What causes you to be hard on yourself? Describe a time when you saw yourself as lacking. Looking back, how were you stronger than you gave yourself credit for at the time? How has your self-image changed since then? How would you give someone the gift of belovedness, as Nouwen wrote? How do you think your self-image relates to your ability to love others?

Community Step

Often churches or small groups focus on the gifts of one person—the leader. If you want to take your group to the next level, notice and employ the gifts of every member. The strongest groups are those in which everyone brings their gifts—whether of mercy, leadership, encouragement, or helps—to the table. Spend some time talking about the giftedness of each person in your group. Ask members to name the gifts they see in each other. What contribution can each make to the life of the group? Honor each person's unique contribution to the group and to the world.

week 6

enough

for years, I did not let my children have video games. We live in a neighborhood where they can play outside with lots of other children. We own a lot of books and regularly visit the library. They enjoy board games. It snows a lot here; they've gotten quite good at building snow forts, sledding, and other winter activities. We've found adventures at the zoo, at the beach, at the nature center, and in our own back yard.

I did let them play games on the computer, mostly educational things like Reader Rabbit. The lack of other options made them think this was actually fun.

I'm not stupid, though. I knew my kids sometimes played the games at other people's houses. Even then, I spoke with parents to do a rating check to screen out violent games.

I've gradually eased my restrictions. When my kids were ten and twelve, they asked if they could buy a Nintendo DS with their own money. The two of them saved their allowances and birthday money for a while, then purchased one player and several games, which they share.

Some of the games require you to play regularly to maintain things. I'll often hear Melanie ask Aaron, "Did you walk Brandy?" There's no Brandy at our house; she's one of their Nintendogs — a virtual dog on the handheld game player. The game allows you to feed, walk, groom, and teach tricks to the puppies.

The other day I told Aaron to put away the DS and pick up a book. "That's fine, Mom; I already did everything I need to do on my game," he said. "I even paid my mortgage."

Paid your mortgage? What? Apparently, another DS game, Animal Crossing, puts you in a virtual neighborhood with a bunch of animals. You might have, say, a raccoon for your next-door neighbor. You buy and sell stuff, trade things, and, every so often, make a mortgage payment.

Aaron explained patiently, as if I were a child, that you had to pay the mortgage. If you paid it off, you automatically got a bigger house.

"What if you want to pay off the mortgage but stay in the same house?" I asked.

"Well, you would ... wait, huh?" he said, looking confused.

"What if you want to be content?" I said, a little more animatedly.

"Then you just don't pay off the mortgage," he said calmly.

And you wonder why I resisted video games for so long. Even the most innocuous ones teach, ever so subtly, the doctrines of consumerism: More is better. Debt is normal. Borrow rather than save. When you pay off one thing, trade it for a bigger thing.

One of the most powerful words in the English language is a term our culture seems to have erased from the dictionary: *enough*. I have enough stuff. I have enough activities. I have enough food, so no, I don't want you to supersize me.

A word you see much more often is *simplicity*. People long for a less chaotic life; they want simplicity. Ironically, we often try to achieve simplicity by buying something. What we don't realize is that the first step toward a simpler life, toward true simplicity, is the word *enough*. To get to enough, you don't have to buy anything. In many cases, the first step toward simplicity is to stop buying. Stop trying to fill that hole in your soul with stuff.

We often think that to live a life of simplicity, we need to move to the country and raise chickens. Or move to the inner city and live in a Christian ghetto commune, as did Shane Claiborne, author of *The Irresistible Revolution*.

Simplicity, once you get clear on what it is, can be experienced anywhere. Christian simplicity begins when we "seek first the kingdom of God" (Matt. 6:33). It's a matter of focus. You have to decide, Is getting a better job, more money, and a nicer house my top priority? Is acquisition going to make me happy? Simplicity is a matter of focus. When we are focused on God, other things fall into their proper place, and we find it easier to be content. No matter how much you've got, it's enough. In fact, it's probably too much. While simplicity may affect you outwardly, it begins as an inner reality.

The apostle Paul wrote, "I have learned to be content whatever the circumstances. I know what it is to be in need, and I know what it is to have plenty. I have learned the secret of being content in any and every situation, whether well fed or hungry, whether living in plenty or in want" (Phil. 4:11 – 12).

For Paul, contentment didn't have to do with how much or how little stuff he had. It had to do with a singular focus, with living his priorities. He explained that the reason for his contentment was Jesus: "I can do all this through him who gives me strength" (Phil. 4:13).

Simplicity comes from living humbly. That doesn't necessarily mean living in poverty; it has to do with trusting that God will be with you and take care of you.

A few verses before Paul's words on contentment, he wrote, "Do not be anxious about anything, but in every situation, by prayer and petition, with thanksgiving, present your requests to God. And the peace of God, which transcends all understanding, will guard your hearts and your minds in Christ Jesus" (Phil. 4:6 – 7).

Even when you have enough, you can still ask God for what you need. Contentment comes when we realize clearly the difference between needs and wants.

My kids wanted a Nintendo DS; they realize it's not a need. It's not bad to have a DS; you just don't need one to be happy. Buying it forced them to grapple with these questions: Was the amount of work they had to do, the spending they had to defer, and the smaller purchases they had to forego in order to get that DS worth it? And while it is fun to play with, did having it make them more content? More fulfilled? Did the Nintendo DS deliver what they had hoped it would? Does accumulating stuff make you less anxious, or more anxious?

Jesus said that a simple life is focused on God. It's a life that is contented and free from worry. No life is free from conflict or struggles; still, when we focus on God rather than on problems, we live in simplicity. We have peace in spite of our trials. Jesus told his followers, "Do not worry, saying, 'What shall we eat?' or 'What shall we drink?' or 'What shall we wear?' For the pagans run after all these things, and your heavenly Father knows that you need them. But seek first his kingdom and his righteousness, and all these things will be given to you as well. Therefore do not worry about tomorrow, for tomorrow will worry about itself. Each day has enough trouble of its own" (Matt. 6:31 – 34). That is the definition of Christian simplicity: to seek first God's kingdom.

So the opposite of worry and fear is to seek God—not an anxious seeking but a joyful, trusting seeking, like a child playing hide-and-seek with a parent. Seek first God's kingdom. I love this promise from God: "Then you will call upon me and come and pray to me, and I will listen to you. You will seek me and find me when you seek me with all your heart. I will be found by you" (Jer. 29:12–14). God longs to be found, like a mother playing with her child. God deeply desires to listen to us, to be discovered by us. When we do discover him, discover that deep relationship of love, we will find that it satisfies us in a way that stuff never can. We will realize we have enough if we have God.

So how do we live a simple life? Seek first God's kingdom, seek to live according to his ways. In other words, walk humbly with God, and all your other priorities will fall into line. This is not a one-time deal. It's a constant journey. Keep seeking God. Seek his kingdom, his will, his love, every day. Seek and you will find. You'll not only find God; you'll find that you have more than enough.

Compassion Step

In what areas of your life is it easiest to be content? Why? How can you bring this contentment to other parts of your life? How might your perspective on "enough" affect your ability to be generous? If you were set free from worry, would you be more compassionate? Why or why not?

Community Step

Do you have stuff you don't need? Does that stuff make you feel more anxious, or less anxious? As a group, make a list of the things you have (that still work) that you'd like to get rid of. Is there anyone in the group who needs something on the list? Consider helping one another by having members share the things they no longer need with members who need them. Check out the website www.freecycle.com, where you can list stuff you no longer need, and where others who need it can find it.

downward

Poking around an airport bookstore last week, I noticed several books on Mary Magdalene. Ever since Dan Brown's novel *The DaVinci Code* came out and people got all bent out of shape because they neglected to notice that it was on the fiction shelf, religion scholars found themselves writing books for the mainstream rather than just academia. As a result, you find books by professors next to *People* magazine and John Grisham novels.

I picked up one book, *The Two Marys: The Hidden History of the Mother and Wife of Jesus* by psychic Sylvia Brown. It's about Mary the mother of Jesus, and Mary Magdalene, who this book calmly asserts was the wife of Jesus.

I did not believe that this premise was supported by the Bible, and wanted to see how the author would substantiate her claim. She does so by talking about her psychic visions of the past. In the first few pages, she asserts that Mary Magdalene and Jesus, both born wealthy, had been friends since childhood. She paints a picture of the two of them hanging out in some sort of luxurious setting as childhood sweethearts. She even gives vivid descriptions of their physical appearance. (Did you know that Mary Magdalene was five feet six and had unruly red hair?)[13]

The Bible (and most reliable historical resources) says Jesus did not live a life of privilege. He grew up in Nazareth, a small village in the region of Galilee. Perhaps we imagine some pastoral little town; it was more of a hole in the wall. When one of Jesus' potential disciples heard that the new rabbi everyone was excited about was from Nazareth, he commented, "Nazareth! Can anything good come from there?" (John 1:46).

Even in his own not-exactly-affluent hometown, Jesus may not have been admired. His childhood was likely tainted by the scandal of his mother's pregnancy, which had begun before she got married. Even though Joseph married Mary, people in their small town knew what had happened. When people first heard Jesus preaching in his hometown, they said, "Isn't that Joseph's son?" (Luke 4:22). The implication was that the supposedly illegitimate son of a blue-collar worker couldn't possibly be anything special.

Jesus wasn't just humble; he was poor. A careful reading of the text shows us that. For example, notice this small detail about Jesus' life from Luke's gospel: "On the eighth day, when it was time to circumcise the child, he was named Jesus, the name the angel had given him before he was conceived. When the time came for the purification rites required by the Law of Moses, Joseph and Mary took him to Jerusalem to present him to the Lord (as it is written in the Law of the Lord, 'Every firstborn male is to be consecrated to the Lord'), and to offer a sacrifice in keeping with what is said in the Law of the Lord: 'a pair of doves or two young pigeons'" (Luke 2:21–24).

This passage shows that Jesus' family carefully observed Jewish law. By including the detail about the substance of the sacrifice, Luke also reveals their poverty. The Old Testament, which records that law, says this about a Jewish mother's duties when she had a child: "When the days of her purification for a son or daughter are over, she is to bring to the priest at the entrance to the tent of meeting a year-old lamb for a burnt offering and a young pigeon or a dove for a sin offering. He shall offer them before the LORD to make atonement for her, and then she will be ceremonially clean from her flow of blood. These are the regulations for the woman who gives birth to a boy or a girl. *If she cannot afford a lamb*, she is to bring two doves or two young pigeons, one for a burnt offering and the other for a sin offering. In this way the priest will make atonement for her, and she will be clean" (Lev. 12:6–8, emphasis mine).

Think about Jesus' parents. They knew this child was the Messiah. They knew his conception was not a sin; it was a miracle. If they could have, don't you think they would have brought the more expensive, more extravagant sacrifice? They didn't. Why? Apparently, they were so poor that a lamb was simply beyond their means. So they relied on the grace of God, which says bring what you can and it will be alright.

Jesus was poor. Jesus was humble. Not just modest in an "aw-shucks," self-deprecating way. He was dirt poor. He grew up in physical poverty.

God the Father did not hand down Jesus' earthly circumstances punitively. Being one with the Father, Jesus must have carefully considered, How do I get close to the people I love? How do I communicate the heart of God toward all people? And then he freely chose a life of poverty and simplicity.

If I say I am a follower of Jesus, what does that mean about how I am to live my life? I have a home, a car, food on the table, money for clothing and even for a few extra things. Is that wrong? If I'm a follower of Jesus, do I need to somehow figure out how to give away everything in order to be physically and monetarily poor? Or do I just need to let go of my fear of poor people, since Jesus was poor?

That depends. God does call some people to live a life of poverty. I don't buy the prosperity preachers' shtick that says God wants everyone to be wealthy. That doesn't fit what the Bible says. I do think money is something we have to be in conversation with God about. For me, it comes down to this: How can I do the most good in this world? How can I best develop and use the gifts God has given me? How can I further his kingdom? Am I aware that all people, rich or poor, are invited to be a part of that kingdom? I need to constantly be checking my attitude about people who have fewer material possessions than I do, and about those who have more than I do. I need to be careful not to let my affluence isolate me. I need to not allow "more" to be the driving value of my life. I need to serve God, not money.

In the late 1980s, I was a yuppie—a young, upwardly mobile professional. It was the thing to be back then. I worked long hours at the third largest newspaper in Illinois, paying my dues, getting promoted, getting noticed. I worked hard at improving my writing. I wanted to impress my editors with my drive and ambition. My job was my identity. I was going to use my writing and reporting abilities to climb the ladder, to get a job at the *Chicago Tribune*, and from there *Time* magazine or *Newsweek*. Career was my highest priority. That and partying with my friends.

Then I went back to church after taking a couple of years off.

I kept hanging around at Willow Creek Community Church, and God used a lot of people there to challenge me to grow. Then my pastor, Bill Hybels, preached an amazing series of sermons on Philippians. When we got to chapter 2, he talked about how Jesus chose "downward mobility" rather than upward mobility. Bill's teaching challenged and stretched my faith.[14] God spoke directly to me through those talks and through those verses, which say, "Do nothing out of selfish ambition or vain conceit. Rather, in humility value others above yourselves, not looking to your own interests but each of you to the interests of the others. In your relationships with one another, have the same attitude of mind Christ Jesus had: Who, being in very nature God, did not consider equality with God something to be used to his own advantage; rather, he made himself nothing by taking the very nature of a servant, being made in human likeness. And being found in appearance as a human being, he humbled himself by becoming obedient to death—even death on a cross!" (Phil. 2:3–8).

I resisted. I liked the idea of upward mobility, of being on the fast track of career accomplishments. A mentor at the time asked me to think about using my talents for God's kingdom. I couldn't at first. My writing talents were mine, not God's. I was not going to give them to him. God patiently persisted. Bill's series on Philippians, along with personal challenges from mentors and ministry leaders, made me realize that ambition, which was so highly revered in my culture, was, at least in my case, selfish. It's humorous to me that today I write Christian books. (Although doing so doesn't make you immune to ambition.) It's probably even more humorous to my former coworkers, who likely remember that my dedication to my career was rivaled only by my dedication to having a good time once work was over.

It's not wrong to do your best in your job. God calls us to excellence, to do our work as if doing it for him. I had made my career my god. I didn't realize that my priorities were killing my soul.

What do these verses say about living humbly? They focus not on the numbers in your bank account but on community. They talk as much about others as they do about poverty. They remind us to look to the interests of others. They tell us how to live in our relationships with others. These verses are a call to community and generosity. We are called to hold very loosely all that we have.

The problem is that it is hard to live humbly when we, well, don't live in humble circumstances. When you have a house and food on the table, you tend to become rather self-reliant. You think you have all you need because of your talent, hard work, and good looks.

Or, if you are struggling financially, you may think that once you have just a bit more, you'll be freed up to be more generous. I doubt it. Either you are generous or you're not. Our generosity does not depend on our financial status; it depends on the condition of our hearts. Some people are blessed financially. Others are blessed in other ways. If you don't have a lot of money, that doesn't mean God is being stingy.

Jesus said, "Blessed are the poor in spirit, for theirs is the kingdom of heaven" (Matt. 5:3). You could write a whole book on what it means to be poor in spirit. For our purposes, let's just say that poor in spirit has to do with humility, with realizing that we are spiritually needy. We need God's grace.

What's been amazing to me is that as I have given my gifts to God, particularly my writing, he's given back to me. That's not to say it's been easy. When I first began writing spiritual stuff rather than business stuff, certain people who allegedly loved me were less than supportive. The cut in income was rather drastic. I wish I could tell you that it has been easy or that everyone was completely understanding and helpful. It wasn't; they weren't.

Downward mobility is not always easy. But it is always worth it.

Compassion Step

What would downward mobility look like in your life? What are some concrete steps you can take to follow Christ's example of humility in regard to your profession and aspirations? How would being down-wardly mobile help you to make a difference in the lives of others? If you ever feel entitled to the gifts God has given you (whether they be talents or possessions), what can you do to transform your thinking? How can you use your gifts for God's glory?

Community Step

How would your group change if you were actually to live out as a group the following verse from this week: "In humility value others above yourselves, not looking to your own interests but each of you to the interests of the others. In your relationships with one another, have the same attitude of mind Christ Jesus had" (Phil. 2:3–5)? What does it mean to look to the interests of others? How can you serve one another in your group? How might practicing service within your group help you as a group to go forth to serve in your community? This week take a step to encourage or serve someone in your group.

wrecked

in an interview with *Discipleship Journal*, Kay Warren, wife of "purpose driven" pastor Rick Warren, asserted that God has "gloriously ruined" her life—that all her plans have been shoved aside because God is calling her to care for the poor. Warren has dedicated her life to trying to help those who are sick and dying of HIV/AIDS, and to eradicating poverty. While I'm impressed with Warren, reading her words makes me a little nervous.

The same day I read Warren's interview, I watched *Oprah*, hoping for something a little lighter. No such luck. Oprah interviewed a couple who claim to be Christians, who say they are "happy having very little"—which is great. To prove their point, they eat food they collect from dumpsters. They go to garbage bins outside of restaurants and find food they say is perfectly fine. They have good jobs. They work. They have a mortgage. And they dumpster dive.

They told Oprah that billions of dollars' worth of food are thrown away by Americans every year, food that could feed whole countries. They asserted that it is wrong to be endlessly and thoughtlessly consuming. Some of what they find in dumpsters, if it is wrapped and clean, they donate to homeless shelters.

I agree in theory with both Mrs. Warren and this couple. We should care for the poor; we should restrain our consumerism. The amount of perfectly good food we throw away, when half the world goes to bed hungry, is outrageous. Would I live it out as radically as these people are doing?

I live a life of outward simplicity, mostly. My husband and I both drive older cars with over a hundred thousand miles on them. We are thrifty. While we live in a nice neighborhood with good schools, our house is simple and in desperate need of updating. We don't even have cable television. We live within our means. Our only debt is our mortgage. So I sometimes think, Okay, is this simple enough? Is it humble enough? Should I move to a poorer neighborhood with worse schools and more crime? Would that make my life simpler?

Our culture is fascinated with simplicity as a concept. It's a topic and word used to sell everything from magazines to makeup. We are not so enamored with living humbly, which is an integral part of simplicity. It's a confusing topic. Rick Warren's bestselling book has made him and his wife millionaires. When Rick went from being an ordinary megachurch Baptist pastor to a bestselling author, the Warrens decided to do what they call "reverse tithing." They reportedly live on 10 percent of their income and give 90 percent away. So they live not just within their means but way below them. Although they live very simply, even that 10 percent is more than most people have. Simplicity is a relative term.

So, in a way, is humility.

The Warrens have decided to use their resources to fight poverty and disease on a global scale. They've visited clinics in Africa, held the hands of people who are dying, helped children who are starving. In the article, Mrs. Warren described visiting a women's leprosarium in the Philippines.

"We can't encounter God and not be radically shaken, disturbed, ruined," she told *Discipleship Journal*. When asked what that meant, she said, "God ruins everything! Our plans, our agendas, our goals, our money, our relationships, our lifestyles, the way we see ourselves, the way we see Him, the way we view our circumstances, the way we look at every person we meet, how we handle temptation, how we fight evil and push back the darkness.... I am gloriously ruined. I'm not the same person I used to be, and I don't want to go back. I can't live the same way I did before. For along with the extraordinary pain and suffering and evil I have seen, along with the amount of sorrow my heart experiences, I know a vibrancy and joy in walking with God and with other people that I never knew before. He really shook things up but in a very, very good way."[15]

Paradoxically, when God shakes things up, we often find ourselves called to simplicity. Christian simplicity is not about organizing closets or decluttering your house; rather it's about seeking first the kingdom of God. It's about the focus of your heart, not how much stuff you have. What would my life look like if I truly lived that out?

What does it mean to live simply? Richard Foster, in his classic book *Freedom of Simplicity*, writes, "Simplicity is an inward reality that can be seen in an outward lifestyle. We must have both; to neglect either end of this tension is disastrous."[16] What steps do we take to move toward that inward reality?

As Foster's title suggests, there is freedom in simplicity, power in humility. The apostle Paul wrote, "As a prisoner for the Lord, then, I urge you to live a life worthy of the calling you have received. Be completely humble and gentle; be patient, bearing with one another in love. Make every effort to keep the unity of the Spirit through the bond of peace. There is one body and one Spirit, just as you were called to one hope when you were called; one Lord, one faith, one baptism; one God and Father of all, who is over all and through all and in all. But to each one of us grace has been given as Christ apportioned it" (Eph. 4:1–7).

It's easy for me to think that people like Kay Warren have just been "apportioned" more grace than I have, to say it works for them but I couldn't do that. However, simplicity also has to do with what Paul mentions in verse 1: living a life worthy of your calling. What does that mean? What calling have we received? We are called to follow Jesus, to live as he would if he were in our place. That will look different in each person's life, because in addition to that general call to being Jesus' disciple, each of us has been given gifts and passions that point toward a specific calling from God. The possibilities are as varied as Christ's followers. You may be called to lead well in the marketplace, to manage people with excellence and compassion. You may be called to provide physical care for people, in your job or in your home. When God calls, how will you respond? It takes prayer to hear God's call clearly. This is part of the complexity of simplicity.

There is great freedom in living humbly, in living in an abundance that is based on abundant love, not abundant stuff. When your life is focused on God and his calling for you, that becomes your priority. In it there is great joy.

I try to make a habit of giving away things my family and I don't need. Outgrown clothes go to friends with younger children; our used clothes, appliances, or coats go to the homeless shelter. We also try to live on less than we earn so that we can support our church financially, so that we have the freedom to give to those in need. Giving is essential to simplicity; it loosens the grip possessions can have on our souls. When you give, God gives in return. Not by sending you checks, necessarily. Sometimes, he sends you furniture.

The other day, my sister-in-law was over, dropping off my nephew so that Melanie could babysit him at our house. My sister-in-law came down into our basement (with the lovely yellow shag carpeting and wood paneling from the 1970s), looked around, and asked where we got such a great TV. A client of my husband had given it to us because he didn't want it anymore. Scot surveyed the basement and said, "You know, almost everything in this basement, people gave us." It was true. The hide-a-bed couch the boys were sitting on, the video game player they were using, the bookshelves, the three desks, the beanbag chair, the pool table — all hand-me-downs from friends. The foosball table had been a gift from my parents, as was the bed and IKEA dressers in the adjacent bedroom (where they sleep when they visit).

We'd bought an inexpensive stand to put the TV on (after a couple of months of having it sit on the floor). Other than that, all of the furnishings in our humble basement had come from the hand of God. It is not a fancy room; the kids can play soccer down there and I don't care if they spill on that old carpeting. That day, I saw my basement with new eyes: furnished with love. It was the outward manifestation of an inner reality. I am content with hand-me-downs, because to me they are symbols of the providence of a generous God.

It is not wrong to buy furniture or other household items. The question becomes, Do we long for God with the same intensity with which we long to redecorate or to get that new television or furniture? Do we live as if we trust that we have enough, that God's provision is enough, that his grace is sufficient?

I don't know if I will go to Africa. I don't think I could get my food from a dumpster, no matter how well wrapped or fresh it might seem. But I can choose to be content and to accept graciously the gifts that God surprises us with. Perhaps choosing to be content is a step on the path to simplicity.

Compassion Step

What gets in the way of contentment for you? How will you determine if you have enough? Contemplate the connection between the ideas of simplicity and enough. One way to do that is to try fasting from unnecessary shopping for an extended period of time. Wear what you already own; eat off the dishes already in your cupboards. Live into the fact that you already have enough.

Community Step

Read Ephesians 4:1–7 out loud. Notice the focus on community. What is this portion of God's Word telling us to do? Brainstorm as a group about some ways that you can live out these verses. Discuss the following: (1) What keeps you from being content? How does that affect your relationships with other people? (2) What do you think it means to live simply? What is one thing you want to do this week to take a step toward simplicity?

hand-me-downs

my job requires some travel. The fall my kids were ten and twelve, I found myself out of town, traveling for work, almost every weekend. I was teaching at retreats, speaking at events, helping women grow closer to God. It's part of what God has called me to do, allowed me the privilege of doing. As fulfilling as ministry is, I missed my family. A lot. Because I'm an introvert, meeting and ministering to so many strangers was taxing. When I'm at a retreat as a teacher, it's not relaxing. It feels like work. Work I'm called to do and enjoy, but work just the same. It drained me.

During that season, when I would describe my schedule to people, I'd find tears in my eyes, even though I'm the one who said yes to these opportunities. Frederick Buechner wrote, "Whenever you find tears in your eyes, especially unexpected tears, it is well to pay the closest attention."[17] So I tried to pay attention. I wondered, Was I doing God's will, or following my own workaholic tendencies? Was I out saving the world at the expense of my family? I had said yes to way too many things, and my life felt out of balance.

When my daughter asked if I'd take her and a few friends shopping after school, I jumped at the chance to try to alleviate my working-mother guilt, to make up for my absence by doing the preteen version of quality time.

Rather than the mall, however, the girls requested a ride to a local thrift shop. One of the few weekends I would be at home, my daughter was the one going on a retreat, with the youth group at church. The kids had been instructed to put together costumes for an '80s dance to be held at the retreat. There's nothing that will make you feel old quite like your kid going to a dance where the theme is the decade that you went to high school. Melanie and her friends had decided that the best place to find appropriately nerdy clothes was at the thrift shop. They delighted in the opportunity to combine two favorite activities: being silly and shopping.

The girls pawed through the racks of used clothes, laughing and screeching at fashions that, frankly, looked a lot like the things which, back in the day, I had spent my hard-earned paycheck on.

They tried on wild combinations, laughing hysterically as they took turns strutting around like runway models, striking poses in — gasp — jewel-toned sweaters with generous shoulder pads. "I can't believe people wore this!" they shrieked. I smiled, remembering a fashionable outfit I'd proudly worn to work twenty years ago that looked very similar to what they modeled.

They took their shopping spree to the next level by deliberately creating mismatched outfits. One girl combined lime green sweatpants (pulled up above her waist to heighten the nerd factor) with a mustard turtleneck and an argyle vest; another found a shiny purple polyester dress and paired it with sensible beige shoes and a brown striped sweater.

For Melanie and her friends, any clothing more than a year old is completely out of style. "That's so yesterday," they'll tell me. She rolls her eyes sometimes when she sees my husband and me wearing clothes that have been in our closet for years. She's not sure what to think when she sees me accepting gifts of used clothes from friends. I'm still teaching her these lessons of simplicity. The fact that she is still growing provides an excuse for quick wardrobe turnover. Melanie is not interested in my hand-me-downs, at least most of them.

Like it or not, however, she's inherited some things from me. She has my blue eyes and my intensity. We all get some hand-me-downs. I'm not just talking about clothes or looks. We also inherit some emotional and spiritual hand-me-downs. Some are treasures; some are rags. Some just don't fit. We try to wear them anyway. Some are ill-fitting to the point of being painful. Others are beautiful, and we want to wear them, yet they don't fit. We need to grow into them.

What did you inherit? When it comes to things like handling conflict, building friendships, trusting others, or relating to God, what was handed down to you? Did you grow up wearing a coat of shame, or dressed in confidence and high self-esteem? When you look in the mirror, do you say, "I'm loved," or do you say, "I'm not good enough"? Spiritually, what did you learn? That God is loving and kind, or angry and demanding?

The way you answer these questions depends in part on what kind of hand-me-downs you inherited, the emotional and spiritual legacy your family gave you. If you don't spend some time looking at that, seeing and naming what is true, you will probably unwittingly pass along the same things to your children.

While we inherit some good and bad things from our earthly parents, the Bible says that if we have become a part of God's family by believing in Jesus, we get a whole new inheritance, and it's all good!

Paul wrote to the church at Ephesus, "You also were included in Christ when you heard the word of truth, the gospel of your salvation. When you believed, you were marked in him with a seal, the promised Holy Spirit, who is a deposit guaranteeing our inheritance until the redemption of those who are God's possession — to the praise of his glory" (Eph. 1:13 – 14).

When it comes to being a parent (if you are one), what are you handing down to your children? Do you want to hand down everything you received, or do you want to do things differently? To take some small steps to change?

While sorting through emotional issues will help you to make some changes, inviting God into the process will result in radical transformation.

The Bible makes this promise: "Praise be to the God and Father of our Lord Jesus Christ! In his great mercy he has given us new birth into a living hope through the resurrection of Jesus Christ from the dead, and into an inheritance that can never perish, spoil or fade. This inheritance is kept in heaven for you, who through faith are shielded by God's power until the coming of the salvation that is ready to be revealed in the last time. In all this you greatly rejoice, though now for a little while you may have had to suffer grief in all kinds of trials" (1 Peter 1:3 – 6).

While we may have inherited some not-so-great things from our earthly families, we have a heavenly inheritance of living hope. We may suffer a bit because of the brokenness of this world, but we can rejoice because God has given us eternal life.

Meanwhile, though, we have to live here on earth and work out our salvation with fear and trembling. We may never get all of this figured out, but it's important to ask ourselves, What legacy am I leaving my kids? What am I giving to the people around me (whether children, spouse, friends, even siblings and parents) that will endure?

In my season of travel, I realized I was absent from my home far too much. It wore me out, and it was not the legacy I wanted to leave.

Talking with my daughter about it, I said, "Maybe I should just not do any traveling at all." She looked at me with the wisdom of her twelve years and said, "Mom, you need to go and speak. Just not every weekend."

She knew that God has called me to teach and to do ministry. She was willing to share me with others but not to give me up entirely. My presence matters to her. So my choices matter.

I'm much more careful now to limit the number of weekends I'm away from my family. The work-family balance had to shift. I still do this kind of work, and I love it. I am also mindful of what kind of legacy I am leaving for my family. I want my kids to have as their example a parent who follows God's call on her life, who tries to make a difference in the world, who knows that her contribution to the kingdom matters. I want them to know they are important to me, that they are precious to me. My children and my marriage are my top priorities, but they're not my only priorities. I need to say that not just with words but also with my actions, and even with my presence.

An important step toward becoming a woman who can make a difference is cultivating self-awareness. Often that begins with the spiritual practice of self-examination.

Self-examination is not an opportunity to put your flaws under a microscope or to list your failings and shortcomings. It is not a chance to beat yourself up or to imagine that God is beating you up.

Rather, it is a look at both our actions and our motives, guided by the Holy Spirit. It's approaching the throne of grace with confidence, tempered by humility. In self-examination we ask God, Have I lived the way a daughter of the King ought to live? Where have I chosen what is right, and where have I chosen what is wrong? Have I followed Jesus' simple directive: love God, love others? In asking these questions, we trust that God will answer us gently, truthfully, without shaming us.

If we want to give good hand-me-downs, it's essential to know ourselves.

If we want to make a difference in the lives of our friends and families — in our neighborhoods, our cities, our world — we must know who we are. We must be willing to see our strengths and our weaknesses and live in the tension of being both flawed and forgiven.

Compassion Step

For centuries, Christians have used a practice called the "Daily Examen," or "review of the day," as a tool for growth. At the end of the day, simply scroll back through the day's major events — your interactions with others, your work, your recreation — almost as if you are watching a video in your head. Ask yourself, Did the choices I made in each situation draw me closer to God, or pull me away? Did I show God's love to those around me? Where was God present in my day? How did I respond? Was I aware of it, or not? Bathe this entire process in grace. You're not telling God anything he doesn't already know. Remember that no matter what you did or did not do today, he still loves you and sees you as his precious child.

Community Step

As a group, discuss the questions from this paragraph: "What did you inherit? When it comes to things like handling conflict, building friendships, trusting others, or relating to God, what was handed down to you? Did you grow up wearing a coat of shame, or dressed in confidence and high self-esteem? When you look in the mirror, do you say, 'I'm loved,' or do you say, 'I'm not good enough'?" Talk about some ways that you can affirm and encourage each other as a group and can help each other to pass down a legacy of love. Try this: affirm each other by having each person in the group describe the strengths of another person in the group. Sit in a circle and have each person complete this sentence about the person on their right: "The thing I love about _____ is ..."

heroes

When Pulitzer Prize–winning journalist and author David Halberstam died in a car wreck, I mourned the loss of one of my heroes.

Of Halberstam's twenty-one books, the two most famous focused on the Vietnam War. Sent as a correspondent to cover the war, he found that his experience converted him from objective reporter to opinionated critic.

As I pursued a career in journalism, even in the 1980s, most of the heroes I had (or more accurately, the heroes given to me) were, like Halberstam, white men: Bob Woodward and Carl Bernstein (the reporters who broke the Watergate story and authored *All the President's Men*), Studs Terkel, Tom Wolfe. My professors held up these writers as examples of great journalistic talent. They were brilliant and inspiring.

Ever since I decided to become a writer, at age nine, I'd loved the work of Madeleine L'Engle. I still do. She was a hero for me, a woman who started with children's books, then grew from there to become an important voice in adult Christian literature. Interestingly, L'Engle was the only female writer we read in my favorite college course, Modern Mythology.

I studied other women writers as well — Flannery O'Connor, Adrienne Rich, Anne Sexton — although our study of them was mostly relegated to the classes on women writers. (They didn't have classes on "men writers" for some reason.) While these women had a lot to say, they didn't offer much in the way of inspiration or role-modeling for a "career," which at the time was a very important question to me: what was I going to do with a degree in literature anyway?

Halberstam, Woodward, and others were changing the world, or at least making meaningful commentary on it. It seemed that many of the women writers (L'Engle being a notable exception) just complained about the world and the raw deal it had handed them. I wanted nothing to do with their whining. Maybe I should have paid more attention.

Back then I thought perhaps my gender wouldn't be a barrier in my career. Well.

I did become a journalist, and later an author. Pre-kids, I had dreamed of being a foreign correspondent, like Halberstam. I'd read *Time* magazine or the *Chicago Tribune* and see reports filed from far-off places and think, Someday. Before someday arrived, I had kids. Being a mother made that career aspiration seem a bit less attainable, and even a bit less desirable. The Christian subculture I lived in made it clear that good moms didn't abandon their children (especially if it meant putting them in—gasp—"day care") to go to work, and didn't work unless they had to. While a lot of my friends worked (and in fact I worked part-time from home), I understood that ideally I should simply be a mom and nothing more. This kind of went against the grain of the you-can-be-anything-you-want mantra my dad had repeated to me as I grew up. In the subculture I was a part of, I got the idea that I was supposed to want to be "just a mom."

I totally love being a mom. My children are my greatest delight in life, and nothing has shaped my soul more profoundly than the struggles and joys of parenthood. I'm extremely close to my kids, who are now teenagers, a stage I am enjoying immensely. But motherhood is just one of the roles in my life. I am also a writer. When my kids were small, most people saw me as an "at-home mom" who "wasn't working." Yet I had somehow gotten two books and dozens of articles published before my oldest child went to kindergarten. My husband had grown up in a family in which both parents worked, and he wondered aloud when I might be able to get a job. Instead of pointing out that I was working, I argued that I needed to be at home with the kids—that was my job. I didn't value the work I was doing. I felt pressure from the Christian subculture I had grown up in and was still a part of that said I should be home with my kids full-time, that said that is what "good" Christian moms do. It was a very confusing season of my life.

Seeing the story about Halberstam's death made me think about the career goals I had dropped when I decided to stay home with my children. I'd thought it would be impossible to be both a mom and a reporter. I chose my children, which I did not regret. I remained a writer, even if others didn't acknowledge that as important work, even if I devoted only a little time to it when the kids were small. I sometimes wondered, though, if I could have done both—been both a mom and a reporter.

That same week, I also saw an article in the Sunday *Chicago Tribune Magazine* about biodiversity in the jungles of Madagascar. The issue contained a profile of the reporter and the photographer who went into the jungle (risking life and limb) to get the story and pictures. The reporter, Laurie Goering, is a mom.

When I saw that, I felt a sense of longing—what if? And I wondered, Who did Laurie Goering look to as a role model? Who told her it was okay to be a foreign correspondent and a mom both? How come no one told me that?

When I posted these musings on my blog, I got a few comments from readers. Then I got an email from Laurie Goering herself; she'd somehow stumbled across my blog post. I was beside myself. She sent me the transcript of a speech she'd given about her career path, about covering the First Gulf War when she was pregnant (but didn't realize it), about how she'd combined (with the help of a nanny and a supportive husband) her adventurous career with motherhood. How she takes her kids with her on assignments all over the world. She took her preschoolers with her to Madagascar! "Since she was conceived, my daughter has been in more than thirty countries on four continents, and my son's quickly catching up," Laurie wrote to me.

It was so cool to have someone I admire take the time to write to me. I find myself looking for her byline in the *Tribune* all the time, grateful for the trails she is blazing for women in journalism. She is a hero to me, because she's figured out a way to do the working mom gig on her own terms.

When I was a new mom, I felt a lot of pressure to create a certain sort of life for my children. I listened to a lot of people who offered strong opinions of what a good Christian mom does. This basically confused me, because everyone seemed to have different opinions.

All people, regardless of gender, are created in the image of God. They need to be part of a purpose greater than themselves. Because it will test their faith, because it will bring them joy, because it will help others, and for lots of other reasons. During certain seasons, for some women, motherhood is enough. I found that as fiercely as I loved my kids, I needed something else to do besides just mothering. I eventually figured out that there is more than one right way to approach mother-hood, career, and combining the two. I'm intense enough that if I put all my energy into my children, it would be unhealthy. Women, especially within Christian circles (unfortunately), tend to think their choices are more limited than they actually are. Which is not that surprising, since much of Christian tradition has been rather male-centric. One of the things that bugs me about the Bible (sorry, it's just the truth) is the elev-enth chapter of Hebrews, which catalogs heroes of the faith. All men, with the exception of Rahab, who is a dubious role model for women, since she was a prostitute. A prostitute with a lot of faith, but still. (See Joshua 2; 6:22–25.)

There are plenty of women in the Bible who could be great role models, if stories were given more attention. They weren't played up very much, at least in my tradition.

I have great hope that heroes and heroines are becoming more diverse, that my daughter will grow up with heroes who look like her. Still, I am realizing that I can't just hope for a hero for my daughter. I need to be one.

Compassion Step

How might your commitment to following the dreams God has put in your heart have a positive impact on the people you live with? If you could let go of your worries about what other people think, what would you be doing with your life?

Community Step

Discuss as a group: (1) During high school or college, who were your heroes? Who did you admire and why? Did your heroes look like you? (2) Are you a role model for anyone (even if you don't intend to be)? How can you encourage and lead younger women by example?

moving

remember the '70s sitcom *The Jeffersons?* The comedy was a spin-off of the successful and, at the time, cutting-edge show *All in the Family.* The Jeffersons, according to the storyline, were an African-American family who had been neighbors of Archie and Edith Bunker. Their hard work and business success afforded them the opportunity to move out of the Bunkers' working-class neighborhood. "We're movin' on up, to the East Side," the theme song went. "We finally got a piece of the pie."

Moving up is a part of the American dream. My husband is a realtor, and real-estate pros have a term for a small, affordable house: starter home. You start here, but it is not your ultimate destination. You buy a starter home, build equity, wait for the value of the property to increase, and then "move on up."

Although I've lived in the Chicago area all my life, I've moved up a few times, with my parents and with my husband, as our family has grown. It's normal, right? Why not move to a bigger house in a better location if you can afford to do so?

I have a couple of friends who have done just the opposite. They've moved down. They've relocated from the suburbs to the city, from an upscale neighborhood to a poor neighborhood.

My friend Nate Heldman, for example, grew up in the suburbs of Chicago. He attended my church for many years, where he served on the worship team for Axis, our ministry to twentysomethings. Eventually, he began to question the very ministry he was involved in.

"Our brand of Christianity is self-seeking," he says. "We put a ton of energy into worship and small groups, in ministering to each other." He took a sabbatical from leading worship and focused on his growing passion for the city.

"I realized I wanted to do justice, rather than not do injustice," Nate says. Like many other young evangelicals who have a growing concern for social justice, he grew up in a church where he memorized Scripture and shared his faith but rarely heard anyone talk about passages like

Isaiah 58, Matthew 25, or Micah 6:8. "I realized that God's heart is for his people to do justice," he says.

After five years of thinking and praying about how to "do justice," Nate helped start an urban church with some friends and moved to Humbolt Park, an inner-city, mostly Puerto Rican neighborhood in Chicago. When he moved in five years ago, he was the only white person on his block. "Now it's almost all white," he says. "I'm considering moving."

That is, moving down. His once-rough neighborhood is gentrifying. Many of the Puerto Rican families who were able to buy cheap homes there have sold them for more than twice what they paid, and moved on. Others have moved out because they can't afford the increasing rents that come with higher property values.

Nate is a picture of a trend of new urban Christians who move into poor neighborhoods. He lives among the people he feels called to. Nate works full-time for an urban ministry. Other Christians who are part of this trend keep their regular day jobs and just try to live their ordinary lives with a "missional" intent. That mission: to live as Jesus would, not just to love their neighbors from a distance but to share in their struggles. The theology behind the movement is simply that Jesus "became flesh and made his dwelling among us" (John 1:14), and these Christians believe they should do the same for the poor.

Much of the movement is inspired by urban ministers like John Perkins, founder of the Christian Community Development Association. The CCDA espouses three Rs—reconciliation, relocation, and redistribution.

One magazine profile on Perkins noted, "The key to Perkins's legacy, and the legacy of CCDA, will surely be replication. There are community development programs in almost every large city now. Can idealistic young people, drawn to the vision of justice and love, stick it out for the long haul, as Perkins and other veterans have? Will their churches, schools, housing projects, and medical clinics endure? Will the CCDA philosophy spread?"[18]

Are you a better Christian if you live in the city? Is it more spiritual to be poor? Over the centuries, many religious people have taken a vow of poverty or chosen to minister to the poor; Mother Teresa is just one example. What does God's Word say about our location?

The Bible warns us against accumulation of wealth and even amassing of land. Through his prophet Isaiah, God told the wealthy,

> *Woe to you who add house to house*
> *and join field to field*
> *till no space is left*
> *and you live alone in the land.*
>
> Isaiah 5:8

Accumulation of wealth, especially land, leads to isolation. Indeed, if you live in a large house on a lot of acreage, you are a bit isolated from your neighbors. Isolation can happen anywhere. I found that condo living was more isolating than living in a neighborhood. Our level of isolation depends, in part, on whether we are willing to build relationships with the people around us.

As I've written about and come to know families that, with the intent of living missionally, have chosen to relocate to poor neighborhoods, I've earnestly prayed about whether God wants our family to do that. What I keep hearing is that he wants me to live missionally no matter where I am. To live and love in a way that points others to Jesus. For now, I am in the suburbs. My husband is very certain God is not calling him to live in the city, and I am certain God would not call me to leave him. Beyond that, after a lot of prayer, I have come to a place where I have moved beyond knowing I'm *not* called to the city, to knowing that I am called to shine right where I am.

God confirmed my decision when I read Al Hsu's book *The Suburban Christian*. He writes, "The missionary impulse for many of us might well be to settle in suburbia in order to have a significant Christian presence, lest we lose our witness there. . . . If we aren't called to go, we must be sure that we are called to stay — not in a passive sense, but to stay with an intentionality of active sending, sharing of resources and participating in global mission even at home."[19]

Sometimes we make following God more difficult than it has to be. He may not be calling us to move to the city or to a foreign mission field. He might be calling us to stay. Maybe you are already in the place where God wants you to be — and all you need to do is to see it that way.

One way to shine whether we live in the city, the country, or the suburbs is to choose to stay and to be content in our staying. What if the place where we are is the place God's called us to be? What if our being here is no accident?

Compassion Step

When you read Nate's story about moving to a poor urban neighborhood, what is your response? Think about the place where you live. Do you feel content there, or do you long for a larger home or one in a better neighborhood? Do you feel called to be where you are? Do you see yourself as a significant Christian presence in the area where you live? What steps could you take to move toward that?

Community Step

While one person can make a difference, having a critical mass of people often allows for more dramatic change. How could your group be a significant Christian presence in the places where you already are: your neighborhood, your children's school, your workplaces? Providing Christian presence does not necessarily mean always talking about God; rather, perhaps, it means showing his love to your friends and acquaintances. Do you know someone nearby who is suffering, whether from illness, injury, job loss, or just discouragement? As a group, brainstorm some ways that you might, without proselytizing, show your neighbors or coworkers the love of God. For now, just make a list. Next week, you'll start working on a specific project.

generous

the world's needs crowd in on our sometimes-unwilling conscious-ness. Images of violence, war, and hunger on CNN unnerve us. We snap off the television to make them go away, but in quiet moments, we know—there is suffering, both here and abroad. Our conviction of our impotence in the face of such insurmountable challenges leads us to ignore injustice rather than to try to change the way things are. This is especially true if we live in relatively comfortable circumstances.

A recent front-page *Chicago Tribune* article told the story of a group of people who could very easily have isolated themselves from others, who had the means to ignore the poor, but chose not to. While they knew that even with their wealth and power they could not right every wrong in the world, they could shine their light in their corner of it.

Families from Kenilworth, a suburb on the city's North Shore, are helping to build a new charter school in Englewood, a poverty-stricken South Side neighborhood. The North Shore is known as a wealthy area of Chicago, and Kenilworth is one of the wealthiest suburbs in the country. Many residents of such places tend to be a bit isolationist in their thinking. Not these folks.

After a few Kenilworth residents met Paul Adams III, a well-known educator who was launching a new charter school in Englewood, they decided to help. Kenilworth has only about eight hundred homes and only one public elementary school, and word of the project quickly spread around the small suburb. According to the *Tribune* article, "Before long, the Providence Englewood Charter School became the cause of the moment in Kenilworth, with families lining up to pledge at least $25,000 each—more than the median annual income in Englewood."

The families didn't stop there. They volunteered to clean the school building over Labor Day weekend so it could open on time. They made plans to keep visiting the school, donating supplies and building relation-ships with the families whose children will attend.

"I was raised with the idea, to whom much is given, much is expected. We are all huge supporters of education. It is the future," the *Tribune* quoted Kenilworth resident Denise Nash as saying. Nash and a neighbor, Frank Techar (who just happens to be the former chief executive officer of Harris Bankcorp), helped launch the project.

While the *Tribune* didn't mention faith as a motive, Nash was paraphrasing Luke 12:48, in which Jesus told his followers, "From everyone who has been given much, much will be demanded; and from the one who has been entrusted with much, much more will be asked."

The article didn't mention whether anyone in this group claims to be a Christian. They certainly are acting the way Christians ought to, and their story is inspiring. They are helping those kids and serving as great role models for the rest of us. Their involvement spoke to the residents of Englewood, telling them without words, "You matter; you are important enough to warrant our time and attention and investment." That's valuing people. I would guess that the experience had to spiritually form everyone involved.

I want to be like this group from Kenilworth — eager to help others. I want to see needs and meet them, motivated not by guilt or "shoulds" but by my hunger for God, my deep desire to walk humbly with him.

"God comes to us not as food but as hunger, not as presence but as distance felt, not as fulfillment but as longing, not as love consummated but as desire enkindled," John Kirvan writes in his book *God Hunger*. "God does not answer our questions but floods our souls with ever-expanding mystery. God does not soothe that 'old ache' but deepens it. God does not open the door but prompts us to go on knocking. For our hunger is a joyful longing. Our hunger is God made present."[20] Kirvan also quotes C. S. Lewis as saying, "God gives his gifts where he finds the vessel empty enough to receive them."

Very few of us in the West know what it means to be hungry — more than just mildly hungry because we skipped breakfast or ate a light lunch. Jesus, and many of his listeners, had likely experienced physical hunger. They knew what it means to get by on very few resources. Jesus and his followers were also first-century Jews and so most likely made a practice of fasting. They regularly went without food for a whole day or longer.

So they knew what it means to be hungry, physically. They also knew a deeper hunger. Racially and economically oppressed, they hungered for righteousness—for justice. In their gut, they longed for things to be made right. They hungered for an end to their oppression. Unless we are the victims of injustice, can we ever be hungry for justice?

Throughout the Bible, we see God's deep concern for the poor. Jesus talked a lot about money and about the importance of being generous. He said you can't serve both God and money. He knew we would be torn between wanting to help save the world and wanting to have a good time. We think there is freedom in just using our money to savor what the world has to offer. The greatest freedom comes when we control our money rather than letting it control us. How? By being generous and using it to help others.

When we have much, it is easy to ignore or forget that hunger in us—our hunger for God. When we respond to what God has asked of those who have much, and we empty ourselves, we open ourselves to the possibility of being filled by God, as the people of Kenilworth did.

The hard part is, What if you don't live in Kenilworth? What if you can't write a check for two hundred and fifty dollars, let alone twenty-five thousand, unless you sell your car? What if you are barely getting by in a not-so-affluent suburb or small town? You're not starving, but your budget is tight. One little unexpected expense—new brakes for the minivan, say, or a trip to the emergency room with your kid—can throw off your whole delicately balanced budget. Maybe you're surviving, but only by incurring debt. What then?

You are not alone. As I write this, the foreclosure rate in America is at an all-time high, and the percentage of income that many Americans save is actually negative. They not only don't save any money; they are slipping farther into debt each month.

One not-so-comfortable truth is that debt is sometimes a prison of our own making. I know of a couple who are both working, making six-figure salaries. They both drive newer BMWs; they own a lovely home. Despite their wealth, they are twenty thousand dollars in debt. They have the means to live comfortably, yet they chose to shackle themselves because they didn't want to drive an older Ford. That and a thousand other choices (from how much they pay for a cup of coffee to how much they spend on new clothes) have created a situation they might not have expected. Choices they thought were an exercise of their freedom actually were bars of a cage.

When we put ourselves into that prison — by living beyond our means — we miss out on the opportunity to change the world. We're restricted in what we can do to make a difference.

There's hope, though. There are countless books on how to get your finances in order. This is not one of them. My hope is to inspire you and remind you that true abundance is an inner reality. True abundance comes when we let God fill us with his Spirit, and that fills us with love, joy, peace, patience, kindness, and so on. (See Gal. 5:22–23.) Happiness does not consist of an abundance of possessions; it consists of the freedom to give away what you have.

As Christians, we have a responsibility to care for the poor. To address their spiritual needs and their physical needs. We ought to see this not as an obligation we fulfill to appease our guilt but as an opportunity to empty ourselves so that we might, as Lewis says, become vessels empty enough to receive God's gifts.

The Bible says, "If any one of you has material possessions and sees a brother or sister in need but has no pity on them, how can the love of God be in you?" (1 John 3:17). Jesus said, "Blessed are those who hunger and thirst for righteousness, for they will be filled" (Matt. 5:6). If we want to be people who make a difference, we will hunger and thirst for righteousness. We will want righteousness (which in the Bible is always linked with justice) in our gut, down deep.

What do I hunger for? What do I long for? God made this world, and the good things in it are a gift from him. How do I live my days? Am I hungry for the wrongs of this world to be made right?

It's not just a question of whether I will spend the afternoon at the shopping mall or serving at the soup kitchen. A subtler, more provocative question is, Where do my thoughts run? What do I want? When I'm at the mall, am I wanting everything there, or just buying a pair of jeans to replace the pair that I have, ahem, outgrown? When I'm at the soup kitchen, do I look at the "least of these" and see the face of Jesus? Am I caring for God's people, or am I feeling pride at my own nobleness, at the incredible lengths I'll go to be charitable?

Regardless of our motives, unless we live within our means, it's hard to give practical help. So perhaps the first step to generosity is frugality.

Compassion Step

Do you live within your means? Does your income exceed your expenditures? If not, what could you do to change that? How could you cut back on your spending, not just for the sake of being frugal but to give yourself the freedom to be generous?

Community Step

The group in Kenilworth decided to pool their resources and make a difference while building long-term relationships. As a group, could you do something similar, even if it is on a smaller scale? Last week you brainstormed about how you might help someone in need. Continue that process by choosing a project and planning specifics. Perhaps you will want to provide groceries and clothes to a needy family, not just once but on an ongoing basis. Or find a teacher who is working hard in an under-resourced school and provide books and supplies for her. Be creative, and plan specific steps. Assign specific tasks (including further research) to group members.

week 13

seeing

O ne of the barriers to becoming a woman who makes a difference is simply this: we don't want to. In many ways, we would like to stay blind and small, like baby mice. We don't realize how fulfilling, how thrilling, being a difference maker can be. Jesus invites us to be people who see and then act. When we do so, our very desires are changed.

"I once was blind, but now I see," proclaims the old hymn. What was it that miraculously gave us vision? Grace.

The Bible talks a lot about seeing. We can be physically blind or spiritually blind. The Bible offers many examples of both. Often those who are physically blind are more perceptive. Our own self-absorption and rebellion blinds us; truth opens our eyes. Jesus said that one reason he came was to give sight to the blind.

In Luke 4 we read the story of Jesus standing up to read Scripture at his home synagogue in Nazareth. Everyone knew him there only as Joseph and Mary's son, now a local carpenter. For the thirty or so years he'd lived there, he'd been a blue-collar worker in a poor village. One Sabbath, Jesus went to synagogue, as he always did. They handed him the scroll, and he read these verses from Isaiah:

> *The Spirit of the Lord is on me,*
> *because he has anointed me*
> *to proclaim good news to the poor.*
> *He has sent me to proclaim freedom for the prisoners*
> *and recovery of sight for the blind,*
> *to release the oppressed,*
> *to proclaim the year of the Lord's favor.*
>
> Luke 4:18–19

He then boldly proclaimed, "Today this scripture is fulfilled in your hearing." At first people were amazed, wondering how this could be. They were awed by his words. Then Jesus continued to speak, accusing them, essentially, of blindness. They were blind to who he was. His words infuriated the crowd, and they attempted to kill him. Somehow he simply walked away untouched.

Throughout his ministry, Jesus often healed people, including the blind. He never healed anyone who didn't want to be healed. Those who acknowledged their blindness received sight. The Christian faith is a journey in which God increasingly improves our vision. One in which we learn to see. Sometimes the first step is asking God not for vision but for the *desire* to ask for vision, which comes only to those who acknowledge their blindness.

When God called Saul, a man who had dedicated his life to persecuting Christians, to be his messenger, he first physically blinded him, knocking him off his horse. The thing is, Saul was already blind—spiritually. Like most of us when we are spiritually blind, he thought he knew and saw everything. He was a man, he thought, with a vision: to stamp out this heresy called Christianity. I know that in many areas of my life, I live with that kind of blindness, oblivious to my lack of vision.

God has some strange ways of changing the world. You'd think he would have selected one of Jesus' followers—say, one of the disciples who had walked with him during his life—to be his "chosen instrument to carry my name before the Gentiles and their kings and before the people of Israel" (Acts 9:15 NIV). Instead he chose a man known for killing Christ followers. He reformed an anti-Christian terrorist. It seems like a crazy plan. God opened his eyes, gave him a new name, and everything changed.

Likewise, God chooses you and me—imperfect, fragile, fallible human beings—to communicate his love. People see the pain and suffering in the world and ask, Why doesn't God do something? Doesn't he see what is going on? God's method, crazy as it may seem, is to use ordinary people, even very unlikely people, to do his work. So the answer to this question is yes, God does see—through your eyes. He wants to do something—through you.

You can read Saul's story in Acts 8 and 9. Eventually God sent another believer to Saul to heal him of his blindness. Here's what happened: "Then Ananias went to the house and entered it. Placing his hands on Saul, he said, 'Brother Saul, the Lord—Jesus, who appeared to you on the road as you were coming here—has sent me so that you may see again and be filled with the Holy Spirit.' Immediately, something like scales fell from Saul's eyes, and he could see again. He got up and was baptized, and after taking some food, he regained his strength" (Acts 9:17–19).

Have you ever had a moment when something like scales fell from your eyes? When you saw truth in a way that you had never seen before? And you said, "Oh, now I get it." And that felt good, for about thirty seconds. Until you realized that seeing more clearly meant you had a responsibility, maybe even a moral obligation, to do something, even if you were not yet sure what that something was.

The Christian faith, a faith that makes a difference, calls us to see with new vision. Jesus says when we pry the plank of hypocrisy and judgment out of our eye, we will "see clearly" to help others. (See Matt. 7:1–5.) What does it mean to "see" someone? Not just to be vaguely aware of them, as some sort of distraction, but to see them?

In Luke 7 the Bible tells the story of a sinful woman who came to Simon the Pharisee's house, interrupting a dinner party with her tears and perfume. What did Jesus say to his host (who was silently judging her)? "Do you *see* this woman?" (v. 44, emphasis mine). He goes on to point out all the common courtesies Simon has *overlooked*. He points out Simon's spiritual blindness. Then he contrasts it with the true repentance and spiritual maturity of the woman. He takes the lowest person in the social hierarchy and makes her a role model for the one who thought himself the highest on that ladder.

And I can feel pretty smug about Simon and how judgmental he is, until Jesus gently helps me to see that I can easily act just like the Pharisees — proud, certain of my grasp of truth, a wee bit superior.

Jesus recently has been challenging me to see even more clearly. In 1 John 3:17, the Bible says, "If any one of you has material possessions and sees a brother or sister in need but has no pity on them, how can the love of God be in you?" This is not a statement of condemnation; it's just a question. In fact, a few verses later John says we need not let our hearts condemn us. It is a question with a challenge. Do we see the underresourced of the world? In our neighborhoods? Or do we work very hard to stay blind to their plight? I think one of the scariest prayers you can pray is, "Help me to see more clearly." God only knows what he might show you.

This might have something to do with why we want, in some ways, to remain small and blind. If we see, we must act. Growing spiritually means seeing more clearly and acting on that vision. The Bible says this about the process of growth: "When I was a child, I talked like a child, I thought like a child, I reasoned like a child. When I became a man, I put the ways of childhood behind me. For now we see only a reflection as in a mirror; then we shall see face to face. Now I know in part; then I shall know fully, even as I am fully known" (1 Cor. 13:11–12).

We don't see clearly here on this earth. Our spiritual vision is like looking in a faulty mirror. Or as the King James Version so poetically puts it, "we see through a glass, darkly." While we can't see perfectly, we still can see, with ever-increasing clarity. "Whenever anyone turns to the Lord, the veil is taken away. Now the Lord is Spirit, and where the Spirit of the Lord is, there is freedom. And we, who with unveiled faces contemplate the Lord's glory, are being transformed into his image with ever-increasing glory, which comes from the Lord, who is the Spirit" (2 Cor. 3:16–18).

God's power is flowing, like electricity. The Holy Spirit is around us and in us, like the air we breathe. God is omnipresent, which is a theological term that means that he is here, there, and everywhere. His power is everywhere, and his love is everywhere. We can receive it.

All of that is great. We can plug into his power, like a lamp. And shine. What if we could receive God's love and power and grace and then be a conduit that others could plug into as well? Like, say, a string of Christmas lights that not only provides light but also passes along the power to the strings connected to it? What if God's power flowed not just into us but also through us?

When we truly see, when the scales fall from our eyes, we become willing to be a conduit for grace—willing not just to receive it but to let it flow through us.

I have material possessions. I see plenty of my brothers and sisters in need. I cannot meet every need. I can do this: I can listen to the voice of love and obey it. I can be willing to let God's love flow through me to even one person he brings across my path. I can let go of some of the resources (not just material but spiritual as well) that God has flowed into my life and let them flow through my hands to help others.

Compassion Step

Read all of 1 John 3, focusing special attention on verses 17 and 18. What do you think it means to love "with actions and in truth"? Ask God to open your eyes, to help you see where you can go or what you can do to more clearly see your brother or sister in need. Make a list of very specific actions that you can take to help those in need. Then start doing the things on your list—one at a time.

Community Step

How can you help each other to see more clearly? Two weeks ago, you brainstormed ways to pool your resources to help someone. Last week, you prayed about and then selected one project of those you discussed and started figuring out details. This week take action. Perhaps you will provide food for a family in need, collect supplies and used books for a teacher in an underresourced school, or engage in another project God has put on your heart. Have each person in the group get involved in the task of showing God's love in a tangible way. When you serve others, try to do so in a way that does not seem condescending. Make it a goal to uphold the dignity of those you serve. You are not committing to this long-term at this point. Your group may choose more than one project, but do them one at a time so that you don't spread yourself too thin.

part 2

compassion grows
in community

bigger

there's a wonderful scene in C. S. Lewis's *Prince Caspian*, the second of his Chronicles of Narnia books. Lucy, the heroine, is reunited with Aslan the Lion, the Christ figure in the stories.

> "Aslan, Aslan. Dear Aslan," sobbed Lucy. "At last."
>
> The great beast rolled over on his side so that Lucy fell, half sitting and half lying between his front paws. He bent forward and just touched her nose with his tongue. His warm breath came all round her. She gazed up into the large, wise face.
>
> "Welcome, child," he said.
>
> "Aslan," said Lucy, "you're bigger."
>
> "That is because you are older, little one," answered he.
>
> "Not because you are?"
>
> "I am not. But every year you grow, you will find me bigger."[21]

I want to grow and find Jesus bigger. As John the Baptist said, "He must become greater; I must become less" (John 3:30). When that happens, and Jesus gets bigger, we realize how little we actually know of him. Then there comes a point, as we are growing in Christlikeness, when we discover that the next step in getting to know Jesus is to begin acting like him. Introspection must be balanced with initiative, contemplation with action. As Lucy's conversation with Aslan continues, he challenges her to follow him, even though it will be very difficult. Her encounter with Aslan is not just for her to enjoy but also to strengthen her to obey him and to help others in that obedience.[22]

Spiritual formation is misunderstood in some circles. It is not "advanced Christianity." Nor is it, as some alarmist conservative website writers seem to think, some strange twist on New Age philosophies. It is simply the forming, via various influences, of our spirits, our inner selves. It is spiritual growth and development. It happens, like a child's growth from infant to adult, whether we intend it to or not. Every person's spirit has been formed—by their upbringing, by their experiences, by their choices—whether or not they are cognizant of it. Dallas Willard explains so well, "Spiritual formation, without regard to any specific religious context or tradition, is the process by which the human spirit or will is given a definite 'form' or character.... Terrorists as well as saints are the outcome of spiritual formation. Their spirits or hearts have been formed. Period."[23]

Christian spiritual formation, then, has to do with inviting Jesus into that inevitable process, letting him form our spirits to be like his. Our openness to God's work in us allows him to change us. As Paul wrote to the church at Galatia, "I am again in the pains of childbirth until Christ is formed in you" (Gal. 4:19). Just as what we feed our body and how we care for it or exercise it will influence the form it takes (fit, flabby, or otherwise), the spiritual food we take in, the spiritual exercises we engage in, will affect the shape of our souls.

We cooperate with God in this process. "Do not conform any longer to the pattern of this world, but be transformed by the renewing of your mind," the Bible says in Romans 12:2 (NIV).

Robert Mulholland adds, "Spiritual formation is the process of being formed into the image of Christ for the sake of others."[24]

And that caveat—for the sake of others—matters. It's easy to allow a deeper, more introspective faith to take you too far inward, to the point where you can become isolated and self-absorbed. Ironically, this takes you farther from God. Richard Rohr, a Franciscan priest, has written several books on spiritual formation. He is the founder of the Center for Action and Contemplation, which, according to its website, is a "training/ formation center that would serve as a place of discernment and growth for activists and those interested in social service ministries." One of the center's core principles is, "We need a contemplative mind in order to do compassionate work."[25] As we reflect and meditate on Scripture, we notice God's overarching concern for the poor as it is expressed repeatedly through the Word.

So far in this book, we've focused on learning about the importance of nurturing our relationship with God, on building our confidence that he indeed loves us. We've focused on our worth in God's eyes and learning to live confidently in light of that love.

At this point, we lift our eyes and begin to look outward. Strengthened for the task by a deep knowledge of our value, we turn our attention to our neighbor. So in this the second quarter of the book (and of the year, if you're reading a chapter per week), we will focus on loving the people around us.

When we start to look beyond ourselves, the first people we see are our families, by which I mean the people we live with—our spouses, children, or in some cases roommates. We see the people in our churches, our workplaces, and those who live in the homes or apartments near us—our physical neighbors. So we'll look at how we can love the people we're sort of stuck with.

If you are being formed into the image of Christ, you will begin to live it out in the world. We don't become more like Jesus just so that we can feel good about ourselves or pride ourselves on being "deep." Jesus had harsh words for the self-righteous. To be like him means to love others the way he did. Our spiritual formation ultimately is not about us but is about loving others, even if they are not easy to love. The choice between discipleship and social action is a false dichotomy. Disciples of Christ grow by taking action—obedient action.

If the goal of spiritual transformation is to become more like Jesus, then eventually we must change our actions. Thankfully, though, we don't have to do it alone. We have a very big God to help us.

As we get to know Jesus better, we will notice that he was deeply concerned for the poor. His heart reflected the heart of the Father. So if we are growing to be like him, we too must become concerned for social justice, for the plight of the poor. It is the natural progression of Christian spiritual formation.

It begins as we become aware of what we have ignored. It continues as we stop ignoring and move forward in our desire for a more complete faith. Our "concern" cannot be genuine if it is only cerebral. Just feeling badly about the plight of the poor, if it does not inspire us to action, is basically the equivalent of not caring at all. I want to cultivate my inner life, yet I cannot ignore God's command to give outward expression to that inner transformation.

A beautiful interplay exists between Christ-motivated action and Christ-centered contemplation. It's a never-ending cycle, and yet a wheel that propels us forward on our journey. We grow, and our understanding of God grows. We know Jesus better; we try to imitate him by living out his call to justice. He enables us to do more than we thought possible, to be bigger than we were before. Those actions, even if we do them imperfectly (which we will), will teach us and change us. We open ourselves up to Christ's work in us, which transforms us. As we grow, we find him bigger.

Compassion Step

Which appeals to you more, contemplation or action? Often our personalities or spiritual temperaments make one seem more preferable. How can you challenge yourself to move toward balance between the two? If you have a tendency to be contemplative, what specific steps do you plan to take this week to live out your inner reality? If you tend to favor action over introspection, spend some time in quiet reflection this week.

Community Step

Last week you engaged in a service project. As a group, talk honestly about how the project turned out. Discuss what you felt went well and what didn't. How did the people who received your help feel? What specific things did you do or say to help them keep their dignity? How did helping someone else affect you spiritually? Do you plan to stay involved with this particular project, or is it short-term? What will that require of the group? How might engaging with those in need help you to grow and help you to find God bigger in your life?

neighbor?

O ur culture has created some ways for us to have more neighbors than we ever thought possible. I have more than four hundred "friends" on Facebook, and I know many people who have over a thousand. Now, some of these folks are people I've spent time with face-to-face. Real friends. Others have read my books or are a friend of a friend of a friend. Some I haven't seen since high school. We interact only rarely, and only online. I may have met them once in my travels.

Our culture is conditioned for superficiality. We have five hundred friends, but we're lonely.

I'm an introvert. I have a limited relational capacity. I'm also not that good at remembering names. Still, I am commanded to love my neighbors. How seriously do I take that command? If I'm not sure who my neighbors are, then how can I love them?

When Jesus was asked about the most important commandment, he said that the whole law hinged on two equally important rules — love God, love your neighbor. (See Matt. 22:35 – 40.) Why is that such a high priority with God? Why do our neighbors matter so much to him? Why would he say, in essence, that part of how we love him is by loving our neighbor? That these loves are two sides of the same coin?

The Bible repeatedly exhorts us to love our neighbors as ourselves. When Jesus was on earth, an expert in Jewish law asked him, "What must I do to inherit eternal life?" Now, if he was an expert in the Scriptures, he probably had an opinion on what he needed to do. He was asking Jesus, "What do *you* say I must do?" Jesus answered that he should love God and love his neighbor. The text says that the man wanted to justify himself, so he asked Jesus to clarify. "Who is my neighbor?" he said. Jesus responded by telling the story of the good Samaritan (Luke 10:25 – 37), which is the story of cross-cultural compassion with a twist: it's the person of lower social standing offering help to the person who hates him. It would be like a black man in the rural South of the 1950s stopping to help a Ku Klux Klan member who'd been beaten up and left for dead.

I don't think Jesus meant that "your neighbor" means only people of other races or people you hate. Your neighbor is anyone who comes across your path. Anyone you live with or live near, work with, worship beside, volunteer with — they are a neighbor you are called to love. Our families, our church communities, our coworkers, and the people who live nearby — all are people who matter very much to God, and people we are called to love.

Two religious leaders passed by and didn't help the man, but a Samaritan — whom the Jews in Jesus' audience despised — helped him with excessive generosity. After telling this parable about love in action, Jesus asked the religious leader, "Which of these three do you think was a neighbor to the man who fell into the hands of robbers?"

The Jewish scholar hated Samaritans so much that he couldn't even bring himself to say "the Samaritan." Jews of Jesus' day would not even use the same dishes as Samaritans did, so deeply ingrained was their racism. So the man carefully replied, "The one who had mercy on him."

Jesus said, "Go and do likewise."

And when Jesus said, "Go and do likewise," he meant so much more than simply loving your enemies or being "tolerant" of those who are different than you. Since he was speaking to a Jewish audience, it's entirely possible that he meant, "Realize that you need others, even those you feel superior to. Accept the mercy of God through unexpected people or means. Admit your own insufficiency."

Mark Buchanan offers this insightful comment on Jesus' parable: "The neighbor is the one *who has mercy*. Did you catch that? My neighbor isn't someone I have mercy upon — *it's someone who has mercy on me.* Which means I'm the one in need of mercy. I'm the one in the ditch.... *Go and do likewise.* Go discover how desperate, naked and left for dead you really are.... What must I do to inherit eternal life? Simple: Realize I'm in a ditch. Realize that I'm doomed unless my Neighbor loves me. Realize I need mercy as much as I need to give it."[26]

What if loving your neighbors is not only for their benefit but also for yours? Part of loving your neighbors is letting them love you, and being humble enough to let them know that you are imperfect, in fact a mess, but you've been rescued by God's generous love.

Who is your neighbor? It's your spouse, your children, your parents, your siblings. According to this story, it is also (although not exclusively) people you feel superior to, people you don't like. It's the guy in the cube next to yours at work, your boss, the people you manage. It's the people you sit next to in worship, the people you argue with in church committee meetings. It's the people who live in the apartment above you or the house next door or the one down the street. It's the people who volunteer on the PTA with you. It's the guy you buy coffee and a newspaper from at the convenience store.

What if Jesus is asking us to love these people and to let them love us? To receive God's love and wisdom through them?

You may think you have chosen to live in a certain place, to work at a certain job, to join a particular church. Or you may wish you lived, worked, or worshiped somewhere else. God knows what he's doing. No matter where you are, it is not an accident. God wants you to look around and notice people right in front of you, who need to experience the love of God through you. These are the neighbors he has given you. God wants to teach you things — maybe like patience, kindness, gentleness — through them. He is able to love you through the people you'd least expect. Over the next few weeks, we are going to look at each of these groups in greater depth and explore what it means to be loving, what it means to shine your light, in each of these circles.

Compassion Step

Is there anyone in your life whom you strongly dislike? A boss, coworker, family member? Read the story of the good Samaritan in Luke 10:25 – 37. Insert that person's name into the story in place of the phrase "a Samaritan." What is Jesus saying to you through this text about this relationship? Journal about your thoughts.

Community Step

Over the last few weeks, your group has begun putting your inner faith into action. Those in need are your neighbors, and while you are to love them, you cannot physically meet every need in the world. What challenges did you face as you have offered help? How did it affect you spiritually? Pray together as a group for those people you are helping. Be sure that everyone in the group gets involved so that you can encourage each other and share the burden.

why?

Why did Jesus tell us to love our neighbors? Was his goal to change our neighbors, or to change us? Did he want us to get to know people so that we could evangelize them? What is the point of loving our neighbors? What do we expect to happen as a result?

I happen to live in a very friendly neighborhood. I have lived here a long time. Plenty of families with young kids live on our street, so my children have friends their age nearby. Most of my neighbors are friendly people. Be assured, we have a few cranky folks around here too. (I am not naming names!)

Because I have known my neighbors for fifteen years or so, I have friends who know me well. Who have seen me at my best and my worst. There's good and bad to that, for sure. I've come to realize that here is where I am called to be. These are the neighbors I am called to love and to let love me.

Why? When we decide to love others (and loving others sometimes requires an act of will), we are formed spiritually. We become more loving people. By obeying God, we become more obedient.

While we don't have to earn God's favor, he does ask us to obey him by caring for others. God's Spirit is at work in us to produce good things, to make us more like Jesus, to transform us from self-absorbed, sinful people to new creatures who bear fruit that reflects God's Spirit within us. The Bible says, "The fruit of the Spirit is love, joy, peace, patience, kindness, goodness, faithfulness, gentleness and self-control. Against such things there is no law" (Gal. 5:22–23). Not the fruit of our own efforts, the fruit (or result, or product) of the Spirit. The *fruit* of the Spirit means the *result* of God's Spirit working in us. Notice that all of these characteristics are difficult to demonstrate by yourself. They're more evident in the context of relationship. For example, it is not that challenging to be patient by yourself. It's when you have to be patient with other people (say, your two-year-old) that the challenge—and the resulting growth—occurs.

Your neighborhood is unique, and it may not be like mine. No matter where you live, you're still called to love your neighbors. The way to begin might be as simple as learning their names.

Maybe you're shy or just busy. If you don't interact with your neighbors, take some simple steps to start. How can you love people you don't even know?

The next time you see one of your neighbors outside, walk up and say hello. Introduce yourself—even if you say, "I know we've been neighbors a long time, but we've never met." Ask their name. That's it. You don't have to invite them to dinner; you don't have to bake them a cake.

And for heaven's sake, please, try to avoid overwhelming them by asking if they know Jesus. Even if you think you'd like to pray for them, don't mention that on first meeting. Save that conversation for another day. I'm all for sharing your faith; I just think you have to build relationships first. Jesus told his followers, "Let your light shine before others, that they may see your good deeds and glorify your Father in heaven" (Matt. 5:16). Let people see your faith lived out. Shining is not, apparently, only about giving a verbal witness. With our words, we often find ourselves pulled into arguments. Our goal seems to be to recruit people or to change them rather than just to love them. God calls us to love people so that *he* can change them. Just as important, so that he can change us.

I've lived in my neighborhood a long time—for seven years in one house, and now nine years in our current home, just two blocks from the first one. We moved here because the area was close to church, was close to our jobs (at the time), had good schools, and was affordable. After sixteen years, something interesting has happened. I've moved slowly into a sense of being called to be here. Even though the winters are long and brutal, and suburbia is not the most culturally rich environment, I'm beginning to see that God has put me here to love the people in my neighborhood. To see that they (like me) may have enough materially but are still needy—spiritually, relationally, emotionally.

Now, some of you are waiting for me to say that you should love your neighbors so you can lead them to Christ. While leading people to Christ is good, seeing them as an evangelistic project is bad. It just is. People can smell you a mile away, and it's not pretty.

Have you ever met a rep for a multilevel marketing company? Whether they are selling vitamins or soap doesn't matter. The products are different; the pitch is the same: they want to share an opportunity with you because they care so much about you. They want you to live the dream. It soon becomes obvious that they are interested in you only as a potential underling in their sales structure. Do they really care about you, or are they just trying to get you into Amway? A lot of folks see Christians this way: recruiters for Jesus. If we come at relationships thinking we have all the answers and can fix others, people will run away.

So what is the goal? The goal is simply to love. To shine the light of Christ in such a way that people are drawn to that light. We sometimes worry so much about getting people to "accept Christ" that we forget what it is that they are accepting. They are accepting his love, grace, and forgiveness. If we don't show them love, grace, and forgiveness, why should they believe?

Just love people. That means both giving and accepting love, as we discussed last week. When we let our neighbors care for us, when we admit we haven't got it all figured out, it draws others to us. Before we can share our ideas, including those about faith, we have to be willing to listen — to hear our neighbors' ideas.

It requires a change in perspective to see saying hello to our neighbors, greeting them by name, as an act of Christian hospitality. If we run ahead of God, aren't we saying that we don't trust him? If we want to be women who make a difference, we might as well start where we are and love the people God has put in our path.

Compassion Step

How many of your neighbors do you know by name? This week, introduce yourself to two neighbors you don't yet know. Pray for an opportunity to at least say hello. Once you've met them, pray for them regularly so that you remember their names. If it helps, write their names in your journal.

Community Step

Discuss the following as a group: How many of your neighbors do you know? What are some ways you can build relationships in your neighborhood? How does it feel to love people without worrying about witnessing to them? How has building relationships in your neighborhood affected your relationship with God?

Then talk about the service project you've been involved in over the last few weeks. How has serving together affected the depth of relationships within your group? In what ways, if any, has it created conflict? How did those you served respond?

family?

i f loving your neighbors means loving the people God has put in your path, then certainly the neighbors we are to love include our immediate and extended families. What would happen to your family relationships if you thought about extending compassion within your home? Our families need to be our first love priorities; if we are called to love others, then the others we live with must be included.

For many of us, the people in our own houses are hardest to love. At home, we let down our guard. As a result, we're not always on our best behavior. When we are in secure relationships, we sometimes take for granted the love of our spouses, children, parents.

The community within your home has a chance to bless your family and to provide an example to those in your neighborhood. I'm not talking about keeping up appearances; I'm talking about cultivating a genuine respect for your family. If you tell your neighbors you're a Christian but they hear you complaining about your spouse's shortcomings or see you screaming at your kids every day, they may wonder why your faith doesn't seem to make you any different from anyone else. I'm not suggesting being fake; it's healthy to admit having struggles. Can we be real without being bitter? It's a fine line to walk.

Throughout the Bible, there is a refrain that prophets and poets use to describe God: "The LORD is gracious and compassionate, slow to anger and rich in love" (Ps. 145:8; see also Pss. 86:15 and 103:8)..

I hold tightly to this comforting description of my heavenly Father, which tells me what I can expect and what I ought to emulate. I meditate on this refrain to remind myself that I ought to freely give what I have freely received: grace, compassion, love. God has, so to speak, a long fuse: incredibly patient, he is slow to become angry. I want to be like that.

The problem is that I am often hurried. I speak first and think second, which means words somehow bypass the filters that would keep me from hurting others. Because of my weakness, I need God to be slow to anger and rich in love. That very love calls me to be more than I think I am capable of.

So the other day, I came home from a run, inspired to write about this verse. As I ran, it had come to mind, and I'd thought of what it means to love this way. Just as I am training my body by running, I need to train myself in godliness, the Bible says. To be gracious and compassionate, slow to anger, and rich in love. As I jogged, I'd been singing those words, praising God. Inspiration poured like sweat, sentences forming in my brain as I stretched for a minute in the front yard.

Except that when I walked inside the house, my husband picked a fight. Interrupted my holy moment, accused me. Never mind about what; it's so ridiculous that you would not believe me if I told you.

My response was neither gracious nor compassionate. I accused right back, blamed and pouted. Told him he didn't appreciate how many responsibilities I have, including writing this great chapter on grace and compassion, which his intrusion had so rudely interrupted.

Slow to anger? Not exactly. Warp speed to anger is more like it. (I got there so fast, I shot right past irony without noticing.)

Remember, I had been thinking about being slow to anger just minutes before I walked in the door, pondering the wise words I would write about it, when my husband started getting on my case.

I live with people who are sometimes hard to deal with. This is not my fault.

I'm richer in excuses than in love, apparently.

The first neighbors God calls us to love is the family he's put us into. Often, living with others allows you to see the flaws that they can hide in public—although it also allows them to see your flaws. Healthy families extend grace and compassion to each other. Our homes are the places where we first learn to practice compassion. If we can't be kind to our children or our spouses, how can we be kind to strangers or neighbors?

This biblical description of God contains four essentially parallel characteristics. Gracious = compassionate = slow to anger = abounding in love. These four aspects of God's character are all interrelated. A compassionate person is gracious. A person who is rich in love will be slow to anger.

The prophet Joel declares, "Rend your heart and not your garments. Return to the LORD your God, for he is gracious and compassionate, slow

to anger and abounding in love, and he relents from sending calamity"
(Joel 2:13).

Rend your heart? Break your heart? Rip it open?

What does it mean to rend your heart? And how is that connected
with God's grace and compassion?

The prophet sets up a contrast between our inner reality (our hearts)
and our outer appearance (our garments). Change your heart, your inner
self, and don't just make a show of false humility. Does your sin break
your heart? Do you feel heartbroken because you've rejected God's gracious love? Or do you defiantly go your own way?

It took me a while, frankly, to see how my response to my husband
escalated the situation. It was almost as if God had been warning me—
get ready, you're going to need to extend grace here in a second. The song
in my head was God speaking, reminding me of what he's like, what he
wants me, his daughter, to be like. Unfortunately, I didn't listen.

Eventually it hit me: my husband is my neighbor. He occupies the
closest circle of relationships in my life. I need to love him, even when it's
difficult. I'm not absolving my husband, but I can't change him. I can
change only me. I can rend my heart. I can break open my stubborn-
ness. I can choose to be slow to anger, even when the people around me
are not.

As God tells his people through another of his prophets, "I desire
mercy, not sacrifice" (Hos. 6:6; see also Matt. 12:7).

So often, in religious traditions, the call to repentance comes with a
warning about God's anger or wrath. To repent means to turn around,
to change direction. The Lord's call to return to him, or to repent, comes
with a reminder of his compassion. We ought to repent not because God
is vengeful but because he is *gracious.*

Likewise, Romans 2:4 says, "Do you show contempt for the riches of
his kindness, forbearance and patience, not realizing that God's kindness
is intended to lead you to repentance?"

God's kindness leads us to repentance. In my relationship with my
husband, I am tempted to wait until *he* shows kindness before I will be
gracious and compassionate. What if I were to follow God's example?
What will happen if I initiate graciousness?

Will my own kindness, my own imitation of God, lead others to
change as well? It may, but even if it does not, I will have been obedient,

and obedience helps us to grow. God shows us how to live, not to avoid conflict but to be difference makers. To be slow to anger does not mean you repress or evade the truth. Rather than demanding apologies, imitate God, who uses kindness to lead us to repentance. Let your kindness, likewise, lead your family to reconciliation.

After urging us to rend our hearts, why does Joel remind us, in the next sentence, of God's grace and compassion, his abundant love, his slowness to anger? If we expose our hearts, if we rend our hearts, they are open to God's compassion and grace.

The psalmist tells us, "The LORD is close to the brokenhearted and saves those who are crushed in spirit" (Ps. 34:18). A few verses earlier David writes, "Turn from evil and do good; seek peace and pursue it" (Ps. 34:14).

Compassion sometimes begins with a broken heart. How can we be gracious unless we have experienced grace? How can we be compassionate unless we have felt the compassion of God?

The first circle of neighbors we are called to love live under our own roof. Whether you live with your spouse, your children, your parents, or roommates, God has put you in this situation to tutor you in love. Such love demands a lot from us, and the only way we can love our closest neighbors — our families — is to trust God to teach us how. We must be willing to admit that it's hard and let God love our families through us.

Compassion Step

Read Psalm 145:8. Is this description of God true, in your experience? When have you seen God's compassion? What does it mean to be slow to anger? Are you slow to anger? How might these two characteristics be connected in your life? If you could be slower to anger, would you become more compassionate? How can you begin to practice compassion in your family?

Community Step

This week take a break from serving outside of your home, and focus on loving the people you live with (your spouse, children, roommate — whoever shares your home). As a group, discuss the following: (1) How did the family you grew up in handle conflict? Did people yell, or did they stuff their emotions? (2) How did your family communicate love to one another? Did they say "I love you" or use their actions? Were they physically affectionate? Forgiving? (3) What was your role in your family? Were you the troublemaker? Did you try to smooth things over for others? How does that play out for you as an adult? (4) How does your experience in your family of origin affect your family dynamics now?

body

i sat in a suburban living room, talking with Joe and Laura,[27] a young couple who led a couples' small group for our church. As their coach, I had visited their group to watch the dynamics and to offer encouragement and help to the leaders. Joe put forth effort, but he needed to work on listening. His wife was much more effective at facilitating discussion. While Joe would simply read the assigned discussion questions and wait for everyone to answer, Laura drew people into conversation by listening empathetically, by asking probing questions, and even with her body language.

"You could learn a lot about leadership by watching your wife," I told Joe. Although he was the official leader of the group, Laura was its true shepherd. We talked about what it means to make your group a safe place, what it means to value people, and how Joe perhaps needed to work on a few things. These were not easy words to say, and in fact Joe was resistant to my coaching that day. His pride, his traditional view of men's and women's roles, made it hard for him to hear me. I wondered if I had been too harsh.

A few days later, Joe and Laura knocked on my door, with their arms around each other's waists, and there was a light in their eyes that I had not seen before. They thanked me for telling them the hard truth and said that my remarks had prompted some deep conversation and an apology. Apparently the group was not the only place where Joe had missed the value of his wife's contribution. God had been working on them, and my coaching had helped not only their group but also their marriage. I felt a sense of joyful relief that I had spoken the truth in love and that, eventually, those words had brought about growth and change in these leaders.

For years, my husband, Scot, and I led couples' groups, which would meet to study the Bible or another book and to build friendships. Eventually, we began coaching other leaders, which involved training, mentoring, and encouraging. Serving as a volunteer coach was a way for me to love the people in my church, to contribute to its growth. It was sometimes scary to confront, but it was gratifying to see people grow.

Coaching provided a chance for us to hone our leadership skills as we helped leaders deal with conflicts that would inevitably arise. Almost every group found that the first few weeks or even months would be a sort of honeymoon phase during which group members were getting to know each other, enjoying being together, building community. But then they would hit a place we referred to as "the tunnel of chaos," where conflict, misunderstanding, and more would begin to take their toll. The only way out of the tunnel was to push through it. The toughest part of coaching was urging leaders not to give up when they found themselves there, helping them to develop strategies to guide their group through this phase and to see how they needed to change in order to be better leaders. At the other end of the tunnel, they'd discover deeper community, forged in the difficult trenches of resolving conflict.

Christians are not immune to conflict. In fact, divorces, lawsuits, and general snippiness are just as common among Christians as they are among those who do not profess faith. Jesus told us to be peacemakers, to love our enemies, to turn the other cheek. We're not so good at that sometimes.

This is nothing new. Paul's New Testament letters often addressed points of conflict within the church. In 1 Corinthians 6, for example, he wrote about lawsuits between believers, as well as sexual immorality that apparently had become a problem in the community. He encouraged unity and respect between people.

Jesus told his disciples to love each other. He said, "My command is this: Love each other as I have loved you. Greater love has no one than this: to lay down one's life for one's friends" (John 15:12–13). He also prayed for us, mostly that we would live in "oneness" and "unity" (see John 17:20–26).

We can stand back and offer commentary, saying that the church has fallen short of these ideals. Or we can become part of the solution. Perhaps the neighbors we are called to love include our neighbors in the pew.

A church is not a building or even a program. It is a body of believers who come together to worship and serve God—in part by serving each other. "There should be no division in the body," Paul wrote, adding, "Now you are the body of Christ, and each one of you is a part of it" (1 Cor. 12:25, 27).

Paul followed this comment with a list of various spiritual gifts. When we accept God's free gift of salvation and adoption, we receive one or more spiritual gifts, divine enablements to serve the body. We're called to use those gifts to strengthen and encourage the body of Christ, the church.[28]

Jesus' disciples (I mean you and me) love God by loving others. One place we find "others" is within the church. Loving them can take many forms. It may be as simple as forgiving others who wrong us. It may mean noticing someone who comes to a service alone and kindly welcoming them. It also means serving where we have gifts and passions (as I do by coaching) and being willing to keep serving there even when it becomes difficult. Just being in a group can be an opportunity to love and serve.

During a heavy storm, my friend Tahna's basement flooded. Overwhelmed by the task of trying to pump out the water and clean up the house, she and her husband called their small group from church. Within the hour, the whole group was at their home—bringing a generator to run a pump, hauling wet and dirty furniture out of their basement. My friend's neighbors were amazed. They asked, Who are these people who are willing to come and clean up a mess? And Tahna was able to say, These people are my church. Their generous help was a clear witness of God's love and inspired the neighbors to begin to help each other. Their love changed the neighborhood.

That is what Jesus was talking about when he said, "Let your light shine before others, that they may see your good deeds and glorify your Father in heaven" (Matt. 5:16), and, "By this everyone will know that you are my disciples, if you love one another" (John 13:35).

Part of how we can "witness" to the people outside of the church is to radically love the people within the church. A church should be a community of forgiven sinners who demonstrate Christlike compassion to one another. If that truly happened within the church, we wouldn't have to put on fancy programs or plan "outreach events." People would want to be a part of our community because it offers what the world does not—love, compassion, acceptance. The church could be a place not only to receive those things but also to learn how to give them to others.

What would happen if we simply began to love the people within our church? If we demonstrated Jesus' values in a radical way? Part of our "mission" is to be engaged in our church communities, while still inviting others into those communities.

I'm not saying we should get involved in every ministry our church offers. I've seen many people who get so busy for God that they burn out and get angry at God. They're often doing much more than God ever asked them to.

We are just one part of the body of Christ. No one person is the head, hands, and feet. Our job is to find out what our gifts are and where God wants us to use them. If we're part of the body, we also rely on others to serve us, even as we serve them. Jesus calls us to mutual service and submission within the body. So often when we try to do everything, we prevent others from stepping up and participating in the church—and that keeps them from the joyful experience of being a part of the body.

No church is perfect, because it is made up of imperfect people just like you and me. Those imperfections provide us with the opportunity to practice loving others as Jesus would, which sometimes means confronting and sometimes means just helping. As we practice loving like Jesus did, we become more like him. And isn't that the point of church anyway?

Compassion Step

How can you serve most effectively and joyfully in your church? Where are you serving now (if you are)? What form of service best fits your gifts and passions? What do you think God is calling you to do or be in your local church? What are some ways in which you could show compassion within your church?

Community Step

Are there people in your church who volunteer every week in the same ministry? Could they use a break or perhaps just some help? As a group, volunteer together to assist in some ministry at your church, just to give the regular volunteers a little time off. You may want to help with the children's program, help out at your food pantry, or help with another ministry. This will not be a long-term commitment, but it will be something you perhaps do one time, or occasionally, to offer respite to those who serve regularly. After you serve, talk together about how your service showed love to the people in your church.

favorites

the transition back into church in my midtwenties after I had stayed away awhile was rough. I loved the worship services, I was convicted by the preaching, but I had trouble finding a place to fit in. It was a large church. I knew a few people, and I sat with them at services. I longed for deeper friendships, so I decided I ought to make a few more connections. Toward that end, I went to a meeting of "the singles ministry."

The singles group was so large that it was divided into about a dozen smaller groups ranging in size from about twenty to as many as one hundred people. Each group tried to recruit people in a process that felt, essentially, like pledging a sorority, except that the groups were coed. I would have given up on it if not for this guy who led one of the groups. Long story short, I ended up marrying him. But I'm getting ahead of myself.

I'd gone to a meeting to find out about how to join a group, and pretty much decided I didn't want to join any of them. What I wanted, and was asking God for, was to get into a Bible study or small group with just women. I wanted community, not a place to meet men. I'd just gotten out of a relationship that had ended quite painfully, and I was ready for a nice long hiatus from dating. That very day, a single friend asked me to be part of a women's small group she was starting—an immediate answer to my frustrated prayers. The group, which was not affiliated with the official singles ministry, was going to read challenging books on spiritual growth. I jumped at the chance. In that group, I found women who had a sense of fun, possessed deep intelligence, and did not fear questions. Women who accepted me with all my flaws yet called me to follow Jesus with my whole self. Those four women and I remain friends to this day.

Anyway, occasionally I'd see that guy around church. Since I'd signed in at the meeting where he was one of the leaders, he had my number, and he was not afraid to use it. He'd call and invite me to various events with the singles ministry. Occasionally I'd say yes.

Sometimes the smaller groups met on their own; at other times they gathered with the entire group for events like concerts, dances, gym nights, retreats—whatever.

It didn't take too much social awareness to figure out that the "beautiful people" (and their hangers-on) congregated in just a few groups. Those of course became the largest groups, being made up of a celebrity core orbited by wannabes. Other groups attracted various types: studious conservatives, geeks, jocks. It was like high school all over again, except sadder and more desperate.

I don't blame the leadership of the ministry for this; it is human nature to segregate according to a social pecking order. It seems impossible to legislate against that tendency. In these cases, human nature aligns with what the Bible calls our sin nature. It was sad that it happened at church. Just as in the workplace or in school, everyone wanted to be a part of certain groups.

That guy I mentioned earlier, Scot, was coleading a group that, frankly, did not have many of the upper-tier people in it. Which I actually liked; I appreciated their kind, authentic faith. I loved their lack of pretension, their seeming indifference to social climbing. It was a ragamuffin kind of group, and it was not that big. As I got to know Scot, I thought, He's a nice guy, fairly normal. He's got a good sense of humor; he's intelligent. Why does he hang around with geeks? What's up with that?

Eventually I realized that Scot chose to do that. He could have jockeyed his way into position in a different group. He could have worked hard to try to fit in with a bigger, better group. He was smart and good-looking, yet he wasn't into games that a lot of other guys were into. In the era of Trans Ams and Cameros, he drove an Oldsmobile Delta 88, a true grandpa car if ever there was one. He didn't care, because he saw a car as transportation, not an extension of himself. I found this extremely endearing.

I loved that he chose to lead people who might not otherwise have had a place to fit in and people who weren't interested in social climbing. Even if he could not have articulated it as a twenty-three-year-old, he saw God in the geeks. This was, in part, because he had moments of geekiness himself—as we all do. He didn't much care about people's outer appearance. He was sort of drawn to the lost and wayward types. He simply didn't play favorites.

Scot saw the richness of faith that some of those young people had, even though at times it was not easy to see. I ended up hanging around with that group quite a bit, as Scot and I became friends and eventually started dating. I appreciated his lack of pretension. And I still do.

In last week's chapter, I talked about loving our neighbors in the pew. While we will find we have affinity with some people more than with others, we are called to love without favoritism.

The Bible says Christians should not show favoritism. In other words, even the poor, even the geeks, are our neighbors. The problems caused by favoritism are nothing new. Look at what James wrote to the early church: "My brothers and sisters, believers in our glorious Lord Jesus Christ must not show favoritism. Suppose someone comes into your meeting wearing a gold ring and fine clothes, and a poor person in filthy old clothes also comes in. If you show special attention to the one wearing fine clothes and say, 'Here's a good seat for you,' but say to the one who is poor, 'You stand there' or 'Sit on the floor by my feet,' have you not discriminated among yourselves and become judges with evil thoughts?" (James 2:1–4).

This seemed to me what was happening in the singles group, and what happens in a lot of churches. Those rich in social standing will separate from those with a dearth of social currency. Those who maybe are not so much financially poor as definitely challenged in the area of coolness shuffle wordlessly into different groups than the movers and shakers.

This didn't just happen then and at that church; it happens now—in neighborhoods, in churches, in ministries. There are inner circles, and not everyone is in them. There is competition between leaders to see who can have the largest group (or church) with the nicest building or the most generous donors. There are beauties, and there are geeks.

I wonder, as I've gotten older, do I show favoritism? I would say no. Truthfully, favoritism can be determined not just by who you are willing to hang around with but also by who you aspire to hang around with. While I am willing to associate with the poor through acts of charity, do I crave their company? Would I choose them as friends?

James writes, "If you really keep the royal law found in Scripture, 'Love your neighbor as yourself,' you are doing right. But if you show favoritism, you sin and are convicted by the law as lawbreakers. For whoever keeps the whole law and yet stumbles at just one point is guilty of breaking all of it" (James 2:8 – 10).

So, favoring the rich over the poor (or the beauties over the geeks) means you've violated God's law? And if you've erred on that point, you've messed up the whole thing? And in fact if you violate any of God's laws (so many of which are about treatment of the poor), you've disobeyed him completely? I wonder what our churches would look like if Christians took this verse literally.

Compassion Step

What are your aspirations socially? Be honest. Do you find yourself longing to be part of a certain crowd? Do you feel left out? Do you have any friends who are from a different social class than yours? Do you feel comfortable with people who are geekier than you? Do you seek out friends who are less popular than you? How much of your time do you spend thinking about ways to get ahead socially? Spend some time in listening prayer, asking God to speak to you about this topic.

Community Step

As a group, discuss the following: (1) Have you ever felt that you were on the outside looking in? That you were not a part of the popular crowd? What was that like? (2) What specific challenges do you encounter when you try to love people who are different from you? (3) Describe a time when you saw a situation similar to the one described in James 2:1 – 4. If that kind of thing happens in your church, what can you do to begin to change things?

enemies

t he neighborhood my family moved to when I was in the fourth grade was semirural, what might be called an "exurb" today. We lived along a river, on a wooded half-acre lot. There was a spring-fed pond down the street, where we'd ice-skate in winter. In summer we'd launch out over the green water on a thick, knotted rope and drop into its cool depths. Although my neighborhood wasn't zoned for horses, several of the kids I went to school with lived on farms or at least kept a pony in the back yard.

The move was difficult for me; I was awkward and shy and didn't make friends easily. I spent a lot of time roaming the nearby woods or perched in a tree, lost in a book. My brother and parents, on the other hand, seemed to befriend neighbors rather quickly, with one notable exception: the retired couple next door.

This couple, whose names I won't divulge, dwelt in an imposing two-story white brick house with strict black shutters, in a neighborhood of mostly brown ranch homes. Their lawn appeared to have been trimmed with nail scissors; the bricks on their curving sidewalk were precisely even in color and size. The house itself was immaculate.

Did I mention that my brother had a dirt bike? And that he and his friends liked to ride, noisily, along the river floodplain behind our house (and of course behind the neighbors' house). He'd also construct plywood jumps in the driveway and launch his bicycle over them as the neighbors peered angrily out their clean windows.

The neighbors would call the police to complain about the noise—or about our existence, it seemed. In our little village of just four thousand people, we were on a first-name basis with most of the police officers, who would stop by or call when the neighbors complained, even though they would roll their eyes at the ridiculousness of their mission. Our neighbors called the police on just about everyone in the neighborhood for various infractions.

Thus began a feud that continued until my parents eventually moved out of the state. At one point, family legend has it, my sweet, Christian, pacifist mother mailed these neighbors two sets of very large-sized underwear, his and hers style, with a note that read, "I thought you might need these, since yours are obviously too tight."

Some people are hard to love.

Jesus repeatedly told his followers to love their neighbors. Then he took it a step farther and told them to love their enemies. The Gospels mention this odd teaching twice (in Matthew 5 and Luke 6). In his famous Sermon on the Mount, Jesus set up this teaching with the Beatitudes, which are about ways we love people.

He said, "Blessed are those who hunger and thirst for righteousness, for they will be filled. Blessed are the merciful, for they will be shown mercy" (Matt. 5:6–7).

That "righteousness" we're to hunger for—in the Greek, the word is *dikaiosune.* Growing up, I thought that verse had to do with always wanting to behave well. Which I didn't, to be honest, despite my efforts to be the very good girl. Sometimes I got tired of trying to be perfect, and I wanted to misbehave. Or I knew what I ought to do, but as the apostle Paul admits in Romans 7, it's often hard to do the right thing.

However, *dikaiosune* is not just personal piety. It also means justice. Righteousness means righting the wrongs of injustice in this world.[29] *Dikaiosune* and the related word *dikaios* are about hungering for justice, for things to be set right. No one hungers for justice like the oppressed. One of the hardest things for people of privilege to do is to hunger for justice, because it may come at the expense of our comfort. Especially if that hunger motivates us to pray, to give, to act. To show mercy, even to our enemies.

English is limited as a language, and the cultural lens we read the Bible through is clouded. *Dikaiosune* means both "righteousness ... the condition acceptable to God" (i.e., purity and virtue) and "justice or the virtue which gives each his due."[30] It is a call to right systemic wrongs in the world. Could it be that these are two sides of the same coin? That when we live rightly, we live justly?

Jesus continues a few verses later with more teaching about how we should respond to our enemies: "Blessed are those who are persecuted because of righteousness, for theirs is the kingdom of heaven. Blessed are you when people insult you, persecute you and falsely say all kinds of evil against you because of me. Rejoice and be glad, because great is your reward in heaven, for in the same way they persecuted the prophets who were before you" (Matt. 5:10–12).

Certainly, people who persecute us and insult us are our enemies, right? Jesus says be glad when those trials come. Then he takes it even farther. Beyond just accepting persecution, he asks us to love our persecutors. He says, "You have heard that it was said, 'Love your neighbor and hate your enemy.' But I tell you, love your enemies and pray for those who persecute you, that you may be children of your Father in heaven. He causes his sun to rise on the evil and the good, and sends rain on the righteous and the unrighteous. If you love those who love you, what reward will you get? Are not even the tax collectors doing that? And if you greet only your own people, what are you doing more than others? Do not even pagans do that? Be perfect, therefore, as your heavenly Father is perfect" (Matt. 5:43–48).

Perfect? Was Jesus telling his followers (including us) to never screw up? Look at the context of those words in Matthew 5. He's talking about loving our enemies. Loving those who don't love back is one of the ways in which God is perfect. For us mere mortals, perfection is impossible, but transformation certainly is possible, with God's help. Jesus' exhortation to emulate God comes at the end of a paragraph on loving our enemies, which is what we will do if we hunger for righteousness.

What if your neighbors are your enemies? Your neighbor in the house next door, or perhaps your neighbor in the next cubicle? The one who is vying for the same promotion you are, who perhaps took credit for your idea? We may not have a feud going on in our neighborhood, but we often feel threatened by our competitors in the workplace.

Who are our enemies? People who have personally wronged us, perhaps, or who seem to want to pick a fight with us, or seem to delight in harassing us. These are the people Jesus calls us to love.

Beyond this, our enemies are people we fear. And in our fear, we judge. We're maybe afraid of people who are of a different race, or people who look, act, or vote differently than we do. We may not have direct conflict with them, but we avoid them. Avoiding and loving are not the same thing.

That kind of love—love that is not necessarily reciprocated—is a step toward justice and righteousness, and that is part of what it means to be a Christian. To admit you are not perfect doesn't mean throwing up your hands and just sinning boldly. To admit you're imperfect just means to invite Jesus into the mess and ask him to help you start figuring things out. If I hunger and thirst for righteousness, it doesn't mean I am a perfectionist. It means I long for justice, not only for myself but also for all people. If there were justice for all—not just for some—that would be a more perfect world, wouldn't it?

Compassion Step

In your journal, list the decades of your lifetime: birth to ten years old, ten to twenty, twenty to thirty, and so on. In each of these eras, who, if anyone, was your enemy? Perhaps it was someone who was unkind to you, or someone you were mean to. What were your interactions like? How did you respond? How do you feel about those people now? Even if they are no longer in your life, what would it look like to love them, to forgive them?

Community Step

Begin by taking some time to have each person share just one enemy story that came out of their journaling exercise this week. Then move on to your current situation and discuss the following: (1) Who are your enemies today? If you think you don't have any, how do you feel about people who vote differently than you do? Or the neighbors who complain about you? (2) What specific steps can you take to love your enemies (not necessarily become best friends with them)? (3) Read Matthew 5:43–48 again. What do you think Jesus meant when he told us to be perfect?

invite

the morning of September 11, 2001, I was meeting, as I did every Tuesday, with my small group—a diverse group of men and women from my church. Halfway through our meeting, one member, Mindy, came in and said something about a plane crash. We said, Wow, that's too bad. None of us knew the extent of it. We didn't turn on the television, just continued our meeting.

On the way home, the radio refused to play music; every station had news about the attack. At home, I found Scot staring numbly at the television, where the image of the plane colliding with the second tower was being played almost continuously. After an hour, I made him turn it off. I closed my eyes but still could see it.

We decided to leave the kids at school until the end of the school day. We gave them a few more hours of innocence, of thinking that the world was okay.

The next day, I called some of my neighbors—the women I carpooled and played Bunco with—and invited them over to pray. Now, if the relationships hadn't been in place before that, would they have come? I don't know. Since many of them come from traditions that use written prayers (or no tradition at all), I wrote phrases from the psalms of lament and turned them into one- or two-sentence prayers that people could read. Things like "God, you are close to the brokenhearted. We are brokenhearted, and we ask you to come close." (See Ps. 34:18.)

A group of about five or six women came to my house. We huddled in my living room, sad and desperate. When you are a mom, you are more keenly attuned to the repercussions of an uncertain future. You question your choice to have procreated at all, to have brought children into this broken world.

So a group of moms, who had previously limited our conversations to potty training, car pools, and mild complaints about our husbands, took our friendships to a new level. We dared to have enough faith to think that perhaps prayer would help. We didn't care if we worshiped in different places on Sundays or didn't go to church at all. In fact, it sort of leveled the playing field. Suddenly, all of us felt uncertain. We were all seekers, looking for answers, stepping cautiously onto the common ground of barely enough faith.

We read the words on our cards. We just sat, quiet and aching yet comforted by the presence of one another. It was a holy moment, even though at the time it almost felt futile. Being together did something: it built community. Suddenly we needed each other for more than just babysitting.

That night, an awareness slowly dawned: it was just as important to be the church to my neighbors as it was to invite my neighbors to church ("church" meaning spiritual community, not institutionalized religion). That little group turned into a Bible study. Many of the women in it had never read the Bible before then. Introducing them to Jesus as we read the book of John, and later the book of Matthew, was the most invigorating ministry I'd ever done. And I have done a lot of ministry.

Eventually, God led me to drop out of my small group from church, which drew from a much wider geographical area. I loved those folks, but I didn't connect with them in my daily life. At the time, this group was one of the many obligations on my plate, and I sensed God asking me to let him do some pruning, to say no to the way I had overscheduled my life. Allowing this discipline in my life would enable me to focus on the things that truly mattered to me. That didn't make it easy. But God never said anything about following him being easy. The book of Hebrews says, "God disciplines us for our good, that we may share in his holiness. No discipline seems pleasant at the time, but painful. Later on, however, it produces a harvest of righteousness and peace for those who have been trained by it" (Heb. 12:10–11).

I sensed God wanting to cut several commitments out of my life at that time, because he wanted to produce a harvest of righteousness elsewhere in my life. I heard him calling me to love my actual neighbors—the people I'd see on the street, at our kids' soccer games, at the grocery store.

Over the years since then, I've occasionally led neighborhood Bible studies. At other times, I just had conversations with my friends about spiritual things. At still other times, I've tried to provide love in tangible ways. Right now I meet with five other moms from the neighborhood (who come from different faith backgrounds) once a week to read and discuss Scripture. Several of them were in that group that met in my living room eight years ago. Our group that serves breakfast at the homeless shelter has been consistently serving for two years. I see amazing spiritual growth in these women—and I'm grateful to be able to lead that group.

Perhaps part of my calling is to invite people into community. I sense God asking me to offer them connection and to be Christian without being obnoxious. Many people in America call themselves Christians but seem to hate in Jesus' name rather than love, to be known for what they are against rather than what they are for.

So I figure those of us who are followers of Jesus but don't buy into the whole hate thing need to speak up, for God's sake. I mean literally, for the sake of Jesus' reputation, we need to honestly love our neighbors before we attempt to correct their theology. We need to live our theology by loving indiscriminately.

Where would that start? What would happen if you lived your days looking for ways to connect with people who live within a few steps of your front door? The old "bloom where you are planted" is still a valid directive. Not so you can proselytize but so you can fight isolation—for yourself and others. So you can love your neighbors and let them love you.

Will and Lisa Samson write compellingly about what they call "theology of place," which basically means that "God has placed us where we are for a reason.... Wherever you are, that is where the kingdom of God is at work. There is no neutral place. That is good news. So doing missions means doing the work of the kingdom wherever you are sent. And the best place to think about where you have been sent is to see where you are.... If you find yourself in the suburbs, welcome to your mission field."[31]

Compassion Step

You probably know a few people who live near you. What could you do to take these existing relationships a little deeper? Ask God for direction as to which person he'd like you to try to get to know better. Ask for his guidance on how to go about building that relationship. Follow as he guides you. If you're a mom, you might invite another mom over to have coffee while your kids play together or to take a walk to the park. Or invite another couple to go out to dinner. Be creative.

Community Step

Have each person in the group share the name of one neighbor they would like to get to know and one step they plan to take to begin building a friendship with that neighbor. Perhaps you will want to invite a neighbor to join your small group. Spend some time praying as a group for each of the relationships mentioned.

If the members of your group live in the same neighborhood, pray together for your neighbors. Plan an event like a block party, a potluck dinner party, or even a multi-house garage sale, at which you can get to know and just have fun with your neighbors. Don't preach. Instead let Christ's love shine through you. If members live in different locations, plan a social event for your group, like going to a movie, going bowling, or engaging in some other fun activity. Invite a few of the people your members have been trying to get to know. Have fun together.

drawn

One of the ways I pray is by drawing. I'm not much of an artist. I don't let that stop me. I sketch and even create simple diagrams, even charts.

It may seem an odd way to pray, but I'm a visual thinker, so it helps. The latest diagram in my prayer journal has a curved line with names along it: Laura and Jon, Colleen and Tony, Bobbie and David, Sarah and Tim, Heather and Jeff, Dan and Joanne, Sue and Ken. The names are placed along the line, which is a map of the street I live on; the names, my neighbors. Their names are placed where they live in relation to me.

Some of the neighbors I know well. I spend time with them, I know their kids, and I know their stories. I've had meals inside their homes or enjoyed a glass of wine on their front porch. Others, I know only their names or just their faces. Like the older woman down the street, for example. We occasionally say hello. She knows my dog's name and likes to pet him if she's outside when we walk by. We first met her when we helped to shovel her driveway after a snowstorm.

Each time I pull out my journal to pray, I flip back to that page and pray for my neighbors. The ones I know, I pray for by name. The ones I don't, I still pray for. God knows their names. I try to figure out a way to fill in more names.

If we are being formed into the image of Christ, eventually his love will not just fill us but also flow out of us and, hopefully, spill out onto the people around us.

Author and pastor Randy Frazee lives this in a way that few other people do. A former workaholic, Randy radically altered his lifestyle when he found he could no longer sleep. He'd overwhelmed his body by denying it rest, and a doctor told him he'd have to either medicate himself nightly to sleep or slow down the pace of his life. He opted for the second choice.

So instead of going back to work after dinner, he began spending the evening hours with his family and with his neighbors. The family's dinnertime went from a quick fifteen minutes to more than an hour, because they had nowhere else to be. What would happen to your family if you cut back on activities so that you could spend time just talking over dinner leisurely? For the Frazees, it brought their family closer.

When Randy lived in Texas, he would sit out in his front yard each evening after dinner, in a lawn chair. At first, to pass the time, he played the banjo. Yes, the banjo. He discovered that his next-door neighbor played folk guitar. They'd get together for impromptu jam sessions.

A pastor plays a banjo in his front yard, it attracts a bit of attention. When his neighbors wandered by, he offered them a chair. It wasn't long before there was a large circle of chairs in the Frazees' front yard every evening, everyone talking, laughing, getting to know each other.

Now, I don't know about you, but I don't play the banjo, or any other instrument, for that matter. I also don't live in Texas; my front yard is buried in snow for about four months out of the year. So I've looked for other ways — from the neighborhood bowling league to Bunco nights — to engage with my neighbors when it's too cold to hang around outside. And the other eight months of the year, I spend time outdoors, walking the dog, gardening, playing with the kids.

And I put chairs in the front yard. Bright blue plastic ones. Colleen and Tony — who live next door with their two kids and Colleen's mom, Bridget — have a front porch. I make it a habit, if they are out there, to go and sit down on the porch with them to visit for a while. Because I really like hanging out with them. Sometimes, even when we enjoy being with people, we skip it because we're so busy. I want to live my life in a way that has margin enough for walking over to sit on the front porch. To share asparagus from my garden, to ask how work is going, to admire the flowers Colleen and Bridget have planted.

When we feel isolated, we tend to withdraw, to wonder a bit angrily why people aren't reaching out to us. This will get us nowhere. The way to cure isolation and loneliness is to extend ourselves, to take the initiative to welcome others. Even if we never mention anything about our faith, simple friendliness is so countercultural that it provides a picture of the radical inclusiveness of God.

"The chief antidote to suburban anonymity and isolationism may well be the Christian practice of hospitality. Hospitality can be a profoundly prophetic, countercultural activity that helps us escape our cocoons, connect with our neighbors and minister to our communities," writes Al Hsu in his book *The Suburban Christian*. "Despite all the challenges and pressure of suburban life, the route to recovering a deeper sense of community is as basic as 'love your neighbor.' The principle may seem simplistic, but living it out in our suburban context will necessarily be as complex, varied and unique as each of us. We can come to see every interaction with neighbors, merchants and strangers as an opportunity to extend hospitality and welcome others in the name of Christ."[32]

Hospitality does not mean entertaining. It means seeing each conversation, each interaction, as an opportunity to love.

One of my neighbors fought breast cancer last year. Watching her pain was awful. Watching her positive attitude was inspiring. Throughout her ordeal, she calmly but purposefully told us, "I'm going to beat this."

At a New Year's party, I saw her, and though she was still bald from the chemo, her doctor had declared her cancer-free. We laughed and cried together. Throughout her treatment, she has had an amazing strength about her. That strength flows from her soul, and from the souls of several of her friends who have stepped up to care for her in very practical ways. They take her kids when she's feeling exhausted by chemo treatments. They set up a schedule for other neighbors to provide meals for her family. They're coming alongside her to share her PTA responsibilities so that she doesn't have to resign her position there. Their goal was to allow her life to be as close to normal as possible.

This, to me, was a picture of what it means to love your neighbor. I'm grateful that I live in a neighborhood where this is normal.

When another neighbor fell and broke her right arm, an email went out that day, and friends from around the neighborhood put together a plan to bring her (and her husband and four sons) meals for a few weeks while she recovered. When I drove past her house one day on my way to the grocery store, I stopped and asked what she needed, then got it for her. These things seem small, even inconsequential. You keep doing them, you'll be surprised at how you'll get a reputation for being loving.

Perhaps you don't have the kind of community I'm describing. How can you begin to change your neighborhood? The only person you can change is you, but if you change, you can start to make a difference. Begin with prayer for your neighbors. Then pray for the courage to change your way of looking at things, for the ability to see every interaction as an act of hospitality.

Compassion Step

Draw a simple diagram of the homes or apartments that surround yours. Fill in your neighbors' names. If you don't know them, ask God to provide opportunities to learn them. Pray for your neighbors. Get a copy of Tommy Walker's song "He Knows My Name" and listen to it. Remind yourself that God knows your name, the name of every person on your street, and the name of everyone on the planet. Try to communicate that love to your neighbors, with your actions rather than words.

Community Step

Talk about your neighborhood. What made you decide to live there? Do you know your neighbors, even those who perhaps are different from you? Al Hsu writes, "Despite suburban tendencies toward isolationism, people still yearn for community. The search for the suburban promised land is not limited to housing; suburbanites long for human connections as well."[33] Discuss your response to Al's ideas. How is that yearning for community expressed in your neighborhood?

welcome

the email came today, as I had expected, confirming that one guest, a woman from Sweden, will be staying at our home for a week while attending the Leadership Summit at our church, Willow Creek, later this month.

For seven years now we've been opening our home to guests from around the world who attend pastor's conferences and training at Willow. Hospitality is a spiritual practice you can do alone or as a family. To welcome strangers is to wage peace.

While some people seem to have a spiritual gift for hospitality, it's an imperative for all believers to engage in. The Bible says simply, "Share with God's people who are in need. Practice hospitality" (Rom. 12:13). What a difference we could make in the world if every Christian did just that.

That these two directives are linked certainly suggests that biblical hospitality is not about entertaining, especially entertaining as a method of social climbing. Hospitality, as spiritual practice, helps us to recognize God in our midst. It is an act of humility. It is welcoming strangers, not just friends.

Jesus said he's right here, in the needy among us. He told his followers to feed the hungry, clothe the naked, visit the sick and imprisoned, because "whenever you did one of these things to someone overlooked or ignored, that was me—you did it to me" (Matt. 25:40 MSG).

Now, the pastor from Sweden who will be staying with us for a week or so this month is not needy in the "sick and imprisoned" sense. She does have a need—a place to stay—which we sense God is calling us to meet. We'll put out a bit of extra breakfast and coffee in the mornings, we provide a place to sleep and shower and rest, but most of what we offer is a friendly haven in a strange country.

We signed on with the Global Hospitality ministry at our church in the fall of 2001. It was a time of global uncertainty. Our children were just five and seven and still trying to make sense of the tragedy of September 11. We'd told them that they were safe, that the bad people who smashed the buildings lived far away, on the other side of the world.

Not long after that, we readied the basement bedroom for our first guest, a young man from Norway. "Where's Norway?" my seven-year-old daughter asked.

"It's very far away," I said. "On the other side of the world."

"Does he *know* Osama bin Laden?" Melanie demanded. We'd told her not to talk to strangers, yet here we were, welcoming a stranger into our home, and not just any stranger but one from that scary place, "the other side of the world." Just preparing for our guest prompted some very interesting discussions at home — and some great teachable moments.

My son went to school the next week and announced to his kindergarten teacher, "I've got a Norwegian in my basement."

Thankfully, his public school teacher attends our church and surmised what was going on. (She called me to tell me what he'd said.)

The Bible talks a lot about hospitality. Our culture understands the word in a completely different way. We think of hospitality as Martha Stewart–style entertaining, where we beautify our home, set an elaborate table with well-prepared food and drink, and welcome our friends. We invite those we know can return the favor. Biblical hospitality is a spiritual practice that requires us to extend ourselves not to friends but to those Jesus spoke of in Matthew 25: the poor, the hungry, the sick, the stranger. The Bible commands us to practice hospitality.

"In the traditions shaped by the Bible, offering hospitality is a moral imperative. The expectation that God's people are people who will welcome strangers and treat them justly runs throughout the Bible," writes Ana Maria Pineda in *Practicing Our Faith*. "This expectation is not based on any special immunity to the dangers unknown people might present — far from it. Rather, it emerges from knowing the hospitality God has shown to us."[34]

God has shown you hospitality by welcoming you into his family, by providing the means for your forgiveness before you even knew you needed it.

Do you welcome others to your home as if they were Christ? Do you welcome people, treating them kindly, even when you are not at home? Being hospitable doesn't mean serving fancy snacks or having handwritten place cards. It means living with the words "whatever you did—you did it to me" in the front of our minds as we interact with others. When we welcome people in this way, especially those we might not ordinarily choose to associate with, we are engaging in the spiritual practice of hospitality. If we let it, this practice will form us into the image of Christ.

The Bible says, "Don't forget to show hospitality to strangers, for some who have done this have entertained angels without realizing it!" (Heb. 13:2 NLT).

Our family has engaged in hospitality in various ways over the years; we've occasionally had single folks live with us for a few weeks or months at a time. As we will do this month, we've had strangers from foreign countries stay at our home.

Having people stay in our home, admittedly, is sometimes an inconvenience. That inconvenience has stretched our family to grow, made us more patient, more tolerant. It has helped our kids realize that our lives are not just about them.

Our accommodations are not perfect. Our basement guest room has yellow shag carpeting and wooden paneling. It is not luxurious in any way. But when guests come, the house is clean and welcoming. Had I waited until I could afford to remodel the basement before we opened our home, I'd still be waiting. And we would have missed out on getting to know some amazing people from all over the world.

At other times, we've practiced hospitality by visiting a shelter in the city and helping serve a meal. Each of these opportunities has been an amazing experience for our family and a way to bless people we don't know. For the last year or so, a group of my suburban neighbors and I have gone to a women's homeless shelter on the west side of Chicago once a month to serve breakfast. This simple act of feeding people who otherwise would go hungry, people who cannot pay us back, has been transformational. Practicing hospitality in this way has strengthened our friendships and grown us all spiritually. We've also realized that when we bring breakfast, we leave blessed by the women we've fed. They teach us so much. Our exchange is not a one-way thing. We bring food and serve it; they teach us about trust, about pain, about love. They have a wisdom that comes only from having struggled and survived.

Every day we have a chance to show hospitality to strangers, to engage in a spiritual practice that can usher us unexpectedly into the presence of God. At home, we can welcome our children's friends. They may not be strangers, but they may be a little strange. They may not be in prison, but it's possible that they are coming to you from homes that are very painful places.

If we can begin to see the things we are already doing as ways to connect more deeply with others, we'll realize that everything we do can be a way to grow and deepen our intimacy with God.

Compassion Step

How has God shown you hospitality, meaning, how has he welcomed you even when you did not yet know him? How do you feel about the idea of letting a stranger into your house for a meal or to stay? Ask God for an opportunity to show hospitality, for the awareness to notice that opportunity, and for the courage to act on it.

Community Step

Discuss as a group: A quote in this chapter states, "Offering hospitality is a moral imperative." Do you agree or disagree? Why? Have you ever invited a stranger to stay in your home or to have a meal with you? Why, in your opinion, does the Bible tell us to practice hospitality (Rom. 12:13)? How is the Bible's definition of hospitality different from our culture's definition of it? How has God shown you hospitality?

Two weeks ago you talked about planning an event to get to know your neighbors, or a step to get to know one person. How is that going? Encourage each other and hold each other accountable as you continue to reach out to your neighbors.

brother

a busy suburban corner near my home — right by the community college and just a mile from the expressway — has become a favorite spot for workers who collect donations for an inner-city mission. They stand on the narrow concrete island, and when the light turns red, they begin working the crowd of SUVs and minivans, smiling widely, waving, holding white plastic buckets with off brand lollipops stuck through holes drilled in the top.

One warm spring day, I was driving with my window down when I approached the corner. I smiled at the man as he waved at me. "Look at you, don't you look great!" he said. "I'm not getting fresh with you! I'm just sayin'! You look wonderful. Would you like to support our ministry to victims of domestic abuse? These babies are *homeless*; we're trying to help them."

I laughed and pointed to the console where I keep change. "You guys cleaned me out last week."

The man smiled, his crooked teeth sincere. "Maybe you could give a five or a ten?" he said. "I can feel the Spirit of God in you." He leaned on the car door. "Look at you, you're so tan you could be my sister," he said, putting his dark brown hand next to my lightly tanned one.

I smiled again. "Well, I am your sister."

That delighted him, and he began quoting Scripture in an excited torrent, including one of my favorite verses from Isaiah:

> *Since ancient times no one has heard,*
> *no ear has perceived,*
> *no eye has seen any God besides you,*
> *who acts on behalf of those who wait for him.*
> Isaiah 64:4

I pulled a dollar from my wallet and stuffed it into the bucket, which caused him to thank me, and God, and rattle off several more Bible verses. I just smiled, since I couldn't get a word in edgewise.

"Take a candy," he said.

"No, that's okay."

"You got kids?"

"Yes."

"Well, take it for them, then!" he said, practically throwing lollipops into the car.

"God bless you!" I said.

"You too!" he said, and scampered off to the SUV next to me, where the woman kept her window shut tight and avoided his glance, talking on her cell phone. The man just grinned and moved on, waving to the next driver as if he were a long-lost friend.

The man on the corner collecting money for the homeless is my brother. He is a child of God, and I am a child of God. When I see that, my whole perspective changes. How I treat him matters much more than how much money, if any, I put into his bucket. Does my dollar make a difference? Does it even go to the ministry he says it does? Is this a scam or legit?

A better question to ask myself is, Does my kindness make a difference? Is there any common ground between us? Can we meet on that ground? If we do, does it become holy ground? Or maybe the question is, Is all ground holy? Are all men our brothers? What if we just need to open up our eyes and see what is true?

Even if this man were not collecting for a legitimate ministry, I would still err on the side of mercy. I would still joke with him, be kind to him. Not just for his sake but also for mine. If I say that all people matter to God and therefore should matter to me, then I need to practice living it out. My being kind to someone I don't know, someone who is different, will stretch me. We grow in compassion by practicing compassion.

Jesus said, "Blessed are the peacemakers, for they will be called the children of God" (Matt. 5:9). His brother and disciple James wrote, "Peacemakers who sow in peace reap a harvest of righteousness" (James 3:18). In this passage, as in others, the word translated "righteousness" is the Greek *dikaiosune*, which means not just personal integrity but also justice. So if we sow peace, we'll not only live with integrity but also reap justice. There is a connection between the two.

What does it mean to be a peacemaker in the way we relate to those of other races? Can you be an activist and a peacemaker at the same time?

One of the greatest social activists of all time, Dr. Martin Luther King Jr., did so beautifully. He once said, "It is not enough to say we must not wage war. It is necessary to love peace and sacrifice for it." King sacrificed his life for peace, which is more than most of us would do.

So often, African-Americans are treated with suspicion and mistrust simply because of the color of their skin. Here in my neighborhood, where they are a very small minority, this is especially true. It's a subtle thing sometimes. Other times, the discrimination is overt.

Racism is a complicated problem. A good place to start is with aligning our sense of humor with God's. God does not laugh at racist jokes. Refusing to tell a racist joke, or even to laugh at one, is to take a stand against racism.

Since the election of our new president, Barack Obama, I've heard a few too many racist jokes. When someone starts telling me one, I try to interrupt. I stop them. I tell them it's not funny. Still, that doesn't feel as if I'm doing much to bridge the racial divide.

I figure rolling down my window and talking to an African-American stranger, affirming to him our common ground in faith and in humanity, is a very small thing. But it matters. To do it is better than not to. Now, I would still roll down my window and talk to him if he were white or any other race.

The street corner, of course, is not the only place where I encounter someone of another race. At work, at church, at the mall, our culture is growing increasingly diverse. My children attend suburban schools with only a handful of African-Americans. But a large percentage of their classmates are Asian-Americans, Mexican-Americans, and Indian-Americans.

In King's "I Have a Dream" speech, he expressed his hope that someday all people would be "judged by the content of their character." How can that dream come true? It begins with every person deciding to pay more attention to character than to skin color, to personality than to stereotypes, and so on.

It comes down to this: will we listen to the voice of love, or the voice of fear? The Bible says that perfect love casts out fear (1 John 4:18). Often we let fear trump our ability to love.

When we interact with people who are different, do we act with love, or with fear? Do we believe that all Christians are our brothers and sisters, or only the ones who look like us and worship in exactly the same way we do?

Another day, my African-American brother and another man stood on the corner, collecting again. It was quite hot, late in the afternoon. On my way home, I stopped at a convenience store and picked up two large bottles of cold water. When I got to the intersection, I rolled down my window and handed the man the bottles. This of course led him to joyfully bless and thank me and, of course, to quote Scripture to me. It was a small thing to offer someone who is thirsty a drink on a hot day. Or was it?

Compassion Step

If you see someone collecting for charity or even panhandling, how do you respond? What could you give rather than money? Which is more frightening—to give a dollar, or to look someone in the eye and say hello? Try this: Keep a small cooler in your car stashed with water bottles and snacks like granola bars. When you see someone begging on the street, give them food or water instead of money. When you give it, smile and offer a kind word.

Community Step

Discuss the following: In the home you grew up in, did you hear racist jokes or comments? Does that happen in your home today? Do you live in an area that is culturally diverse, or are most of the people you encounter of your own race? Do you have relationships with people of other races? What are some ways you as a group can begin to bridge cultural and racial divides? How do you think God feels about this issue?

elders

the kids and I were driving home from my in-laws' house in Wisconsin late in the afternoon on Memorial Day. Rather than take the interstate home, I decided to take Route 120, a two-lane country road that begins in the town square of their small town. It's more direct and more scenic but can sometimes take longer, especially if you get caught behind a slow truck or, say, a corn combine.

We hadn't gone far when I saw an elderly woman walking along the gravel shoulder. Not long ago, I would have driven past and thought only, *That's an odd place for an eighty-year-old to be strolling.*

But when you are writing a book on living more compassionately, and when you are telling others to "act justly, love mercy, and walk humbly with God," you begin to see opportunities to show compassion all around you. God, in his good humor, often provides these opportunities, which you will notice if you just slow down a bit.

So I pulled over, lowered my passenger window, and leaned past my shocked fourteen-year-old daughter, who was in the passenger seat.

"Hello there," I said. "Are you alright?"

The woman turned to study us, trying to mask her confusion. "What? Oh, yes." She had to be eighty-five or older. She wore a flowered cotton top, denim-colored polyester slacks with an elastic waist, and blue Keds-style sneakers.

The look in her eyes was that of a child, both scared and stubborn. In one hand, she clutched a stone the size of a baseball.

"Where are you headed?" I asked gently. It was a warm day, and there was nothing but farms for the next several miles of the road she was headed down. My daughter, still speechless, watched us carefully.

"Well, I'm going to my daughter's house," she said firmly.

"Really? Where does she live?" I asked.

"Somewhere," the woman said. "I can't remember exactly."

I could see that she had very little idea where she was or where she was going. It was suddenly obvious to me what I had to do. This woman is my neighbor; she lives in the town where we spend our summer week-ends. She was a stranger in need of some help.

"Well, it's pretty hot out here to be walking," I said. "Would you like a ride?"

She looked at me warily. I told my daughter to hop into the back seat, which she quickly did. "I can take you to your daughter's house," I said. I couldn't leave her out there.

The woman opened the door and climbed in.

"What's your name?" I asked.

"Peggy," she said, quietly, so I had trouble hearing her.

"Maggie?" I asked.

"No, Paggie. I mean Peggy," she said. "I get mixed up sometimes." Apparently.

"What's that rock for, Peggy?" I asked.

"In case anyone tries any funny business," she said, looking as men-acing as a one-hundred-pound eighty-five-year-old can.

"Don't worry, Peggy. We'll help you find your daughter's house."

We drove down Route 120, past widely spaced farmhouses sur-rounded by acres of rolling hills of corn and soybean fields. "Is her house on this road?" I asked.

"I think so," Peggy said uncertainly.

What had I done? I was in too deep now. I couldn't just dump her out on the side of the road, miles from where I'd picked her up. I began to think that perhaps she'd wandered away from someplace in town, and I was carrying her in the wrong direction. I didn't look at my kids, but I could feel their incredulous stares boring into the back of my skull.

Every time I would ask, "Does this look familiar?" she'd obligingly reply, "Oh yes, very familiar." Sigh.

Okay, God, I prayed silently. Help me out here. We reached an inter-section with a farmhouse on the corner. I saw a man, woman, and child in the yard. They glanced at us curiously but stayed where they were.

"They're going to pretend that they don't know me," Peggy said softly and suspiciously. "That's how they are."

I waved at the man and rolled down Peg's window, which was closest to him. As people in rural Wisconsin tend to do, he came over and rested his arms on the sill of the open window in a familiar way. Unfortunately, he didn't know my passenger. He did affirm my decision to take Peggy back into town, to the police station.

"Peggy, we're going to find your daughter," I told her, although by then I was doubting said daughter's existence. "I think God sent me to help you." She nodded in agreement, accepting my words like a child.

On the way back into town, we passed a low-slung brown building with a modest wooden sign in front: "Brolen Park Assisted Living." She stared at it. "That's Brolen Park," she said.

I asked if she lived there.

"Yes, but I live in the other one. The one in town."

Fifty feet past Brolen Park, we *were* in town, at the police station. When she got out of my minivan to go with me into the station, she left her rock on the floor. Guess she figured if I was taking her to the cops, she didn't want to be caught packing.

We had a short conversation with a friendly police officer, who deduced that Peggy had wandered away from Brolen Park. The officer promised to get her back where she belonged.

On the way home, my kids and I had a short conversation about what had happened. I simply said, "When you see someone who needs help, don't just pray for them. Pray for the strength and courage to help them. Then do it. Prayer is action." I didn't need to elaborate. My actions had already said plenty.

Living a life of compassion isn't hard, but it can be a little inconvenient. Our little detour added twenty minutes to our trip home. That rock had my daughter worried a bit. If I want to love as Jesus loved, I will pull over and help someone like Peggy every time.

What if I had taken a different route, as I often do? Someone else might have helped her. We often think this way; someone else will do it, so I don't need to get involved. Then again, someone else may have tried some "funny business" that a small rock would not have been able to deter.

A few days later, I read a newspaper article about an elderly woman in Florida who mistakenly drove her car down a boat ramp into the Gulf and drowned. The article said she suffered from dementia and that as the Baby Boomers age, the number of Americans with Alzheimer's disease is expected to grow from the current five million to sixteen million by 2050. It noted that six out of ten Alzheimer's patients will wander, and "if they are not found within 24 hours, as many as half will suffer serious injury or death."[35] Which means that opportunities to help widows in their distress will only increase in the coming decades. If you do the math, it's obvious that you and I might eventually be those in need of help.

Do I think God sent me to help Peggy? Yes. Oddly, I found myself thanking God that he let me do it. Thanking him for the chance to practice compassion. It's only by practicing things that we get better at them. The Bible says that "pure religion" is not just about studying truth; it's also about living it out. It means to "look after widows and orphans in their distress" (James 1:27). Peggy may have qualified as a distressed widow.

So on Memorial Day, God took care of Peggy, keeping her out of harm's way. He did it by using me and a kind police officer. He stretched my faith, strengthened that little mercy muscle I'm developing. I got a glimpse of the fragile lives so many elderly people live—and how they are in need of our compassion.

Compassion Step

Do you have elderly neighbors? How might you show love to them? What about elderly people within your own family? Do you visit with them, invite them to spend time with you? If so, what is that like? How do you feel when you are around elderly people? What do you think causes that feeling? Look for opportunities to show kindness to strangers, especially the elderly.

Community Step

This week go out into your community to serve your elderly neighbors. Decide as a group whether you will visit a local nursing home or offer assistance to one of the elderly people in your neighborhood. If your church has a list of shut-ins, offer to visit someone on the list. Bring them a meal or a dessert; offer to read to them. Ask them what they need, and listen carefully. While you cannot meet all their needs, you can offer simple kindness. Again, this does not have to be an ongoing commitment.

biblically

I remember the chairs: molded from a single thin slice of orange fiberglass, bolted to shiny curved chrome legs—a study in modern design efficiency. Easy to clean, hard to tip over, and best of all, stackable: the quintessential primary Sunday school chairs, their concave seats barely a foot from the floor.

I recall sitting in those chairs, arranged in rows divided by a middle aisle, in my Sunday school room, where a large woman, ironically named Mrs. Smalls, whipped us into a frenzy, conducting us like a choir. Leaping from our orange chairs, we'd shout at the top of our lungs, "Genesis! Exodus! Leviticus! Numbers! Doot-a-ron-o-MMEEEEE!"

Sitting in those chairs, or jumping in and out of them, I memorized the table of contents for both Testaments, along with hundreds of verses and stories. Whether via Bible memory drills, flannelgraph stories, or boisterous songs ("The B-I-B-L-E, yes that's the book for me! I stand alone on the Word of God, the B-I-B-L-E!" was a favorite), Mrs. Smalls and other teachers imparted the knowledge of God's Word to us. They loved us; mine was a church that felt like family.

In high school I attended Campus Life and church youth group, where we studied the Bible more. I went to a Christian camp, where we lived our faith by not wearing bikinis or short shorts and by memorizing as much of the Bible as possible. The reason for memorizing, we were told—remember, this was the 1970s and the height of the Cold War—was that if the Communists came and confiscated our Bibles, we would have them memorized. One summer our guest speaker was Josh McDowell. He gave us lots of evidence, which apparently demanded a verdict.

And then I went to Wheaton College, a bastion of academic pressure and evangelical fervor, where I learned even more about the Bible, whether I wanted to or not, since you had to take four semesters of Bible to graduate, regardless of your major. I also learned how to argue just about anything, whether I believed it or not. I learned ontological proofs, and didn't even stop to consider the audacity of such an endeavor. I had deep philosophical discussions about everything.

Except for a couple of years in my twenties, when I was recovering from Wheaton and found sleeping in on Sundays much more appealing than any form of spiritual accountability, all my life I've been attending church, reading my Bible, and talking to other people about how to live out my faith.

Despite all this training, I still find myself asking, What does the Bible say about how we're to live? Why do people disagree so strongly about what it means? And why did so much of what the Bible says, especially about justice and about the poor, not show up on my flannel-graph radar? (Okay, we heard the story of the widow's mite and the good Samaritan, the takeaways for which were, respectively, put your offering in the basket and be nice to people.) Why did it not even show up in my Christian college years, when the verses that apparently were most important were the ones that prohibited smoking, drinking, and dancing? Oh, wait, there aren't any verses prohibiting dancing? Or smoking? Huh?

What does it mean to "live biblically"? At the surface, an easy question, right? You live according to the precepts of the Bible. You follow its rules, embrace its truth.

The Bible is an interesting book with a lot of information. It's a collection of forty-four scrolls, written in three different languages (Hebrew and Greek mostly, with a little Aramaic sprinkled in). It was written on three different continents, over a period of fifteen hundred years or so, by forty different authors, mostly Middle Eastern Jewish men (although many scholars, and I, believe Hebrews was written by a woman mentioned repeatedly in the New Testament, Priscilla). It contains history, poetry, allegory, prophesy, biography. Many of its stories are true both literally and symbolically. Some only symbolically.

The religious tradition you grew up in handed you some lenses through which to view Scripture. You interpret its meaning, in part, based on those lenses. Often we come to a point where we question those teachings, and the ensuing crisis of faith causes us either to give up on them or to embrace a new and deeper understanding of this book. This is not necessarily a bad thing. Often it is the point in our lives where our faith becomes our own.

Well-meaning people can disagree about what the Bible means and how to live it out. That's one reason why we have so many denominations within the Christian faith. We're all saying we believe in the Bible and may even agree on a very few major points. We differ on the minor ones enough that we want to meet in different buildings on Sunday morning. (Or, for those who interpret those Sabbath laws in the Bible differently, *Saturday* morning. See?)

A. J. Jacobs tackled this whole issue in his brilliant book *The Year of Living Biblically*, which is part satire, part memoir, part investigative journalism. Jacobs devotes a year to trying to follow every single command in the Bible. The book is funny; for example, he wanders New York City looking for an adulterer to stone and ends up throwing pebbles at a man who readily admits to being one. It is also touching; for example, he faces honestly his struggles with prayer and with disciplining his two-year-old. Jacobs is Jewish but had not done a lot to practice his faith until he began his "research" for the book. He tried to follow both the Old and the New Testaments, which got interesting because some of Jesus' teaching seems to contradict some of the Old Testament edicts (especially when taken out of context).

Jacobs' point is that living biblically is no easy task. To follow every single rule, all the time, is impossible and often impractical. Some of the Bible's commands were directed toward a specific group of people at a certain time in history. For example, most Christian women feel no guilt about blatantly disobeying 1 Corinthians 11:2–16. A few (Mennonite and Amish, for example) wear a head covering, not only when praying but anytime they are in public. So who lives biblically?

I was talking with an acquaintance who is a wacko right-wing conservative, NRA member, racist, extremist Republican, not to put too fine a point on it. She also considers herself a Christian, and in fact to prove it, she'll tell you how much she hates Muslims. So I asked her about that verse in Luke, where Jesus says his mission is to release the oppressed and preach the good news to the poor. (See Luke 4:16–22.) What did she think that meant? How do we live that verse out?

"Liberation theology," she snorted.

"What?" I asked.

"Yeah, that's liberation theology."

Gee, thanks for slapping a label over my mouth. "Well, the text says he came to release the oppressed," I said.

"He's speaking figuratively," she said. "The *spiritually* oppressed."

I wanted to ask her who was spiritually oppressed, and didn't she think those trapped in physical poverty also struggle spiritually, but I was afraid she might shoot me.

What do we make of the thousand or two thousand verses in the Bible that talk about the poor? Do we even know they are there? Sometimes our justice journey leads to that crisis of faith because we wonder if the Bible we grew up reading has anything to say about the atrocities of hunger and poverty that plague our world. Doesn't God care? And then, if we're brave enough to read Scripture with new lenses, we realize he does very much care, and the crisis becomes, How did I miss these verses? Why didn't I hear a sermon on the sins of accumulation and greed?

Scripture goads us to action, if only we would read it. Unfortunately, many of us grew up reading the Bible through lenses that focused on certain parts of it but ignored others.

Will and Lisa Samson, in their book *Justice in the Burbs*, note, "We tend to read Scripture selectively, applying as direct commands those things we agree with and understand, while we outright ignore those elements that make us uncomfortable. For example, we apply the Ten Commandments and the Old Testament ideas about sexuality as rules for living. But why do we not have the same approach when we read commands in Leviticus about relieving debts or providing rest for the land?"[36]

Sitting in those orange chairs, I learned so much about God's love for me. I heard very little about his love for the poor. I memorized countless verses, but there were many we never even read.

I want to live biblically, which means living justly. For me, the first step to living biblically is to admit that I don't do so. Still, I can't stop there, depending on cheap grace to excuse me from pursuing truth.

I do think you have to get up out of your orange chair. You appreciate everything you learned there, but eventually you have to go live it. To put into practice all those verses you memorized. To live it as courageously as you can, even the parts that seem difficult. To go on an adventure with God, one in which he holds the map and navigates.

Compassion Step

When you were growing up, what did you understand to be the central message of the Bible? Which aspects of God's Word were emphasized? Has your perspective on what it means to live biblically changed? What caused it to shift? What do you think it means to live biblically?

Community Step

Begin by having group members share their responses to the questions in the compassion step. Then discuss the following with your group: Do you agree with this chapter's assertion that living biblically means living justly? Last week your group encountered your elderly neighbors. What was that like? How did you show biblical love to those people? What does the Bible say about how we are to treat our elders?

part 3

compassion extends
beyond our comfort zones

urban

Oﬀne summer a few years ago, our household budget was, to put
it mildly, squeezed. My husband and I are self-employed, which
means neither of us has a regular salary. It had been a slow year for both
of us. To say we've learned to be thrifty doesn't even give you the half
of it.

Cutbacks included vacations, which was frustrating to me. My most
precious childhood memories are of camping trips and vacations all over
the country, and I longed to give my children the same thing.

When I complained to God about it, he gently brought to mind a
fact I'd overlooked: we live about forty minutes away from one of the
most wonderful cities in the world—Chicago. We didn't have to travel
very far to see that. So that summer, I decided the kids and I would have
weekly "urban adventures."

Chicago is a very cool city. Especially in summer, when you can go
to the beach, the zoo, the museums, or Millennium Park. One week, we
threw our bikes into the back of the minivan and went biking down the
trail along the lakefront. Another time, we took the architectural boat
tour (Aaron aspires to be an architect) that chugs along the Chicago
River.

The first time I took my kids to Foster Avenue Beach, we drove
across the north side on Lawrence Avenue. My kids asked why so many
signs were in foreign languages. I said, Why do you think? We talked
about how when people emigrate, they often want to be with people who
are familiar, and so various neighborhoods tend to have clusters of different ethnic groups. When one group moves in, I explained, sometimes
people who are different from them get scared and move out. We talked
about how sometimes people don't get along, especially with those who
are different from them.

In the park just adjacent to the beach, the kids noticed that large
extended Hispanic families gathered to play soccer, relax on blankets
and lawn chairs, cook on grills, and picnic in the shade of tall trees. My

kids swam and played in the sand next to kids with a wide variety of skin colors, heard various languages being spoken. Occasionally we saw a homeless person sleeping on a park bench.

It is healthy for my kids, who live in a neighborhood that is mostly white, with a few Asians and Indians, to visit places where not everyone looks like them, especially when those places are less than an hour's drive from home. It's good for them to see that not everyone has grandparents who have a lake house, to see people who "go to the lake" by gathering in a public park. My aim in visiting the city is to get all of us, including myself, to lift up our eyes, to become aware of what a different world lies in our own back yard. To see and interact with those who may not live right next door but are still close enough to be considered our neighbors. A life that matters requires a broader vision, a willingness to embrace the unknown and unfamiliar. To love people who are not necessarily just like me.

God wants me to love mercy, act justly, and walk humbly (Mic. 6:8). What does that mean when I look at the city and its violence and chaos? Compassion, if we live it out, requires risk. It requires us to move out of our comfort zones, to show God's love to strangers. If that's true, how am I to engage with the city?

I love Chicago, especially the cultural stuff, the upscale, safer neighborhoods, the lakefront, the architecture, and the vibrancy. The shopping. The nice parts.

I've read a lot of books about urban social justice, about God's heart for the poor, and I'm still trying to figure out what to do with the information, how to live it. I'm asking God. He hasn't given any easy answers yet. The Bible, I've noticed lately, is full of directives about how we are to treat the poor.

The Bible says we are to be generous to the poor. The book of Proverbs says, "Whoever oppresses the poor shows contempt for their Maker, but whoever is kind to the needy honors God" (14:31); "Those who are kind to the poor lend to the LORD, and he will reward them for what they have done" (19:17); "The generous will themselves be blessed, for they share their food with the poor" (22:9); and perhaps most compelling, "Those who shut their ears to the cry of the poor will also cry out and not be answered" (21:13).

You can argue that poor is a relative term or that we are all spiritually poor without Jesus. But even when my budget has been tight, as it was that summer, my kids have never gone hungry. We have a home and food and clothes. We go to the city, in part, to remind ourselves that this is not the case for everyone. There are rich people in the city, of course, but also there are people who have less than we do. Something changes in our hearts when we are among the poor.

I've started getting involved with an urban ministry and talking to people who have chosen to live in the city among the poor. I am raising my awareness and understanding.

I grew up reading the Bible and hearing about missionaries to Africa. I was scared to death that God might send me there, and I basically told him, "Here am I; don't send me." I had never thought about the city as a mission field. So I am still assimilating a lot of new information. My paradigm, as they say, is still shifting. Maybe you feel this way too.

You can't be anywhere besides where you are, as my friend Sibyl likes to say. So I try to add small actions to my learning. Because otherwise it all feels theoretical. I serve breakfast at a women's shelter once a month and rally my neighbors to come along. We're building a little community with each other by serving together, and hopefully helping each other as we each journey toward compassion and justice. Is it enough? Maybe not. It's something, which is better than nothing. It's molding us, to rub shoulders with homeless women for a few hours on a Saturday morning. We cook for them, then go out into the dining room and chat with those who are willing. We work with them to clean up the kitchen after the meal.

Do I understand the urban experience? Not really. What does God want me to do about the city? How do I love my neighbors who live twenty miles away yet seem to reside on another planet? Mother Teresa, who ministered to the poorest of the poor in Calcutta, India, would tell people who wanted to join her work that they didn't need to go to India. They could find Calcutta in their own back yard.

Is Chicago the Calcutta in my back yard?

Some parts of the city are so affluent that I could not afford to live there. There are some very beautiful neighborhoods and some downright dangerous neighborhoods. Every person in my city matters to God and needs to know his love.

So let's spend the next three months thinking about how to make a difference in our cities, whether they're big or small. We'll look at practical ways to practice simple compassion beyond our immediate families and neighborhoods. (If you live in a rural area, you can apply these chapters to interactions with the poor in your county or township.) To extend ourselves in this way requires a sort of courage, a fresh kind of awareness. Our hearts must expand a bit if we are to even care about what is going on beyond the confines of our neighborhoods. It's scary, but we have to trust that God will grow our hearts of simple compassion as we follow him out of our comfort zones.

Compassion Step

Take out a map of your town, city, or region. With a highlighter, mark places where you know the poor and marginalized live. Spend some time praying for the people who live in those areas, including those who minister by living among the poor. Ask God to show you how you might be able to show compassion to those people. Again, if you live in a rural area, is there a neighborhood near you that is home to people who have fewer resources than you do?

Community Step

Show your map to your small group. Ask everyone to pray with you about the areas you've marked. Ask them if there are other areas they feel led to pray for. See if you have any areas in common and consider the possibility that God may be using that to lead you. Do some research, then visit a church or parachurch ministry in an area highlighted on at least two members' maps. On your first visit, simply go to learn as much as you can. Don't assume you know what people need or want. Ask those who live and serve there how you can help. Listen and ask questions before doing anything.

week 28

hungry

i t wasn't yet noon, but it had already been a busy working-mom mul-titasking day.

I was up at 6:05 to nudge the kids out of bed, to prod them as they had breakfast, brushed their teeth, packed their backpacks. I'd signed notes to the teacher and quizzed Aaron on his spelling words, reminding him that I'd pick him up at lunch hour for an orthodontist appointment.

The kids waved goodbye by 7:00. I was working in my home office five minutes later. It was one of those mornings when I asked God, very briefly, as the coffee was brewing, to help me through the day. I didn't linger. I wish I could tell you differently, but that's what kind of day it was.

I wrote for an hour, answered emails and organized files, then left the house at 8:50 for Starbucks to meet Wendy, who helps me with administrative stuff. I gave her a long list of tasks; she gave me updates on the things she's working on. We drank cappuccinos, worked, and laughed for more than an hour. Knowing I had to get Aaron at 11:15, I ran over to the gym for a short workout.

I picked up Aaron from school and offered to take him through the Wendy's drive-through for lunch. He requested both a chicken sandwich and a bowl of chili. "Wow, you must be hungry," I said.

"I'm starving," he replied.

We'd had a lighter than normal dinner of baked fish and vegetables the night before. He'd had a bowl of cereal in the morning, but my fast-growing boy burns fuel like a race car. He's tall and thin, standing a head above most kids in his sixth-grade class. I was a little hungry myself. I'd had only a biscotti and coffee that morning. (I know, not exactly healthy breakfast choices.)

I asked Aaron how his morning at school was, and he replied, "I was hungry!" He said it had made it hard to pay attention in class. Talk about a one-track mind.

After picking up our lunch at the drive-through, I cut through a shopping-center parking lot to head for the orthodontist. Aaron finished his chicken sandwich in the time it took me to take one bite of mine.

As I went to drive past the furniture store, I saw an older African-American man in a parka, walking slowly. He shuffled at a snail's pace, watching me, and I had to stop to avoid running him over. Because I'd been handing Aaron food and putting my change in my wallet while driving, my window was still down from going through the drive-through, even though it was a chilly winter day.

He motioned to me. "Hello there!" he said, walking up beside the van. He peered inside to see Aaron sitting behind me, then smiled widely. "Hello there, young man!"

I felt only slightly nervous. He wasn't very threatening—just a little old man, not drunk, not incoherent. I was in my minivan near a busy strip mall. If I felt threatened, I could simply drive away. Hardly a compassionate thought, but I was just being practical. "Hello?" I said, wondering what he wanted, wondering what had made me decide to cut through the parking lot instead of taking the roads that went around the shopping center.

"I'm just wondering, do you have any change? So I could maybe get myself a sandwich or something? I just walked here, all the way from Barrington Road," he said. (Barrington Road was about two or three miles away.) He explained he was homeless, and the shelter would not open until dinnertime that evening. "I'm just so hungry," he said.

I'm careful about giving money to panhandlers, because I sometimes fear the money will be spent on things less healthy than food, and it keeps them in a cycle of dependency. I'm used to encountering them in the city. In suburban parking lots? Not so much. Sitting in the car with my son, I took a moment just to stop my hurried day. I felt pity for the man. Without stopping to think about it, I said, "Here, if you don't mind sharing mine, I'll break off the part where I took a bite." I messily divided my chicken sandwich, giving him the larger portion and the wrapper. You'd think I had given him filet mignon on fine china, the way his eyes lit up. He tore into the sandwich. I gave him some of the change so he could go get coffee and sit in a nearby restaurant to warm up. "Thank you," he said through a mouthful of mayonnaise and chicken.

"You take care," I told the man. We drove away.

"That was really nice of you," Aaron said quietly.

As a preteen boy, Aaron is not big on deep conversations with his mother. I try not to push. But this was a teachable moment. I explained why I'd given food instead of just money, and then I said, "Aaron, the Bible says, 'Don't withhold good when it is in your power to act.' And I had the power to do something. Something small, but something."

A few minutes later, as we sat in the parking lot finishing our lunch (a few minutes early for his appointment), I added, "Jesus once said, 'I was hungry and you gave me something to eat.' So when we feed hungry people, we're actually doing it to Jesus." I turned to smile at him. "I bet you didn't think Jesus was an old black man."

He flashed a grin, but I could tell he was still chewing on his thoughts.

My boy, who had experienced only moderate hunger that day, trusted me to feed him. And that old man—his heavenly parent fed him too.

It brought me joy to eat less for lunch that day, knowing I'd fed Jesus. Eating less than half of a ninety-nine-cent sandwich was strangely satisfying. I wish I'd had time to do more, to go and get the man a table at Wendy's and a couple more burgers.

Isaiah 58 talks about the discipline of fasting. The point of this practice is not to impress God but "to share your food with the hungry." God says that religious activities, even disciplines like prayer and fasting, are meaningless if our hearts are hard. Such disciplines are meant not to be ways to demand God's attention but rather to be ways to humble ourselves and soften our hearts.

Sometimes the best fasting is unplanned—to fast when God provides you a chance to share your food with the hungry, to go without food, or with less food, so that you can help someone who needs it. Fasting is simply delayed gratification. Opportunities are all around us, and you'll find them only when you can pay attention enough to stop hurrying, to slow down, and to notice Jesus waving to you on a street corner.

I know that a tattered sandwich and a little money didn't solve this man's problems. I don't know his story; I can't see the bridges he's maybe burned or know the pain that has been a part of his journey. I'm not so sure I loosed the chains of injustice much at all. Isaiah calls us to do a lot more than I did that afternoon. Still, I did something, took a baby step, and caught a glimpse of God in the face of a hungry person.

I didn't think I had time to spend with God in my busy day; I'd brushed past him on my way to meetings and workouts that morning. Undeterred, he tracked me down—that's how much God loves me and wants to be with me.

Being available to God, even in such a small way, can be a transformative experience. Simple compassion begins with paying attention, noticing opportunities to share love or a sandwich.

God told his people, "Love the LORD your God with all your heart and with all your soul and with all your strength. These commandments that I give you today are to be on your hearts. Impress them on your children. Talk about them when you sit at home and when you walk along the road, when you lie down and when you get up. Tie them as symbols on your hands and bind them on your foreheads. Write them on the doorframes of your houses and on your gates" (Deut. 6:5–9).

My kids and I rarely "walk along the road," except when walking the dog. We do spend a lot of time on the road, in the sanctuary of our minivan. Sometimes we talk about matters of faith, sometimes listen to Christian music. Sometimes we talk about school or friends and listen to rock and roll or pop. Sometimes I'll ask them to tell me what the lyrics of a certain pop song are about, and we'll have a discussion about values. I try to be on the lookout for teachable moments as we go through our day, as we walk (or drive) through the world.

The suburban homeless are often invisible. This one came into view as we went along the road. I helped him, and he helped me: to pay attention and to impress on my child what it means to love the Lord your God with all your heart, soul, and strength.

Compassion Step

Memorize Proverbs 3:27 (NIV): "Do not withhold good from those who deserve it, when it is in your power to act." Ask God to bring you opportunities to share your food with the hungry, and for eyes to see those opportunities. Think about fasting, if you have tried it before. Was it an act of personal piety, or something you did in order to share with others? How could you use fasting as a way to bless others?

Community Step

Last week you visited a ministry or church in a poor neighborhood. Talk about how that went. What needs did you notice or hear about?

How does what you saw or experienced impact the way you read Isaiah 58? What do you think it means to "loose the chains of injustice" or to "satisfy the needs of the oppressed"? In past weeks you've reached out to people in your neighborhood. While you don't want to abandon those people, how could you as a group connect with people outside of your neighborhood, perhaps quarterly or monthly? God does not call one person to meet every need. But where do you sense he is calling you and your group to show compassion? Consider fasting and praying as a group to seek God's direction as to where to allocate your time and resources.

shoes

my house tends to be a bit cluttered, although I like to point out that I am not the only one who lives there, not the only one leaving things all over the place.

My family is a "take your shoes off when you come in" family, mostly because the weather in Chicago often means you will be walking in with snow, mud, or both on your shoes. So just inside each door, you'll find a pile of shoes and boots.

The hall just inside the front door even has a throw rug, where we line up everything from flip-flops to snow boots. Since it's April, both are there now. The dog for some reason loves to nap there. I've seen him gently pawing the footwear on the rug, rearranging the shoes to make a nest where he can lounge, his chin resting on a sneaker, surrounded by the smells of his family. For reasons only a dog could understand, he will sometimes forsake the large cushy dog bed on the laundry room floor so that he can lie on the uneven surface of a pile of shoes in the front hall. I don't know if he is guarding the shoes, keeping an eye on the front door, or just enjoying a doggie version of aromatherapy.

The other day I got an email from a global charity, telling me the story of a fourteen-year-old girl who has no shoes. She gets hookworm, repeatedly, from running around barefoot.

This makes me sad, frustrated. How is it that this girl has no shoes? Not even flip-flops to protect her?

I had just bought my own teenage daughter a pair of running shoes because she's on the track team at school this year and had worn out her old sneakers. Dropped fifty dollars or so to make sure her feet are well supported.

Most women love shoes. Some women seem to love expensive and impractical shoes. I'm more of a comfort shoe sort of person. In my pre-adolescent years, I had big feet. Size nine wide. I ended up being almost five foot eight, so I pretty much caught up to my feet. At age twelve I was an awkward tomboy with thick glasses and big feet. I hated buying shoes. I went barefoot whenever I could, although I didn't have to suffer health issues because of it.

In my twenties, I became a bit more fashion conscious. I was glad to learn that big feet are sometimes part of a genetic package deal that also includes long legs, and that contact lenses are a wonderful invention. I was still in denial about the width of my feet, though, so I squeezed them into pointy-toed torture chambers.

This abuse of my metatarsals led to surgery before I turned thirty. I became acquainted soon after with the Naturalizer shoe store, where my mother had shopped for years. Sigh. So now I make sure my shoes fit properly. I wear tennis shoes or flats a lot of the time.

Yesterday I was getting dressed for church. I'm pawing through the pile of shoes on the floor of my closet, and nothing goes with the navy blue pants I have put on. I'm grousing to myself that I have no shoes that go with this outfit.

Then I remember the email about the girl with no shoes—while I am complaining about having no shoes *that go with this particular pair of pants.* I feel privilege guilt for a minute. Why does it matter so much to me what I wear to church? It's not a fashion show. I'm there to worship, not to see and be seen.

So I say a quick prayer that the "glamour don't" photographers won't be lurking around the church lobby, and go to church with imperfect shoes on. Actually, our shoe problems are the result of our clothing problem: we have too many clothes, so we need plenty of shoes to find the right ones to go with all our outfits. I could have solved my shoe problem by choosing another of my dozen or so pairs of pants for church.

I cannot blindly accept the systemic injustice that allows some people to get sick with preventable diseases because they lack shoes, while others of us have overflowing closets. Just because some people in the world don't have shoes, should I feel guilty for having shoes at all? Guilt gets me nowhere and doesn't get shoes to those who need them. So what can I do?

I search the internet and discover that I'm not the first person to wrestle with this issue. I find a website called www.shareyoursoles.org, through which you can donate gently used shoes to those who need them.

The book of Proverbs calls us to be generous, as we've seen in previous chapters. It also makes much of the connection between hard work and generosity. If we work hard and are wise, we're able to be generous.

Proverbs 31 is a passage that some women hate; they feel intimidated by this "Proverbs 31 woman," as if the passage describes one overachieving superwoman—Mother Teresa, Martha Stewart, and Hillary Clinton all rolled into one. I don't think this chapter offers us the description of one woman. Rather it's the answer to the rhetorical question, "A good wife, who can find her?" The passage lists various careers and callings that a woman might pursue: she might be in the import-export business (v. 14); she might be a real-estate developer (v. 16); she might be an entrepreneur in the textile industry (v. 24).

This passage notes that a hardworking woman can afford to be generous; it also notes that a hardworking woman can be fashionable. She does not let her own family go about in rags. She is both generous and well dressed. She doesn't spend frivolously, but she apparently gives some attention to her wardrobe and that of her family. Not undue attention, just enough. She works hard and then uses the resources she's earned to care for the poor, but she doesn't neglect herself or her family.

> *She sees that her trading is profitable,*
> *and her lamp does not go out at night.*
> *In her hand she holds the distaff*
> *and grasps the spindle with her fingers.*
> *She opens her arms to the poor*
> *and extends her hands to the needy.*
> *When it snows, she has no fear for her household;*
> *for all of them are clothed in scarlet.*
> *She makes coverings for her bed;*
> *she is clothed in fine linen and purple.*
>   Proverbs 31:18–22

It's interesting that the verse that mentions her care for the poor and needy is sandwiched between the description of her hard work and the way she and her family are dressed—in the colors and rich fabrics of royalty. She works hard, is successful, and is able to dress her family warmly and well. A woman who is clothed in fine linen probably has the shoes to go with it.

I'm guessing she probably had a healthy attitude about shoes. Shoes do not change who you are. It is okay to have shoes. The answer to the problem is not for me to go barefoot but for me to limit my consumption so that I am able to help provide shoes for those who don't have them.

What if every time I bought a pair of shoes, I also donated some money to a charity that provides shoes for someone who doesn't have any? Or if I saw a pair of just totally cute shoes, wanted them, then chose not to buy them but instead donated the money I would have spent? What if I donated the shoes I don't wear? What if I decided how many shoes are enough and then stopped buying shoes until the ones I have wear out?

It may seem like a small step, but for many of us, getting a grip on our shoe addiction may be the first step toward living a life of simple compassion.

Compassion Step

Small steps like donating money instead of buying another unnecessary pair of shoes may seem insignificant. Do it anyway. Start a shoe fund, and anytime you pass up a pair of shoes, take the money you would have spent and put it in a jar. After several months (depending on how shoe crazy you are), donate the money to a charity that provides shoes to impoverished children (for example, www.worldvision.org).

Community Step

As a group, collect gently used shoes from your members to donate to www.shareyoursoles.org, another charity, or a local homeless shelter. If you need it, go on a shoe fast and stop buying shoes for a period of time you know will be difficult for you. Express your solidarity with the poor by wearing last year's shoes another season. Hold one another accountable: when you are tempted to buy shoes you don't need, call another person in the group and let them talk you out of it. Consider carefully how you define *need* versus *want*. What longing are you trying to fulfill by buying another pair?

ground

Why is it that we pick certain sayings of Jesus and turn them into benchmarks for faith, while we twist backward other things he said? For example, he told one person, who already believed in God, that he had to be born again (John 3:1 – 21), and we say that's what everyone must do. I'm not arguing against being born again — I've done it myself — but I am against selecting certain verses while ignoring entire themes.

One time Jesus said, "Be on your guard against all kinds of greed; life does not consist in an abundance of possessions" (Luke 12:15). Why is greed not the deal breaker when it comes to who is in and who is out of God's kingdom? What if — I know this sounds crazy, but what if — greed is a deal breaker? Jesus mentioned that born-again thing to only one person, who came alone to talk to him, at night. He talked about greed a whole lot more, in front of crowds. So why do we not say, you have to give up being greedy? I'm just wondering.

Certain prosperity gospel types seem to be saying the exact opposite of this verse, promising that Jesus *will give you* an abundance of possessions, along with a tax deduction for your gift, if you will just call the number on the screen with your credit card ready.

I don't agree with that. Who are we to predict what God will do, to assume that we can manipulate his blessings? God may bless us, but there are no guarantees that those blessings will be material ones. While Jesus said he came to give us life to the full, he also said life is not about lots of stuff. So life to the full is, apparently, not about more and more stuff.

Luke writes,

> Someone in the crowd said to him, "Teacher, tell my brother to divide the inheritance with me." Jesus replied, "Man, who appointed me a judge or an arbiter between you?" Then he said to them, "Watch out! Be on your guard against all kinds of greed; life does not consist in an abundance of possessions." And he told them this parable: "The ground of a certain rich

man yielded an abundant harvest. He thought to himself, 'What shall I do? I have no place to store my crops.' Then he said, 'This is what I'll do. I will tear down my barns and build bigger ones, and there I will store my surplus grain. And I'll say to myself, "You have plenty of grain laid up for many years. Take life easy; eat, drink and be merry."' But God said to him, 'You fool! This very night your life will be demanded from you. Then who will get what you have prepared for yourself?' This is how it will be with those who store up things for themselves but are not rich toward God."

Luke 12:13–21

Look at the first sentence of Jesus' parable (Luke 12:16): "The ground of a certain rich man ..." His story doesn't say, "The excellent agricultural techniques of a certain rich man ..." Jesus doesn't attribute the abundant harvest to the man's efforts, his intelligence, or even God's blessings on the man. It's just the ground. And it has a good year.

Part of the reason why some people have more stuff than others is because of the ground. The ground they live on. The ground they just happen, by accident of their birth, to occupy on this planet. I am lucky enough (certain people would say blessed) to occupy ground in a comfortable suburb in middle America. If I had been born in Africa, or even the south side of Chicago, my life would be different, no matter how hard I worked.

Jesus points out, right after his words about greed and possessions, that the ground is often the determining factor in our lives. Not God's favor, not our hard work. Just the ground. When we have a lot of stuff, or we've been blessed, depending on how you tend to view that situation, sometimes it's just that we happen to live on good ground. Jesus says if we are that lucky and end up with an abundance, then we should not hoard it, or we'll risk the wrath of God.

Rob Bell notes that poverty was a reality for many of Jesus' listeners: "Jesus told this story at a time when many of his countrymen were losing family land and having trouble feeding their families. Being hungry was a very real issue for a lot of people. In the story, God is so offended by the man's selfish actions that his very life is taken from him that night. It is one of the only places in all of Jesus' teachings where someone does something so horrible in Jesus' eyes that they deserve to die right away.

And what is this horrible thing the man did? He refused to be generous. He brought hell to earth."[37]

What if refusal to be generous makes God mad? What if simply believing Jesus died for your sins and being born again is only the first step? What if making him Lord of your life also means making him Lord of your financial portfolio?

Having a lot of stuff can tempt us to put our faith in the stuff rather than God. That's what the man in Jesus' parable did. He not only didn't share; he decided that his future was secure because of his stockpiles of grain.

So much of our striving has to do with building financial security. Saving is a good idea. Giving is just as good an idea. Apparently, Jesus is saying that greed doesn't just make us unhappy or make people dislike us; if we are greedy—if we hoard instead of being generous—God becomes angry.

How do you become a generous person? The first step toward generosity is realizing that anything you have is in part because of the ground you are on—the family you happened to be born into, the color of skin you landed in here on earth, the opportunities you received.

When you realize that, you can begin to stop saying "Mine!" What happens to us spiritually when we are able to hold loosely our material possessions? The things we have can easily be lost, so we shouldn't put our faith in our stuff.

As Luke's narrative continues, he records Jesus' teaching on, of all things, worry. "Do not worry," Jesus said (Luke 12:22). How are these connected? We'll talk about that in the next chapter.

Compassion Step

Reread the quote from Rob Bell in this chapter. Do you agree or disagree with him, and why? Of the possessions you have, which are the most valuable to you? Do you ever worry about losing those things? What would it look like to hold loosely those possessions?

Community Step

As a group, read the parable in Luke 12:13–21. Study the context. Jesus often told parables to answer a question or make a point. Discuss your observations about the story and its context. Where was he? What was going on? Why did he tell this story? What do you think Jesus' audience thought about this parable? What does it mean for us today?

In chapter 27, you visited a ministry or church in a poor neighborhood. This week, visit again and provide help in a tangible way.

anxious

i need to confess a sin. I've tried to confess it to others, but no one will hold me accountable on it; no one will even name it as a sin. Ready? I worry.

I'm working on it, but I can't seem to give it up. I have a worry addiction.

I used to be worse. But, oh, sanctification is a slow process on this one. I used to have almost constant irrational fears that something bad was going to happen. If Scot was late coming home, I imagined a car wreck. When I got on an airplane, I was sure we would crash. I lived with a layer of vague fear under everything, like blood surging just below bruised skin. I felt uncertain, even though I hid it well. I pretended to be confident. Most people thought me brave. Ha.

You may not think worry is a sin, but Jesus said don't do it. (See Matt. 6:25–34.) Many of us do. Sometimes we worry about ourselves, at other times about others. A lot of times the latter comes across as being judgmental. Or just annoying.

I haven't always been like this; having babies did it to me. My children: so vulnerable, so needy. Who would care for them if I were not there? And they quickly discovered so many ways they could get into trouble — fatal trouble. Toddlers are like a disaster waiting to happen, and baby-proofing offers no guarantees. Melanie, when she was a toddler, would run under our dining room table. She was short enough that she could go right under it without ducking. Then one day, she wasn't short enough. Bam! The table caught her smack in the forehead. She landed on her behind, silent for an agonizing moment, then wailed. I hadn't even thought to worry about that happening, which made me worry about whether there were other things I'd neglected worrying about. There are so many dangers out there lurking for little people who don't know better than to fall into swimming pools or drink the dish detergent. My kids have survived into adolescence, which brings me new and fresh opportunities for anxiety.

My husband also wrestles with this sin. He tends to worry about money, which is something I'm not inclined to worry about. I know he's got it covered. He once got mad at me for not worrying enough. I'm not joking.

With God's help, my healing is coming along. Like someone in a twelve-step program, I had to admit I was powerless, and that admission brought great power. I realized worry is a sin and named it such. Worry was stealing my joy, making life, well, maybe not unmanageable, but at least not very fun. I also realized that (1) when your husband is a realtor, he's almost always late for dinner, and (2) I get on a plane several times a month, and I needed to get over it.

I would like to say that I just turned over my fears to God. Not exactly. It felt more like he came looking for me, hand held out, like a parent with a child, asking her to hand over the scissors before she hurts herself. "I'll take that," he'd say, prying my worries gently from my clenched fist, reminding me that his most often repeated commandment is "Do not be afraid."

I was glad God brought it up, frankly. I was a bit weary of living my life waiting for the other shoe to drop. I want to be present, to live in the moment, to be mindful of all the good things that are right now. As Jesus said, tomorrow has enough worries of its own. Fear is an expression of worry, of anxiety. God whispered gently, "I can't use you to make a difference if you're cowering in fear. So trust me. I've got something for you to do, and you're slowing yourself down with this anxiety thing." (Some of this he communicated through a good Christian therapist. Which I highly recommend, if your anxiety is more than moderate.)

Compassion is incompatible with worry.

My deep desire is to live a life that matters, a life lived to the full. I want to be a generous, lavish, joyful, exuberant person. I want to be fully present, mindful and kind. I want people to see how I live, and shake their heads in wonder, not because I'm so great but because it is just so obvious that the only explanation for any of it is Jesus. I want to let go of being anxious. Jesus is telling us that the path to freedom from anxiety is generosity.

Last week we read the first part of Luke 12, where Jesus talked about greed. The next section records Jesus' teaching on the sin of anxiety. The words are nearly the same as those in Matthew 6:25–34 (part of the

Sermon on the Mount). I wonder if Luke or Jesus, or both, were perhaps making a statement about how greed is just a form of anxiety. The text says that after telling the story about the man who wanted to build bigger barns, Jesus says to his disciples, "Therefore ... do not worry." The word *therefore* points us to what just happened. He tells a parable and then says "therefore" to preface his explanation of the parable, his teaching on the topic.

People who struggle with anxiety are not necessarily greedy. Still, greed can be a particular manifestation of anxiety. By greedy, I don't mean always trying to get more. I mean refusing to be generous.

So if you want to be generous, give up your worry addiction. Conversely, if you want to be less anxious, be generous. Greed takes root in a soul that believes far too strongly in scarcity, a soul that is afraid there is not enough. Anxious people tend to grab and hoard. People who believe in abundance simply are less tempted to get greedy.

The Greek word translated "worry" or "be anxious" in these texts is *merimnao*. It means to be troubled with cares, to be anxious, or, according to one lexicon, it can also mean "to seek to promote one's interests." In other words, *merimnao* is self-protection that becomes anxious selfishness. Worry is selfish.[38]

Paul uses the same word when he talks about being free from concern in 1 Corinthians 7:32 – 34, and also in Philippians 4:6, where he writes, "Do not be anxious about anything, but in every situation, by prayer and petition, with thanksgiving, present your requests to God."

Lois Roberts is a woman who has reason to be anxious. After forty-five years of marriage, her husband left her. She had been sponsoring a child through World Vision but could no longer afford it after her divorce. Rather than wallowing in self-pity, Lois decided to minister to the people around her — something she'd been doing all along.

Lois lives on a farm down the road from Pleasant Vineyard, a Christian children's camp. The camp didn't have room for its horseback riding program, so the program had been housed at various farms over the years. A few years ago, the camp director asked if he could move it to Lois's property. She and her husband ended up building a larger barn and a new hay barn and clearing more trails for the kids to ride on. "I just said yes," she says.

Lois says she is always looking for people to pray for and to help. When she gets up in the morning, she simply prays, "God, show me what I can do to help someone today."

Sometimes that means simply praying for people who cross your path, even if you don't speak to them. "If you keep your eyes open, God will bring things to you," Lois says. "It becomes a way of life. You become more observant." She remembers driving one day and noticing a young man and woman in a park. The man looked odd and scruffy, like a hippie. She wondered if he might be on drugs. She felt God tugging at her heart to pray for him. "I simply prayed, 'Lord, save him and fill him with your Holy Spirit,'" Lois remembers. She drove past the couple and didn't see them again. Until a year later, when they walked into her church. The man and his wife became Christians, and the man even worked in a Christian bookstore.

"God wants to use everyone," she says. "We're it. He doesn't have a plan B. Even doing little bitty things really can make a difference." In the summer, Lois likes to buy fresh vegetables at a farmers market. When she does, she always buys an extra bag of corn and whatever else looks good. She takes them to a trailer court in town (where she knows the residents are poor) and knocks randomly on the door of someone she doesn't know. "I just ask them if they need food, and if they need me to pray for them," she says. "Often they'll invite me in, and I will pray for whatever they need." She does not invite them to church; she just tells them that God loves them, "no strings attached."

The Bible says, "Whoever oppresses the poor shows contempt for their Maker, but whoever is kind to the needy honors God" (Prov. 14:31). If we say we want to honor God with our lives, here's a way to do it — be kind to the needy. The needy don't live only in the developing world. They might live in a trailer court or an apartment complex not far from your home.

Compassion Step

This week, try a seven-day experiment. Each day, before you get out of bed, pray the prayer that Lois recommends: "God, show me what I can do to help someone today." Then be on the lookout for people or situations that God brings across your path. Like Lois, you may have to venture over to a trailer park or a poorer section of town. When God provides an opportunity for you to help or pray for someone, do it.

Community Step

As a group, discuss the following questions: What are some things that you worry about? In what ways is worry a sin? What do you think is at the root of your worry? Is it fear or a desire to control things? What keeps you from trusting God or trusting other people? How might worry hinder you spiritually? How might it keep you from being compassionate? Worry keeps us from generosity; how might generosity keep us from worry?

legacy

If you were to die today, what sort of legacy would you leave behind? What are you doing that matters to someone other than yourself?

The book of Acts tells about a woman named Tabitha (or, in Greek, Dorcas) who had dedicated her life to providing love and practical help to a group of marginalized people—the widows of her town. In those days widowhood was a sentence of suffering. While all women had very few rights, widows had even fewer. Donald Kraybill notes that in Jesus' time, "a widow in Palestinian society was an outcast. She had no inheritance rights from her husband's property. When the husband died, the oldest son acquired the property. If there was no son, a brother of the deceased husband might marry the widow. If the brother refused or there was none, she would return to her father's house or to begging."[39]

By the time Acts was written, widowhood had improved only slightly, depending on the woman's station in life while she was married. It still often meant poverty and struggle. *The IVP Women's Bible Commentary* notes, "The widow's legal status improved in the Roman Empire. Roman widows functioned as independent, legal parties if their finances allowed. They could inherit from husbands and manage their own property."[40] Still, their rights were limited.

The text shows us that widows were assumed to be poor. Acts 9:36 says Dorcas "was always doing good and helping the poor." A few verses later, in describing her death, the text says that "all the widows stood around him [Peter], crying and showing him the robes and other clothing that Dorcas had made while she was still with them" (Acts 9:39). The widows were the poor whom she had helped. They had depended on her for such basic necessities as clothing.

The text doesn't tell us whether she herself was a widow, although some commentaries indicate that she was. It does say she was a disciple. There's no mention of her husband, so one might assume she was a widow, although she appears to have had some financial means, by which she was helping others.

I have to guess that Dorcas was not a wealthy woman. I imagine her as one of those people who believed that she had enough, even if it wasn't much, who embraced abundance rather than scarcity. I've known people who say that they cannot afford to be generous or even to tithe. I disagree. Giving, in my experience, is more contingent upon your level of trust in God than upon your net worth.

Dorcas apparently didn't let lack of resources restrict her impact. She not only loved the widows around her; she left them with tangible evidence of that love. They held robes, clothing—things that Dorcas had made for them to meet very practical needs.

Dorcas put her faith into action. She didn't let her lack of resources keep her from being generous. She lived out the truth later recorded in the book of James: "What good is it, my brothers and sisters, if people claim to have faith but have no deeds? Can such faith save them? Suppose a brother or sister is without clothes and daily food. If one of you says to them, 'Go in peace; keep warm and well fed,' but does nothing about their physical needs, what good is it? In the same way, faith by itself, if it is not accompanied by action, is dead" (James 2:14–17).

When I was growing up, that passage bothered me. I'd been taught that Christianity was about cultivating personal piety. The "action" that went with my faith was rules-keeping and witnessing. I was a good little evangelical and knew I was supposed to give an answer for my faith. I was to "get out of the saltshaker" (sorry, Rebecca Pippert) and lead people to Jesus. Mostly by arguing with them (thank you, Josh McDowell) and being so happy that they would wonder what my secret was. When they asked, I was supposed to tell them it was Jesus. I'd compare that passage with the declaration in Ephesians 2:8: "It is by grace you have been saved, through faith—and this not from yourselves, it is the gift of God—not by works, so that no one can boast." Which, if you look at the context, does not contradict James at all.

James' example of action goes far beyond verbal witnessing or being a light for Jesus with my positive attitude. He illustrates his point by talking about very practical works, such as feeding and clothing people. Huh. I never heard a sermon about that. Of course, in my little world, none of my brothers or sisters in Christ actually lacked food or clothes, so maybe that verse didn't pertain to us. We were a well-dressed and well-fed bunch.

In Matthew's story of a miraculous feeding of a crowd that likely numbered more than fifteen thousand (Matt. 14:13–21),[41] Jesus took the meager offering of five loaves and two fish, thanked God for it, and then broke it. Once broken, the food was used to feed many.

Dorcas may have been a woman who was broken. Widowed and alone, she undoubtedly knew doubt and suffering. She chose to focus elsewhere, to find community by reaching out to others. She shared herself with other women, meeting them in their suffering, which she herself had experienced. She was a loaves-and-fishes kind of disciple who brought her little bit to help others. She let God break her and then bless her. Instead of being known as a poor widow with few resources (even if that was what she was), she was known as a generous woman.

A legacy of generosity is not contingent upon great wealth. Rather, it simply requires trust and action. Dorcas helped the other widows in Joppa with practical things like clothing. Beyond that, she brought together the isolated and formed a community.

Peter heard about Dorcas when he was in Lydda, which was ten miles away. The people of Joppa sent for him, begging him to come. One commentary notes, "It is hard to tell whether they hoped he would raise Tabitha from the dead or whether they wanted him to conduct the funeral."[42]

The story in Acts continues, "Peter went with them, and when he arrived he was taken upstairs to the room. All the widows stood around him, crying and showing him the robes and other clothing that Dorcas had made while she was still with them. Peter sent them all out of the room; then he got down on his knees and prayed. Turning toward the dead woman, he said, "Tabitha, get up." She opened her eyes, and seeing Peter she sat up. He took her by the hand and helped her to her feet. Then he called for the believers, especially the widows, and presented her to them alive. This became known all over Joppa, and many people believed in the Lord" (Acts 9:39–42).

I love that phrase, "especially the widows." In God's kingdom, those who would ordinarily be considered unimportant are honored.

Dorcas had a legacy, but she was also given several more years of life, apparently, to continue building that legacy. What an amazing way for God to affirm her, to say through her life, "This is what it means to love your neighbor." She lived, more than once, a legacy of compassion.

Compassion Step

Read James 2:14–17 again. Spend some time reflecting on this passage, reading it slowly several times. Read its context in James 2. Ask God to speak to you through this passage. What word stands out? What does that word (or words) have to do with you and your journey? What do you think God wants you to know or do as a result of your reflection?

Community Step

Read the story of Dorcas aloud together. How could you as a group follow Dorcas's example, especially as you serve the poor? Talk about the question posed at the beginning of this chapter: what sort of legacy do you want to have?

What could you do to provide not only clothing or other practical help but also community to people who are isolated? Decide on one action you as a group will take this week. Perhaps you will want to continue connecting with neighbors you've served in the past weeks. Consider "adopting" someone you've met in your outreach projects and providing simple, tangible help to them on an ongoing basis (meals, visits, a bag of groceries, transportation to doctor appointments). Pray before acting; ask God to lead you in this endeavor. Set a time limit of a few months or so, and then decide whether to continue. If you choose to take this on, make sure to divide the work between all members of the group.

boss

there are some verses I wish had been left out of the Bible. They hit a little too close to home; they sound a little too intense. For example, the first six verses in James 5. This passage feels like a bit of fire and brimstone. It's politically incorrect.

The passage is a rant against the wealthy, actually. Which makes me just a little uncomfortable. I mean, I live in America. I'm a homeowner (well, technically, a mortgage holder). I have a comfortable and safe place to sleep at night, a job, clothes, and food. Which makes me, by global standards, outrageously wealthy. Even by American standards, I'm doing okay.

I have friends who have more financial resources than I do. I can think of several whose net worth is probably ten times mine. I can honestly say I would not trade places with them. I grew up having plenty and knowing people who had a lot more than that. They're just people, and frankly, they struggle, because even though they say that they know money can't buy happiness, they keep trying to find it on sale someplace. People with a lot of money don't necessarily have happier marriages, children who are better behaved, or less stress. They don't necessarily lead more interesting lives.

I have friends who have much less than I do. I sometimes think that God would like me to have a little more financial diversity in my circle of friends. My friend Arloa lives in East Garfield Park, one of the poorest and most violent neighborhoods in Chicago, because she serves the poor there. Another friend, who recently reconnected with me, is a single mom living in a trailer in an aging farm town. I suppose you're expecting me to tell you that my less-wealthy friends are happier or smarter or something. Not necessarily. Poverty doesn't necessarily make you more noble.

On the other hand, the Bible doesn't cut the rich much slack, especially if their wealth is combined with a lack of generosity. I wonder if God was thinking of me or my friends when he dictated this memo to his scribe James: "Now listen, you rich people, weep and wail because of the misery that is coming on you. Your wealth has rotted, and moths have eaten your clothes. Your gold and silver are corroded. Their corrosion will testify against you and eat your flesh like fire. You have hoarded wealth in the last days. Look! The wages you failed to pay the workers who mowed your fields are crying out against you. The cries of the harvesters have reached the ears of the Lord Almighty. You have lived on earth in luxury and self-indulgence. You have fattened yourselves in the day of slaughter. You have condemned and murdered the innocent one, who was not opposing you" (James 5:1–6).

Ouch. What is this passage saying to me? Is it even talking to me? (I'd like to hope not.) Am I aware of the source of my stuff? Am I deaf to the cries of the harvesters or the factory workers or the people I interact with every day, like the employees at Wal-Mart or the servers at McDonald's? Do I realize the implications of buying clothing made in sweatshops, toys made in foreign factories where there are few labor laws? Do I even know where the junk I buy comes from?

Every day, I eat food that has been harvested by someone. I wear clothes sewn by someone else. It could be that my bread was made with wheat harvested by an American farmer driving an air-conditioned combine through his fields. Or not. The fruit I select from the produce section at the grocery store might be harvested by a migrant worker in the United States or a person in South America earning a subsistence wage, if that. If I can buy a shirt for less than it would cost me to buy the fabric and make it myself, what does that tell you about the wages paid to the worker who made it?

Many of the world's agricultural workers are held in virtual slavery. Many workers in the United States, though they earn much more than people in the developing world, have trouble earning enough to live on because our cost of living is out of whack with minimum wage. (A great resource on this issue is Barbara Ehrenreich's bestselling book, *Nickel and Dimed*.)[43] How do I show God's love to workers I see every day—the waitress, the cleaning crew at the health club, the woman stocking shelves at the discount store? Even if I don't think I'm hoarding wealth, what does this passage tell me about God's concern for subsistence-level workers?

Like Jesus' story about the man who wanted to build bigger barns, this passage warns against hoarding. Does it also warn against wealth?

Some of the Bible's heroes, like Solomon or Abraham, were wealthy. What if you are wealthy but also generous? Or if you are generous, is it impossible to be wealthy, because you give it all away?

Should I give money to everyone who has less than I do? To everyone who asks? I don't think that's a responsible use of what God's entrusted to me, but I can use my resources to help others. I can do small things, like leaving a generous tip for the minimum-wage worker who serves me in a restaurant or cleans my hotel room. I can limit my consumption. I can trust that I have enough, and by so doing tap into the abundance of God.

What does God accuse the rich of? "You have hoarded wealth." Why would we hoard stuff when we know, as this passage says, that treasures on this earth eventually wear out or corrode or get stolen? Jesus said, "Do not store up for yourselves treasures on earth, where moth and rust destroy, and where thieves break in and steal. But store up for yourselves treasures in heaven, where moth and rust do not destroy, and where thieves do not break in and steal. For where your treasure is, there your heart will be also" (Matt. 6:19–21).

God warns us against hoarding, storing up, accumulating. Does that mean we should not have a 401(k)? That we ought not to have a savings account? The Bible also lauds good money management and thriftiness. Our thrift ought to enable us to be generous.

Jesus continues, "No one can serve two masters. Either you will hate the one and love the other, or you will be devoted to the one and despise the other. You cannot serve both God and Money" (Matt. 6:24).

Whom or what do you serve? What do you spend more time thinking about—God or money? What do you arrange your life around? Is your money a tool, or is it your taskmaster? Are you the boss of your money, or is it the boss of you? Is your goal to save in order to do good for others, or is your motive simply to have more?

If you serve God, your money will serve him. That doesn't mean giving it all away. It means managing it without hoarding it. I've got two kids, and in just a few years I want to send them to college. So how do I save for their education yet still be generous? Is saving for college the same as hoarding? I'm saving up so that I can be generous to my children. Can I find ways to be generous to strangers at the same time? Would I do that? These are questions I still wrestle with. I invite you to wrestle with them as well.

Compassion Step

What is your response to James 5:1–6? Do you think of yourself as rich? Do you think this passage was written to a specific group of people at a specific time in history or to all people? What keeps you from being more generous? What is one way you can choose to be generous?

Community Step

Talk about your ongoing relationships and the serving you are doing as you read through this book. Share both the triumphs and the struggles. Spend some time in prayer about that. Ask God for direction as to where he wants you to spend your time and resources. Then as a group discuss the following: What are the responsibilities of having financial resources? How can you let your money serve God? What barriers get in the way of being generous? What do you think God is saying in James 5:1–6 to people who would consider themselves "middle class"? What do you think it means to store up treasures in heaven?

overfed

at 6:30 a.m. Saturday, a group of suburban moms gathers in my driveway, carrying egg casseroles and cartons of orange juice. We load the minivan with breakfast foods and drive about forty minutes or so to the west side of Chicago, to Breakthrough Urban Ministries' Joshua Center, to cook and serve breakfast.

Our monthly trek to the city has been an eye-opening experience for me and for many of my neighbors, almost a dozen of whom have come to the shelter. We rotate so that three or four of us go each month. It's amazing how difficult it can be to give up three hours of your month. All of us have good intentions. Living them out is strangely difficult, especially when our kids have sporting events on Saturday mornings.

Some women who live in the shelter are homeless because they have been rescued from domestic violence or prostitution. Others have, to put it mildly, emotional issues. Breakthrough Urban Ministries requires its guests to be sober and to be working toward a goal — sobriety, employment, getting an apartment, and so on.

Some of these women look as if they have not missed any meals. I'm always surprised at obesity in the poor. If they don't have enough, how did they get to be overweight? Then I watch the way they come back for thirds on the sausage, the way they eat the meal we serve as if it were their last. I see the fear in their laden plates. Their overwhelming mindset is scarcity — you'd better fill up now and stick a bagel in your pocket, because you don't know when you'll eat again.

Their addictions and emotional issues also play a role. It's complicated. I can't even pretend to understand. Realizing my ignorance is the first step toward empathy. So I bring food, but I also try to bring myself and my concern for them. I try to listen. Some talk shyly; some eat in stony silence. Others weave amazing stories, which may or may not be true. That's not for me to judge. I just offer the gift of listening.

Going to the shelter reminds us that our lives are not the only definition of normal. I don't do it to assuage anyone's privilege guilt, although the first few trips do sort of remind you of how lucky you are to have a roof over your head and food on the table. Beyond this, I want to build community within my own neighborhood. Serving together has created a deeper bond between us.

I also go because I want to embrace my city. Chicago is my hometown. I want to give back to my city in some small way. I want to love it more holistically. I feel called to live in my suburban neighborhood, for now. I also want to care for the city, not just avail myself of its benefits.

One Old Testament prophet, Ezekiel, delivered a scathing message from God, not to an individual but to a city. He compared his own people, whom he called by the name of their city, Jerusalem, to other cities that had incurred God's wrath. Through Ezekiel, God reminded his people that he had destroyed one city because of its arrogance and lack of concern for the poor. Which city? Sodom.[44]

For years, I assumed that Sodom's only sin was homosexuality, because, well, that's what I heard preached. It's true that there is a reference to homosexual rape in Genesis 19. The etymology of the word *sodomize* traces back to the biblical story.

However, Ezekiel 16:49–50 says, "Now this was the sin of your sister Sodom: She and her daughters were arrogant, overfed and unconcerned; they did not help the poor and needy. They were haughty and did detestable things before me. Therefore I did away with them as you have seen."

Will and Lisa Samson write, "You have no doubt heard homosexuality condemned as a sin from the pulpit. How often have we heard a sermon about the sin of not sharing what we have with those in need?"[45]

I too never heard a sermon on Ezekiel 16. Why have Christians created a hierarchy of sins? The Bible says that if you break just one part of the law, you've broken all of it. (See James 2:10, which, interestingly, is in another passage that condemns ignoring the plight of the poor.)

So many Christians fear the "homosexual agenda" but apparently ignore the greed agenda, which is just as real and has, arguably, way more potential for destruction.

Arrogant, overfed, and unconcerned — there have been times when I have been all of these things. Even if you are not overweight, do you have more food and stuff and clothes than you need? Does it bother you, or are you unconcerned about it?

While half the world goes to bed hungry, many Americans wrestle with the opposite problem. More than half of Americans are overweight. The factors are many; as we noted earlier, even the poor in our country often wrestle with obesity, in part because healthy food costs more than unhealthy food. To eat organic, low-fat, whole-grain, and so on is a luxury. If you have limited funds and you're not sure when you will eat again, will you choose a seven-dollar organic salad or a two-dollar Big Mac?[46]

Weight loss programs are a $55 billion U.S. industry. Some analysts expect that figure to balloon (pun intended) to $68.7 billion by 2010.[47]

I know wrestling with weight can be a difficult battle, which often is about so much more than food. Our culture uses food like a drug, to numb and comfort. Eating disorders range from overeating to anorexia, and both can bog us down in self-absorption, blinding us, keeping us from practicing simple compassion, preventing us from making a difference.

If our "concern" for the poor does not lead us to action, it's not authentic concern. If we merely observe, "Wow, it's too bad people are hungry," but don't do anything about it, we are disobeying God. The Bible asks, "If any one of you has material possessions and sees a brother or sister in need but has no pity on them, how can the love of God be in you?" (1 John 3:17). If God has entrusted us with any possessions and with his love, he asks us to extend both to those who are hungry or in need. Our pity cannot be merely theoretical.

Throughout the Bible, God uses the symbol of a feast to describe his relationship with his people. It is a picture of abundance and generosity and grace—where we get what we don't deserve. Through Isaiah, God declares,

> Come, all you who are thirsty,
>   come to the waters;
> and you who have no money,
>   come, buy and eat!
> Come, buy wine and milk
>   without money and without cost.
> Why spend money on what is not bread,
>   and your labor on what does not satisfy?

Listen, listen to me, and eat what is good,
and you will delight in the richest of fare.
Isaiah 55:1 – 2

I go to the shelter on Saturday mornings to live this verse. The pancakes and eggs are a symbol of the abundance of God, an edible prayer for these women. In serving the meal, I delight in the richest of fare.

Compassion Step

Spend some time with God in self-examination. Remember, self-examination is a look at your actions and motives, guided by a God who loves you and wants you to grow. Be honest about your attitude; are there times when you are arrogant, overfed, and unconcerned? How can you be more humble? How can you perhaps reduce consumption and increase action fueled by your concern? Or are you overly concerned with others, to the point that you do too much for others and neglect yourself?

Community Step

In week 27 you looked at a map of your region or city and made plans to visit a church or parachurch ministry in a poor area. Over the last few weeks, you've done that. How is that going? Talk this over with your group. Consider making a monthly visit, if only to keep yourself from becoming unconcerned. What are some things you are learning as a result of your visits? What are the needs of the people in that community? Are there people there who are hungry? What challenges have you encountered?

refuge

Laurie and Scott Pederson didn't need to add anyone or anything to their busy lives. Scott works at our church, Willow Creek, where they were founding members. Laurie manages investments for a family business and had served as an elder at Willow for years. They have a large extended family in the area and spend lots of time with them.

While they don't have kids of their own, they've focused on work and ministry for the thirty-plus years of their marriage. They have close relationships with their many nieces and nephews.

Then five years ago their hearts were unexpectedly stolen by a bunch of little kids from Africa, and life has not been the same since.

In 2002 friends invited Laurie and Scott to a banquet put on by Exodus World Services, where they learned about this organization's work with refugees. "For the first time, our eyes were opened to the plight of refugees fleeing persecution and to our call as believers to 'welcome the stranger,'" Laurie says. They enthusiastically decided to support Exodus financially.

Until then Laurie had never heard much about refugees — those who flee their homeland, leaving everything behind and running for their lives because of racial, ethnic, political, religious, or even gender-based persecution. An estimated twelve million refugees live all over the world, and seven million of those have dwelt in squalid refugee camps for more than ten years.

When God led his people out of Egypt, he gave them some guidelines for living in relationship with him, which extended to their relationships with strangers. He told them, "Do not mistreat an alien or oppress him, for you were aliens in Egypt. Do not take advantage of a widow or an orphan. If you do and they cry out to me, I will surely hear their cry. My anger will be aroused, and I will kill you with the sword; your wives will become widows and your children fatherless" (Exod. 22:21–24 NIV).

Whoa. Those are harsh words. God promises harsh punishment to those who take advantage of aliens or the poor.

The heart of God is compassionate toward aliens, widows, and orphans. If we are God's people, we will share his concern and love for the oppressed and work to set them free from oppression. We will become aware of how our mindless consumption oppresses others. We will welcome the stranger.

Each year, the United States allows between fifty thousand and sixty thousand people from war-torn areas to enter the country as refugees. The U.S. State Department website notes, "Reflecting the best humanitarian traditions of the American people, the U.S. Government funds protection and life-sustaining relief for millions of refugees and victims of conflict around the globe. The United States also admits tens of thousands of refugees annually for permanent resettlement. PRM (Bureau of Population, Refugees and Migration) administers and monitors U.S. contributions to international and non-governmental organizations to assist and protect refugees abroad."[48]

Chicago has become a resettlement destination for many refugees. In 2004, more than thirteen hundred refugees landed at O'Hare Airport. World Relief helped nearly 170 of them resettle in the western suburbs of the city.

Beyond financial support, the Pedersons found themselves getting more involved with Exodus World Services. A year later Laurie and Scott, with a team of friends, agreed to host one of the first Somali Bantu families coming to America. (Somali Bantu are a people descended from former slaves in Somalia, who are now mostly subsistence-level farmers. As African-Americans do here, the Somali Bantu face racism and persecution within their own country.) The Petersons were to have the family live with them for a few weeks to learn some very basic life skills—like how to use electricity and indoor plumbing—before moving into an apartment. A week before the family arrived, Laurie and Scott learned that it consisted of a mother, a father, and nine children—ages four months to twenty-one years!

The team scrambled, securing the finished basement of Dick and Beth Anderson, another Willow family, to turn it into a dormitory for the family. The team quickly shopped for parkas, hats, gloves, boots in every conceivable size, clothing, car seats, diapers, and more.

The Petersons and a few other families had planned to help only until the families got settled into their own apartments. "By then, we were too attached to the kids," Laurie says. When the children went to public schools in the suburbs, "it was just a train wreck. The schools weren't ready for them, and the kids had never experienced school and didn't know how to behave," Laurie says. "We had to teach them what a shower and toilet are, how to use them. They spoke no English, and we did not speak Birundi. They had no schooling; they didn't know what it means to sit in a chair and hold a pencil. Until 1976, they had no written language in their home country."

So the Pedersons and a few other families started a summer program for the kids called Sonlight, in which the children would receive tutoring to try to prepare them for school the next year. Refugee children from Somalia, Rwanda, Sudan, Liberia, and other countries attend the classes, which are run by volunteers. A church in Wheaton provided classroom space, and despite the challenges, Laurie and other volunteers provided space in their hearts for these children. She was nervous at first and later wrote, "We were simply trying to put together an eight-week summer school program—*for twenty-five* kids, spanning five grades, representing five nationalities . . . blacks and whites, half Muslims, half Christians, all who had been in America for six months or less, with little, if any English spoken by any of them!"

The team wanted to help the children adapt to their new culture, but also wanted to share God's love with them. This was a challenge because they did not want to offend the parents of these primarily Muslim families. But because they appreciated how the program was helping their children, the families didn't seem to mind its Christian tone. "The parents know that we're Christians, and that name of the program, Sonlight, is a reference to Jesus," Laurie says.

While the volunteers don't teach directly about Jesus out of respect for the families, they do teach Christian principles like love, kindness, and forgiveness. The songs they sing with the children are often Christian songs.

"The kids are just really cute," Laurie says. "Working with them is very tiring, but very gratifying."

After the first session of Sonlight, she and the other volunteers met Mohamed (not his real name)—a seventh-grade Somali Bantu boy. The Bantu are typically small. Mohamed was tall and too old for the class.

The next day, Taroh (one of the teachers) stopped by Mohamed's apartment to explain that this class was for little kids, not for him. "I little! I little!" he protested, scrunching his heavyset body toward the ground. His parents agreed he was too old, or so Taroh thought.

The next morning, however, he returned, looking hopeful. Laurie and Taroh felt God nudging them to let the child stay, as long as he promised good behavior.

What he lacked in academic skill, he made up for with effort and enthusiasm.

On the last day of class he wrote "I love Miss Laurie" in his journal, which delighted Laurie, especially because eight weeks prior he would not have known those words, what they mean, or how to write them.

One day, as the leaders distributed snacks, Mohamed raised his hand to point out that they'd forgotten to pray, as they usually did before snack.

Laurie, deciding to take a risk, asked this Muslim boy if *he* wanted to pray.

"Yes," he responded. He bowed his head, folded his hands, and then looked up. "I don't know how to pray."

"Just tell God what you're thankful for, Mohamed," Laurie prompted him.

"Dear God. Thank you for the good food and thank you for the swimming pool. Amen!" (He was anticipating the group's weekly outing.)

On the very last day, when Taroh dropped Mohamed off at his apartment, he asked, "Miss Taroh, do you go to church?" She responded that she did. "Can I come too? Can I go to church?"

By providing a place for these refugees to experience the love of God, Laurie and the other Sonlight leaders also experienced God in a fresh way.

The Bible often refers to God as a refuge. It also says, "The righteous care about justice for the poor, but the wicked have no such concern" (Prov. 29:7).

Laurie and Scott have impacted African children by engaging in a long-term relationship with their families. They have been agents of justice—of providing practical help to allow these kids a chance for success in school, and so on.

While I have not volunteered at Sonlight, I have had a chance to connect with a refugee family. One Thanksgiving, we agreed to host a family for dinner. We invited another family from church as well, so we ended up with fourteen people around the table. It was an amazing day. When we explained that Thanksgiving was a holiday first celebrated by pilgrims who had fled to our country to escape persecution, the Sudanese couple at our table, whose children had grown up in refugee camps, nodded knowingly.

As some of the boys outgrew the Sonlight program, Scott and another volunteer started a junior high boys group. These children now do service projects here in the states, including a project at church in which they packed "hope boxes" to send to kids living in refugee camps in Africa, as they had done.

The Pedersons and several other families continue to put on Sonlight each year, creatively teaching the kids, forging relationships with the families. They have a core of committed volunteers, and each year, serving teams from other churches around the country come to help for a week or two at a time.

The Bible says, "Speak up for those who cannot speak for themselves, for the rights of all who are destitute. Speak up and judge fairly; defend the rights of the poor and needy" (Prov. 31:8 – 9). Seems to me that Laurie and Scott have not only spoken up for these families but also, by teaching them American culture and language, taught them to speak for themselves.

Compassion Step

Educate yourself about refugees and their plight. Browse the websites of both World Relief and Exodus World Services (which is based in the Chicago area) at www.worldrelief.org and www.e-w-s.org, and watch their videos on YouTube. Spend some time this week praying for refugees. As you pray, listen for the Spirit's promptings.

Community Step

As a group, consider helping a refugee family by providing school supplies or clothing. While relief organizations often get help during the holidays, they need it year round, especially as families try to begin the school year. Many African families are not used to cold weather and have fled their homes with just the clothes on their backs, so they need coats and other cold-weather clothing. Or consider hosting a family for a meal. World Relief or Exodus World Services can help connect you with a family who are new to the United States.

forgiveness

O n the morning of October 2, 2006, Charles Roberts, a thirty-two-year-old milk truck driver, walked into a one-room Amish schoolhouse in rural Pennsylvania, armed with a shotgun, a semiautomatic pistol, a rifle, and what appeared to be supplies for an extended siege. Roberts barricaded the school and began lining up students in front of a blackboard. He dismissed the boys and a few teachers, then started shooting. He killed five schoolgirls execution-style, injured several others, and then shot and killed himself. The news shocked the world. If these pacifist, simple people weren't safe, who was?

Even more shocking to most was the reaction of the Amish community to this tragic affront. They immediately forgave Roberts. That evening, the Amish community whose children had been terrorized and killed sent a representative to Roberts' home to offer forgiveness to his wife and three children. Within a few days, the community set up bank funds for the families of the five murdered children, and one for Roberts' family. They knew that his wife mattered to God just as much as their daughters did and that his children needed God's love now more than ever. This man, who had seemed like a loving husband and father, had snapped. The man they'd loved and trusted had suddenly become completely unloving and untrustworthy. If anyone needed to be reminded of God's grace, it was that family. If anyone would be hard to show grace to, it was that same family. That didn't seem to matter. The shattered community swept together the pieces of its broken heart and extended grace and forgiveness.

When asked how they could forgive, they simply said that it was what Jesus would do. Jesus helped them to forgive. They believed that God was in control and that they would see their children someday in heaven.

Is the response of the Amish community radical? Or is it simply Christian? Could it be that if we lived the life Jesus told us to live, this kind of radical would be normal? Might we be able to make a difference in someone's life if we offered this kind of radical forgiveness?

Jesus told his followers, Love your enemies, pray for those who persecute you. In fact, he said if we want to be forgiven, we have to forgive others, even if they don't apologize first. Look closely at what he said: "If you forgive others when they sin against you, your heavenly Father will also forgive you. But if you do not forgive others their sins, your Father will not forgive your sins" (Matt. 6:14 – 15).

While God's love is unconditional, his promises are sometimes conditional — they are embedded in an "if ... then" statement. If you forgive, then you'll be forgiven. If you condemn, then you'll be condemned. Jesus said, "Do not judge, or you too will be judged. For in the same way you judge others, you will be judged, and with the measure you use, it will be measured to you" (Matt. 7:1 – 2).

I have found that Christians can be just as judgmental as atheists. Jesus told us to forgive someone not just once but over and over. He said we are not only to tolerate people we don't like; we are actually to love them.

Women who make a difference in the world love mercy. They embrace it. They love to forgive. The Bible says, "He has shown all you people what is good. And what does the Lord require of you? To act justly and to love mercy and to walk humbly with your God" (Mic. 6:8).

Do I love mercy, enough to show it to my enemies? Or do I just think it's a good idea for others to show mercy to me? Mercy means, among other things, forgiveness. I love being forgiven; do I love forgiving others, showing them mercy? Am I really in love with that idea if I'm the one who's been wronged?

If we want to become women who make a difference, if we want to live free and strong, we've got to shed some things. Many of us walk around with anger and bitterness velcroed like ankle weights on the legs of our faith. We can't figure out why we're in pain and why it feels as if our progress, spiritually, is plodding along.

We may not have to forgive something as awful as what that Amish community had to forgive. So perhaps we'll start with smaller things. When someone gossips about you, when your spouse is annoying, when people at your church don't treat you the way you think they should — are you able to forgive these things? Unforgiveness blinds us.

When we refuse to forgive, we think we're showing that person who hurt us how terrible he or she is. When we withhold the grace of forgiveness, we often think we are punishing the offender, making the person live outside of the light of our approval. Unfortunately, the only one we are punishing is ourselves. To forgive is to access the power of God. To forgive is to enter into deep community with Jesus, the ultimate forgiver. To forgive doesn't let the person who wronged you off the hook. It lets *you* off the hook.

Lewis Smedes, a former professor at Fuller Theological Seminary, said, "When you refuse to forgive, you are giving the person who walloped you once the privilege of hurting you all over again—in your memory.... The first person who *benefits* from the forgiving is the person who *does* the forgiving. Forgiving is, first of all, a way of helping yourself to get free of the unfair pain somebody caused you."[49]

Mercy also has to do with understanding people's pain. As we become women who increasingly love mercy, we become more compassionate toward everyone. Toward people who, perhaps, have made a mess of their lives and now need our help. We're more tolerant of their mistakes, more empathetic with their humanity. This happens when we become more aware of our own frailty. I wish I could tell you an easier way to get at this mercy thing, but I don't know of one.

The Amish community clearly showed the world what it means to love mercy. Amish are known for living without modern conveniences, such as electricity and, for some reason, zippers. They're also known for not proselytizing. They don't try to convert anyone to Amish ways or even to Christianity. They are quiet, simple people—pacifist farmers in quaint horse-drawn buggies. They don't "evangelize," which bothers some Christians who think that is important. At least, they don't evangelize with words. They share the gospel, though, with their actions, which points people very clearly toward God. Or at least it did in October 2006, when people all around the world heard about a forgiveness that defied logic.

Who makes a difference in the world, someone who talks about faith, or someone who just lives it? In our violent world, we have many opportunities to choose to love mercy, to forgive. While our decision may not be broadcast on CNN or discussed in the blogosphere, it's still a powerful, radical choice. And it's a choice we can make every day, because people around us are going to screw up. They are going to hurt us, even if it's unintentional. Opportunities for forgiveness abound.

I hope none of us will ever have to forgive someone for something as absolutely unthinkable as what Roberts did. The truth is, life produces some dings and dents on our hearts. We get hurt, slighted, giving us opportunities to forgive. What will we do with those opportunities? We have to choose: forgive or hold on to the grudge. We have to choose to make the world a more loving, peaceful place, or join in the fray of hate and venom.

We'll often have to forgive more than once, which is hard. Jesus had a conversation with one of his followers, Peter, about this. The Bible says, "Peter came to Jesus and asked, 'Lord, how many times shall I forgive someone who sins against me? Up to seven times?' Jesus answered, 'I tell you, not seven times, but seventy-seven times'" (Matt. 18:21–22). Some translations say that Jesus told him "seventy times seven." Does this mean that after someone wrongs us 490 times, we no longer have to forgive? I don't think so. Jesus was not instructing us to keep score—just the opposite.

And we have to forgive not only those who wrong us personally but also those who wrong us on a wider scale. To live compassionately in the world begins with our most intimate relationships and then extends to the world. Maybe a step toward living a more compassionate life would be to forgive people we don't even know but we're afraid of. Forgive them for their violence and strangeness, their otherness. And in forgiving, set ourselves free.

Compassion Step

Is there someone who has wronged you? Are you allowing that person to continue to hurt you over and over by not forgiving him or her? What steps could you take today toward forgiveness? Perhaps you could write a letter spelling out how you've been wronged, then burn it or tear it up. Or make a phone call to tell the person you forgive them. Or simply ask God to help you love mercy enough to forgive.

Community Step

Stories like the one in this chapter often evoke strong emotions, because they bump up against our own stories. Our sense of outrage when others are hurt often comes, underneath it all, from our own hurt. Ask group members to share about a time when they were wronged and how they chose to respond. Did they forgive, or are they still holding on to that pain? Without judgment, listen to each other. Talk about this: how does forgiving those who've wronged us help us to grow in compassion toward the world at large?

cross-cultural

Last summer my friend Arloa, who founded and directs Breakthrough Urban Ministries, a ministry to the poor on Chicago's west side, suggested that I take a class her ministry offers. The BUILD (Breakthrough Urban Institute of Leadership Development) class is a six-week seminar that brings together people of different races and social classes to discuss racial reconciliation, urban community development, and so on. Our class had a couple of women who lived in Breakthrough's women's shelter, a variety of people of different ethnic backgrounds who worked in urban ministry, a couple of businesspeople. It was designed to educate people about urban issues and to provide a cross-cultural group experience in the class itself.

I was a little nervous. Arloa had told me it would be a life-changing experience, and I wasn't sure I wanted my life changed. I had already started visiting Breakthrough's women's shelter once a month to serve breakfast. I'd already started donating used clothes and sports equipment. I'd written a few checks. I'd even organized a coat drive and collected one hundred coats for the poor. I'd sent in occasional donations. Wasn't that enough? I knew inside that it was only the beginning of a journey. I wondered if I could be brave enough to take the next step on that adventure.

The Bible says, "Do not deny justice to your poor people" (Exod. 23:6). I had read enough to know that I needed to learn about the differences between charity and justice, and I felt this class might help me with that.

I called Sibyl, a spiritual mentor and friend, and asked if she would take it with me. She wisely declined but told me that Allison, a young woman she knew, would probably be interested. Sibyl suggested that another step in my journey might be to be a friend and mentor to someone twenty years younger than me. So Allison and I decided to sign up for the class. Because of our schedules, we chose a daytime class. This also made the idea more palatable to Scot, who didn't like the idea of my driving around Garfield Park, even during the day.

Allison and I drove into the city once a week to visit various urban ministries in Garfield Park, in Lawndale, and in other sites in poor neighborhoods on the west side. We have become good friends. Our urban adventures were a chance to learn and also to build a friendship. We laughed about how obviously suburban we were, driving my minivan (with the Mickey Mouse soccer ball antennae decoration and the vanity plates) through the mean streets of Chicago.

Anyway, the class required us to read a number of books on the urban experience, on racial issues. These were both enlightening and depressing, truth be told. Our group had some lively discussions, which made me realize just how complex the whole thing is. Some people in the group probably wondered why I was there. Was I trying to appease guilt?

I was very aware of the fact that I am a child of white privilege. Born and raised in the suburbs, I had been surrounded by positive role models — in family, in church, in the neighborhood. I'd been sheltered from violence, attended great schools, enjoyed luxuries, and been told repeatedly that I could accomplish whatever I dreamed of. I was simply born into a family that had opportunities and believed that working hard would bring financial success. Because for us it did.

It began to dawn on me during the class that the "hard work = success" formula wasn't everyone's experience. Some people had been so beat up by life that the idea of working hard seemed pointless. As I've gotten to know the Breakthrough staff, who are amazing, one challenge they say they face is this: many of the young people they work with will tell them, "Why should I work hard to do anything? I'm just going to end up dead or in prison in a few years." Hope is a rare commodity in East Garfield Park.

So as someone who was given the gift of hope, and the gift of a supportive community, and the gift of parents who believed in me and provided for me, it might be easy to feel guilty when comparing my lot in life with that of those less privileged. I don't. Lucky, yes. Guilty, no. I don't live in guilt, but neither do I fool myself into thinking I have accomplished things only because of my hard work. Yes, I have worked hard. I also had advantages that others might not have had. Such privilege comes with responsibility.

One class session, we did an exercise which demonstrated just how those advantages have impacted my life. We started by lining up in the middle of the classroom. The leader read statements and asked us to step either right or left if a statement was true of us.

"If you were ever called names because of your race, class, ethnicity, or gender, move one step to the left.

"If there were people of color who worked in your household as servants, gardeners, et cetera, move one step to the right."

The group began to shuffle with each statement.

"If you were often embarrassed or ashamed of your clothes, house, car, et cetera, move one step to the left. If your parents were professional, doctors, lawyers, et cetera, move one step to the right.

"If you were ever stopped or questioned by the police because of your race, ethnic group, or gender, move one space to the left." Every black and Latino man in our group immediately stepped left when they heard that. I knew that happened; I'd heard people talk about it. But seeing those men step in unison was chilling.

"If there were more than fifty books in your house when you were growing up, move one step to the right." I stepped right—Allison and I were the only ones. I thought having that many books was just good parenting. I felt my prejudices and privileges being exposed.

"If you were encouraged to attend college by your parents, move one space to the right." I stepped to the right, along with a couple of other people. Not only had my parents talked with me about college since I was about five; they'd paid for it, 100 percent.

"If you were ever denied employment because of your race, ethnic group, or gender, move one space to the left." That was a tougher one. In various jobs over the years, I may have earned less or received fewer promotions because of my gender, but could I prove it? I'd applied for a couple of jobs I had not gotten. Was I the victim of subtle discrimination because of my gender? Just considering that possibility made me sort of angry. I looked at my African-American brothers in the class and thought, What if that always happened to me? What if that happened so often, I just assumed the world was against me? How would that affect my motivation? How would that shape me?

Eventually, the class was spread out across the room, with mostly white men to the far right, and black and Hispanic women on the far left. We saw the strata of society laid out for us, and what separated us was not what we had done but what had been given to us or taken away from us. How others had treated us.

During the class, we sometimes visited other ministries and heard leaders talk about their work. Some of them were facilitating change, and others, frankly, didn't seem to be making much progress in the face of huge challenges. They seemed to be treading water rather than getting anywhere. As a class, we argued with each other, tried to explain our own experience and hold it up to the experiences of others.

When Jesus said, "To whom much is given, much is required" (Luke 12:48), he was talking about me. That doesn't mean I have to give everything away. If I want to be a woman who makes a difference, I need to first examine the small ways in which I allow myself to discriminate. One thing I learned in the class is that I need the poor more than they need me. Part of loving well is not just doing things for others but also believing that they have something to offer to you.

One black pastor we visited shared honestly about the frustration he'd feel when white suburban churches would call him up, wanting to do a "service project" at his inner-city church. When he would push back and say, Okay, you can do a project here if we can come out there and do something for you, they resisted, hemmed and hawed, or outright refused. The underlying assumption, he felt, was that the white suburban churches didn't think they needed anything from a poor urban church. That's not exactly valuing people.

Conversely, I have met pastors of very underresourced congregations who seem interested only in getting money from more affluent churches.

One thing I'd been ignorant of is how the urban culture sometimes sees the accomplishments of others as a threat. African-American kids who try to avoid trouble and who work hard in school are accused by their peers of "acting white." Their accomplishments are seen as an affront. "Why are you getting straight A's? You're trying to make us look bad." When we discussed this in the class, I was enraged. These kids were trying to better themselves, and their peers were trying to pull them back down? How do you help a group of people who disdain success? And then complain that white people don't care about them?

The cultural pressures were so complicated. The wealthy have a responsibility to the poor, but the poor need more than charity. They need a new perspective. They need hope. Donating money, while important, is only part of the picture. Somewhere, somehow, systemic change is necessary. How can I begin to facilitate that?

I realized that before a culture can change, we have to understand it for what it is. That's one reason I took the class, to try to understand. I need to understand other cultures and realize (duh!) that the goal may not be to get other people to look and act like me; it may be to help them find hope.

Compassion Step

What desires or feelings does this chapter stir in you? Do you wish you could take a class like the BUILD class? Do some investigating — there are a growing number of classes like this at churches and ministries around the country, and a number of national conferences on compassion and justice. Consider the possibility of attending such a conference or class. If you can't find a class like this, here's an easy baby step: rent the movie *Freedom Writers*, starring Hilary Swank. Write down some observations about race relations and educational opportunities that you glean from the movie. What stands in the way of increasing your understanding of racial and social divisions?

Community Step

As a group, do the privilege exercise described in this chapter. How diverse is your small group? Do you know anyone who would step left in this exercise? Discuss your thoughts on the purpose of such an exercise, what it shows. How does it promote understanding? How might it create conflict?

lawrice

W hat have I gotten myself into? If you are a comfortable suburban-ite thinking about writing a book on compassion, all I can tell you is turn back now before it is too late.

God is pulling me inexorably into a deeper faith, and it's so messing with me, because it is challenging me to move beyond prayer and contemplation to action. Not just neat and tidy acts of charity that I can fit into my schedule, that are merely blips on my Day-Timer or minor line items in my checkbook. Those acts are a part of my journey, a necessary part, just as paddling through the calm waters of a river is the beginning of white-water rafting. I'm feeling like the current is starting to move a bit faster. While I'm aware it's too late to turn back, I also think I didn't know the exhilaration of faith until now.

Before I even started writing this book, I read Shane Claiborne's book *The Irresistible Revolution*. Shane lives in a community called the Simple Way, a radical group of Jesus followers in the slums of Philadelphia, fighting injustice and poverty. His book rocked my world, but at least for now, God is not calling me to live in the ghetto.

Clarity on what he's *not* calling me to gets me only so far.

So what is he calling me to do? What if he is calling me to love people who do live in the city and to connect them with people who live in my world? What if he wants me to challenge the people around me to get out of the comfort zone? My friend Arloa, who lives and ministers in the ghetto, says I am a bridge-builder. In order to connect the affluent and the poor, I have to get to know some of the poor. I know very few. And I'm not the only one. Claiborne writes that "the great tragedy in the church is not that rich Christians do not care about the poor but that rich Christians do not know the poor."[50]

That was true of me. Despite my concern about poverty as an issue, I had insulated myself from poor *people*, except perhaps for the World Vision child I sponsor. But that is slowly changing. God has put several people of very limited means in my life since I read Shane's book, and he keeps challenging me to add more to the circle.

One small step, which seems like wading in with your baby toes, is this: when I have lunch with Arloa, I meet her in her neighborhood. To walk among the poor, even for a few hours, is a spiritual discipline that has begun to change my perspective. I see that my city has some dark corners, but it's not as scary as I once thought.

This month brought the biggest challenge. I got an email from a young man named Lawrice. In a way, Lawrice's story, and its intersection with my story, shows you how God is working in this area of my life. How he's worked even since I started writing this book.

I wrote about Lawrice in my book *Listen: Finding God in the Story of Your Life*. I found Lawrice's inspiring story in an article by Ofelia Casillas in the *Chicago Tribune*. Lawrice had grown up on Chicago's south side, near 86th Street and King Drive, which, if you know Chicago, is a pretty tough neighborhood. Unlike his peers, Lawrice was into classical music, and his talent had earned him a spot in the prestigious Chicago Children's Choir. His schoolmates let him know that he didn't fit in, by throwing rocks at him or beating him up.

Despite his difficulties, Lawrice listened to God through his struggles and his joys. He was going on a trip with the choir to Japan, the article had said, but was five hundred dollars short of the funds to do so. The day after the article appeared, someone donated the money for his trip.

I never spoke to Lawrice; I just cited the article. I loved his story. I could see his faith shining from the pages of the newspaper. He was inspiring, from a distance.

Last month I received an email from Lawrice. He had Googled his name, looking for a copy of that *Tribune* article, and because the Amazon.com page for *Listen* includes his name as a key phrase in the book, he found out I had written about him.

We had an interesting conversation on the phone. I asked what he was up to these days, and he told me he had been accepted at a small college in Los Angeles, but just as had been the case with his trip to Japan, the financial aid and scholarships he had received didn't cover all of his costs. He wanted to study musical theater, to get a degree in fine arts. At first, I have to admit, I thought he was asking for help, rather boldly. I told him to email me the details of his situation and I would pray about it. I honestly didn't have the money to help him.

He didn't email me. (Perhaps he was discouraged by my initial response.) I tried to forget about him, but God would not let go of me. I kept thinking about this kid and his dreams.

The odds for an African-American male in Chicago's public school system are not good. Several reports put the overall graduation rate at Chicago Public Schools at just over 50 percent, and the graduation rate for black males at around 40 percent.[51]

A *Chicago Tribune* article noted that "of every 100 freshmen entering a Chicago public high school, only about six will earn a bachelor's degree by the time they're in their mid-20s. The prospects are even worse for African-American and Latino male freshmen, who have only about a 3 percent chance of obtaining a bachelor's degree by the time they're 25."[52]

Lawrice, who for his senior year had moved to Milwaukee, where the schools are not much better, was defying those odds. He had not succumbed to the violence or drugs that plague his neighborhoods. He had graduated and been accepted to college, a major accomplishment considering the challenges he faced. He'd continued honing his skills in music all through high school, singing in the Chicago Children's Choir, and had now been admitted to a four-year musical and dramatic arts school. He'd applied for and received scholarships, loans, and financial aid. He was just a little short.

I argued with God, What can I do? I can't pay for this kid to go to college. He was about four thousand dollars short. I did not have the money to help him, and besides, I have kids of my own who will be heading for college in a few years.

God kept challenging me. I tried to just do research for this book (not completely oblivious to the irony, but trying to ignore it) and found this verse: "He raises the poor from the dust and lifts the needy from the ash heap; he seats them with princes and has them inherit a throne of honor" (1 Sam. 2:8). I prayed, telling God what I thought he ought to do: God, here's a person of limited financial means. Raise him from the dust. God gently asked me to remember how he accomplishes his work on earth. He inspires and equips those who are a part of his kingdom to do it. He's the King, and we are his loyal subjects, who carry out his will.

And God came near and whispered to me, you have something this young man does not, something you can share. Lawrice needs more than money. You have what he lacks and doesn't even realize he lacks. You have a network.

He also whispered, Honor me.

And I said, God, I write Christian books; I'm basically in full-time ministry. I do honor you.

And he whispered the words of Proverbs 14:31: "Whoever is kind to the needy honors God."

One glaring difference between the rich and the poor is that the rich (and often the middle class) have connections. We know people who know people, and those networks serve as a net for us, to hold us up, to help us, to provide opportunities. When we are applying to a school or for a job, we often do better if we have recommendations from those who know us, who can make an introduction, put in a good word for us. The poor typically don't have access to those connections.

I tried to ignore God. I had work to do. Didn't he realize I had a deadline? For my book? My book about—oh yeah, compassion. God kept after me. He kept saying, I'm giving you another chapter, not just for the book but for your life. I'm giving you the opportunity to know someone who has less than you. I'm giving you the opportunity to grow.

Finally I talked to Arloa about it. She recommended that I talk to Kevin Gwin, who runs a scholarship program for kids coming out of the Chicago Public Schools. Kevin told me to have Lawrice get in touch with him, so I emailed Lawrice.

I put a post on my blog, telling Lawrice's story, asking people to make donations to his school in his name. My friend Wendy and I paid a deposit to his school that was overdue, so he could move forward with his application.

I realized that what I have to offer Lawrice, he didn't even know how to ask for. I have that network. I got on Facebook and found Ofelia Casillas, the reporter who first wrote about Lawrice in 2005. She told me to have Lawrice get in touch with her.

In a few hours, I will drive downtown to meet Lawrice and his grandmother. I'm nervous, a little. Mostly I'm excited to hear more about his story, to actually get to know this person.

I happen to be in a place where I can't just write a check and walk away. So God is asking me simply to get to know this young man a little bit, to love mercy just enough to be willing to extend myself to him and to his family. This could get messy. The water is flowing a little faster. The amazing thing is, I feel closer to God than I have in a very long time. I feel as if Jesus is right there beside me, laughing with joy as the current begins to move, and the fun is only just starting.

Compassion Step

John Ortberg writes, "Is there any challenge in your life right now that is large enough that you have no hope of doing it apart from God's help? If not, consider the possibility that you are seriously underchallenged."[53] How would you answer his question? What steps could you take to up the challenge level (and therefore the growth level) in your life?

Community Step

This chapter quotes Shane Claiborne: "The great tragedy in the church is not that rich Christians do not care about the poor but that rich Christians do not know the poor." As a group, discuss this idea. While you have served the poor, do you feel you've gotten to know them? Rich and poor are relative terms. Are you friends with anyone who is poorer than you? What could you do as a group to actually develop friendships with people who have fewer resources than you? How might actually getting to know someone on a deeper level affect you spiritually?

radical

Lawrice went to school. He could not have gone without my help, and I couldn't have done it without God's help. I mess up repeatedly in other areas of my life, but I said yes to a step of crazy radical adventure.

Dozens of people stepped up with donations ranging from ten dollars to four hundred dollars. One of my friends, who used to be a travel agent, found him a cheap ticket to Los Angeles. Raising money for Lawrice's tuition and meals gave me the opportunity to experience the presence of God in a whole new way. I had to trust that money would come in, that I was hearing God right on this assignment.

Before Lawrice went to school, my kids and I had lunch with him and his grandmother, Delores. After about five minutes, I felt so comfortable with them it was almost scary.

Dolores and I just clicked, like old friends. She's only about ten years older than me, and I totally loved her sense of humor. I thought, I could learn a lot about faith and perseverance from this woman. "God bless you," she kept saying. In phone conversations since, we've covenanted to pray for Lawrice.

Lawrice told me more about his life, about having to move to Milwaukee the first day of his senior year of high school, when his mom came and simply signed him out of school, in spite of the fact that he was going to be class president and had been accepted into the National Honor Society.

He told me that part of the reason that his mom wanted him to move was because he'd gotten mugged in his Chicago neighborhood. Another day, he was walking along and a tiny snake crawled up his pant leg. On a city street! "I wouldn't mind having a snake as a pet," he said. "It didn't hurt me." His grandmother and I looked at each other, raised our eyebrows, and simultaneously said, "No!" And we both laughed. His mother saw the mugging and the baby snake attack as God's way of telling her to move away from Chicago.

His first school in Milwaukee was worse, he said, but when the teachers there heard him sing, they transferred him to the Milwaukee School of the Fine Arts, a public high school for artistically gifted students.

I got an email a few days later from Lawrice, telling me, "I think that you have been sent to me as an angel from God," and that he loved me. A few days later, he asked if he could put my name on a form for school (which would give me permission to get his school records) and put "godmother" on the line indicating how we were related.

It made me cry.

This project threw me off balance. I felt as if I were in the white water, hanging on. I found solace in God's Word, which says, "Those who are kind to the poor lend to the LORD, and he will reward them for what they have done" (Prov. 19:17). I would tell God, I don't know what I'm doing. I'd hear him say, Keep paddling; you're in for the ride of your life. Above the roar of the rapids he'd yell, Do you trust me?

I did trust God, but here's the thing: Lawrice started strong at school, but he struggled. His grades at the end of the first semester were pretty low, for many reasons. His mom told him to just come home. He lost his focus, even stopped attending some of his classes at the end of the semester. To my dismay, he decided to leave the school in LA to attend a community college in Chicago.

I'd poured a lot of time, energy, and money into this child. When I was on a business trip in LA, I went to visit him, to take him shopping and to dinner. I tried to give him advice, encouragement, and more. We talked on the phone a lot. I asked my friends to donate money, and they did. When they ask how he's doing, it's hard for me to explain the choices he made.

At the beginning of the semester, I wrote, "I believe God will provide for Lawrice and for me. I want to be the kind of person who will obey regardless, not just for the promised blessing but because I love God. Even if this doesn't turn out the way I'd hoped, I still want to obey him, to trust him. I believe that his Word is true when it says, 'Those who give to the poor will lack nothing, but those who close their eyes to them receive many curses' (Prov. 28:27). I've got a long way to go, but the way to become that kind of person is to take a risk of radical obedience."

Things did not turn out exactly as I'd hoped—yet. I still am expecting Lawrice to succeed. I still talk to him and his grandmother. I have grown to love him, even though I don't like some of the choices he made. I wonder if I should have given more guidance, even though I was thousands of miles away. Who knows what will happen in the next few years?

What if the "reward" for helping Lawrice is just the adventure of obedience? An interesting thing about the Bible's directives on compassion is that they don't focus on how helping the poor will help the poor. The Bible says generosity will benefit the person who provides the help. Read Proverbs 28:27 again or Isaiah 58. God wants us to help the poor not just for their sakes but also for our own sakes. God wants us to love others in tangible ways, because it will form us spiritually, because it will enfold us into the heart of God in a way no other spiritual practice can. He wants to form us into his image, his radically compassionate and indiscriminately loving image. He doesn't just want us to know him; he wants us to be like him. More and more, even though it's scary, that's what I want too. I want to be like Jesus.

Will Lawrice eventually graduate from college? If he does, he will beat tremendous odds. I don't know what will happen. I'm hoping and trusting and praying and walking forward. I am checking in with him periodically, calling Delores now and then to pray. I don't know how things will turn out. In a way, that's not the point. The point is to keep going, to let the journey form me into who God wants me to be.

In the Old Testament book of Daniel there's a story about three young men in exile: Shadrach, Meshach, and Abednego. They refuse to worship the idols of King Nebuchadnezzar of Babylon, so the king threatens to throw them into a fiery furnace. Undeterred, these young men calmly reply, "O Nebuchadnezzar, we do not need to defend ourselves before you in this matter. If we are thrown into the blazing furnace, the God we serve is able to save us from it, and he will rescue us from your hand, O king. But *even if he does not*, we want you to know, O king, that we will not serve your gods or worship the image of gold you have set up" (Dan. 3:16–18 NIV, emphasis mine).

"Even if he does not." Those are fighting words. They are words of radical obedience. Summoning the courage to say those words formed those young men. I wonder if they had doubts in the back of their minds. I wonder if they had to hold hands to steady each other, to keep their voices from quavering. I kind of think they might have, because I know I would. My prayer is that God will give me that kind of courage.

That courage is found not in contemplation but in action. Even if God does not work this out in the way I would suggest to him, I will trust him. I am praying that God will rescue Lawrice. I'm grateful that he allowed me to assist in some small way, because it brought a new vigor to my faith to step out in obedience. It also softened my heart for the poor. I cannot go back to a faith that has no action associated with it. I'm in too deep, and I'm on the ride of my life.

Compassion Step

How can you show compassion to a college student? If there is a college in your city, consider helping the students there in some way. For example, you could mentor a student, open your home to students for a meal, or drop off care packages with cookies and other supplies. You could make a donation to an organization that provides scholarships. What is God calling you to do to show compassion and kindness to the next generation?

Community Step

Read and discuss the story in Daniel 3. Have group members share about a time when they demonstrated radical obedience. What happened? Talk about the following as a group: What keeps you from taking steps of radical obedience? Was there a time when you obeyed God but things did not turn out as you had hoped? How did that experience affect you spiritually?

compassion offers God's love to the world

together

It's one thing to make a difference in my neighborhood, or even in poor areas close to home, be they urban, rural, or even suburban. But what about the big wide world, where millions of people live on less than two dollars per day? Where children sometimes eat dirt because there is nothing else to fill their bellies? Where families knowingly or unknowingly sell their children into slavery so they can feed the ones they still have at home? What about Africa, where HIV/AIDS is ravaging an entire country and ignorance is so ingrained that many people still believe that having sex with a virgin will cure them of the "big disease"?

It's enough to make you scream and run away. To zone out, put on some loud music, pour yourself a stiff drink, and just say, I can't think about this; it's hopeless. There is nothing I can do. I've got problems of my own, and thinking globally just exhausts me. It feels like a formula for compassion fatigue.

That is exactly what the architect of all this evil, Satan himself, wants us to do. To be overwhelmed by the sheer numbers, the magnitude of suffering. Or to think, This has nothing to do with me, so there's nothing I can do. The fact is our patterns of consumption, our insatiable appetite for cheap clothes and out-of-season foods and a disproportionate amount of the world's fuel, are part of the problem, though certainly not all of it. We are leaving a messed-up planet to our children, and we have to live here for a while too. We are a part of the problem, and when we're blind to that, we only make things worse.

I cannot change the whole world, but I can make small changes to make a small difference. To show simple compassion on a global scale, we must quietly and firmly refuse to let the magnitude of the world's problems overwhelm us. For the last quarter of this book, we will learn about some global justice issues and explore practical ways in which we can begin to make a difference for our neighbors all over the planet. Be open to just learning; be ready to be surprised by how you can make a difference.

One of my pastor's favorite sayings as Willow Creek was growing from a small group of idealistic high school kids into a very large church was this: "We come together to accomplish what none of us could do alone." In other words, the whole body of Christ is greater than the sum of its parts. When we look at global issues, we wonder if just one person can make a difference. God's people, when they come together, can do what no one can do alone. That's the adventure we're called to be a part of, and I for one don't want to miss it.

I've been inspired to make small but significant changes by some college students I met recently, who belong to a group called Live2Free, at Vanguard University in California. They are a troop of Davids taking on the Goliath of human trafficking, of modern-day slavery. They are coming together and inviting their fellow students to join them, to try to do more than any of them could imagine doing on their own.

They're trying to educate their peers and change their buying habits to make a difference. Live2Free is the student chapter of Lydia Today, an organization focused on rescuing and restoring women and children who are victims of domestic abuse, human trafficking, and other abuse. Their focus is on educating people about how their lifestyles and choices affect others in the world and can either enslave people or set them free.

Lydia Today was founded by Sandie Morgan, a registered nurse who served as a missionary in Greece for ten years and is currently the administrator of the Orange County Human Trafficking Task Force.

While she was teaching at Vanguard (the only Christian college in America with a women's studies department, which Morgan headed), a number of the students heard her speak about human trafficking. They decided to join the abolitionist cause — trying to educate fellow students about how their buying choices affect the world, to teach them about sexual trafficking, Fair Trade, and social justice.

More people in the world are trapped in slavery today than at the height of the slave trade of the 1800s. Most are virtually invisible.

God hears their cries. They are not invisible to him.

Centuries ago God's people ignored the plight of the poor. God's prophet Amos let the people know of God's anger about this: "For three sins of Israel, even for four, I will not turn back my wrath. They sell the righteous for silver, and the needy for a pair of sandals. They trample on the heads of the poor as upon the dust of the ground and deny justice to the oppressed" (Amos 2:6–7 NIV).

Does God still care about how our way of life, our insatiable use of resources, denies justice to the oppressed? Of course he does.

"As Christians, we haven't paid attention to what our purchases mean," says Lance Trueb, a communication major who volunteers with Live2Free. "People can make a difference with the things they buy. It's good that we have choices, but it's bad that we often take the cheapest available and don't realize what that means. There's a huge potential to raise awareness."

Drew Zimmer, a religion major and business minor at Vanguard, said he was motivated to join the group "because of my faith. Being a follower of Christ means we're called to care for and serve people. But beyond that, a life lived just for yourself is pretty dead. I just don't think it's that enjoyable. A life serving others is a more valuable life. I'm really getting into rebellion against low expectations."

"You can do a lot of things for yourself, but it's not that fulfilling," agrees Melissa Dang, another Live2Free member, who attends the University of California at Berkeley.

"Students don't want to have just another rally," Morgan says. "They really want to do something."

Dang and Alicia Woodard decided to do an outreach project. They visited seventy-five medical clinics near their school to provide health and human services information that would help clinic workers recognize victims of sexual trafficking. As a result, several trafficking victims were rescued almost immediately, and more are being discovered because health care workers know what to look for.

"It was overwhelming in a lot of ways," Woodard says. "When the public attorney told us, I wanted to cry. I was both sad and happy. Just one person getting rescued is exciting. I love being a part of this."

They also try to raise awareness to encourage students to purchase clothing, food, and other items made by companies that do not exploit their workers. They invite fellow students to join them in Live2Free.

The information they offer about human trafficking is startling to many students. "A lot of students receive it well, and some start coming to meetings," Zimmer says. "But so many people are so busy. I've found that people are afraid of it. They like their little bubble, and they want to stay in it."

"The premise is not about disengaging from the life you're in but realizing that what we do impacts somebody else," Morgan says. "We don't want people to give up their lives but to incorporate personal responsibility into their lives. We challenge them to put the brakes on consumerism and become aware of the impact of their choices."

Compassion Step

What do you think it means to value and protect all people? When you think about global issues such as HIV/AIDS, human trafficking, extreme poverty, and so on, which do you feel most compelled to try to change? Do you experience "compassion fatigue" when you look at these issues? What can you do to feel compassionately energized?

Community Step

One of the students said, "A life serving others is a more valuable life. I'm really getting into rebellion against low expectations." As a group, talk about your response to this idea. What would it look like for you to rebel against low expectations? In what ways have the projects you've engaged in over the last few months helped you to do just that? Do some research as a group on the impact of your buying choices. How can your choices about which kind of clothing, shoes, or food to buy serve others?

sold

amber Beckham has traveled the world. In 1999, newly graduated from Middle Tennessee State University, she took a job with World Relief. That position soon led her to Rwanda, where she helped to develop a microenterprise loan program for refugees. She also took a trip to Indonesia, where she simply followed other workers around, shooting photos and writing up stories for World Relief's brochures.

Her travels opened her eyes to problems she'd never even heard of. The devastating tsunamis that have hit Indonesia, for example, do so much more than destroy property. They create a chaos that provides opportunity for evil.

"In Indonesia, I first heard of human trafficking," she says. The confusion resulting from the destruction of a huge tsunami often scatters families, leaving parents to search for their missing children and to fear the worst. "People were worried that their kids would be taken and sold into slavery," she explains. In fact, that often happens. "It got me thinking about the problem. I guess I knew it happened, but it was hard to believe."

In the developing world, trafficking is a huge problem, especially among uneducated populations. Young women, children, even men are promised jobs in another country or town and leave their families, hoping for a better future. When they arrive, they find there is no job, except the job of prostitution or manual labor. They're told that they have to work to pay off the cost of their transport or their housing. They're often abused, not paid what they were promised, and held against their will. Other times, desperate families will sell their children into slavery.

What many people don't realize is that human trafficking is a problem not just in remote places like Indonesia; it is happening in the United States. The U.S. Department of State estimates that more than fourteen thousand people a year are being trafficked into this country. Many more are trafficked within its borders.

Amber just followed the path in front of her and says it slowly became obvious that she was doing what God wanted her to do.

"Some people have a moment where they realize, 'Wow, this is my calling,' but I didn't have that moment," Amber admits. "I simply began following the steps. I just started learning about the problem. It took a year before I even talked to a victim."

Eventually, she began working to fight trafficking in Nashville, Tennessee.

Nashville? Home of country music, barbeque, and ... sexual slavery? "We have a large international population," Amber says. "People are brought through ports of entry, then move quickly into other cities."

Often women brought into the country illegally are surprised to find, upon arrival, that a promised job of waitressing or house cleaning does not exist. Their captors offer them two options: become a prostitute (to earn money for their captors) or be killed. Because of their illegal status, these women don't seek the help of police.

In the Old Testament, God spoke to his people through the prophet Jeremiah and let them know that they had gotten completely off track. He said,

> *"Like cages full of birds,*
> *their houses are full of deceit;*
> *they have become rich and powerful*
> *and have grown fat and sleek.*
> *Their evil deeds have no limit;*
> *they do not seek justice.*
> *They do not promote the case of the fatherless;*
> *they do not defend the just cause of the poor.*
> *Should I not punish them for this?" declares the* LORD.
> *"Should I not avenge myself on such a nation as this?"*
>   Jeremiah 5:27–29

When this text was written, what evil had God's people done? They had become rich and powerful, and in so doing ignored the poor. They had not promoted the case of the fatherless—those with no one to protect them or provide for them. What does this mean to us? What if God still wants his people to seek justice, to promote the case of the fatherless, to defend the cause of the poor?

Sexual trafficking victims are separated from their families and have no one to protect them or advocate for them, as a father should. They are fatherless. In some cases, their families have betrayed them and sold them into slavery, or have been duped into such action, thinking that their children could get a job and support the family.

Amber decided to try to work with local law enforcement to find trafficking victims. "At first they'd say they'd never seen it," she says. Then one detective started coming to some of the meetings Amber held on the topic. He gave her some tips on how to work within the police community, including a suggestion that she get certified to teach continuing education classes for police officers.

"Eventually, I trained twelve hundred officers in Nashville on how to recognize sexual trafficking and to help victims," she says. "That was a huge victory. My passion is to help victims and get them out, but to do that, I had to communicate truth to those who would find people. If our police don't know what to look for, we're all up a creek."

In late 2007, police answered a call to a rundown apartment complex for another problem. Because of Amber's efforts (which also included riding along on patrol with prostitution and gambling vice squads), police quickly recognized that two women in the complex, one of whom was a minor, were likely to be trafficking victims. They called World Relief, and "my two volunteers were there within an hour," Amber says. "By that night, they had a place to stay."

Amber is a woman who values and protects all people. Although she has traveled the world, she is making a difference right in her hometown, in Nashville, Tennessee. She says there is more work to do, especially with setting up systems to make sure victims are found, rescued, and helped. "My biggest strength is perseverance," she says. "I'm like a bulldog that won't let go. When I work with victims, that is rewarding; it gives me the energy to keep going."

You don't have to be a full-time social services worker to make a difference, Amber notes. She has plenty of volunteers in Nashville who help out in other ways. "It's always best when people come up with their own idea" of how to help out, she says. "Just ask yourself, 'What am I good at?'" For example, a doctor, nurse, or EMT might be able to address victims' health needs. "But if you're a mom, you might volunteer to transport victims when they need a ride. If you love art, maybe you'd offer to give art lessons to victims." Amber recalls one victim who, when offered art supplies, began painting and creating artwork, a therapeutic exercise that allowed her to express some of her deeply held pain. "It was a great outlet for her."

Many of these victims need tutoring in basic skills or need to learn English. Victims also need the people around them to be aware of what's going on and to report suspicious activity.

Amber now works with another organization that fights trafficking, defending the just cause of the poor.

While it takes a lot of training to work directly with victims, there are many ways to help fight against slavery—from changing our buying patterns to volunteering our time.

Human trafficking is a vast and complex problem. It can feel a little overwhelming. It's important to give ourselves permission to take it slowly, to start simply by learning more about this. Often, hearing about someone else's victimization bumps into our own stories, our own pain. When we keep walking, we realize that our common ground with victims is empowering. We admit it's not a problem any of us can solve alone, but we can certainly be part of the solution.

Compassion Step

Pick up the book *Sold* by Patricia McCormick. It's a quick read but profoundly moving. This story of a young victim of sexual trafficking will help you understand this issue more deeply than any number of statistics. Pray as you read the book, asking God what he would have you do. If you suspect that slavery or trafficking is happening near you, report it to the U.S. Department of Health and Human Services Trafficking Information and Referral Hotline (1-888-373-7888), the U.S. Department of Justice Trafficking in Persons Complaint Line (1-888-428-7581), or the FBI field office nearest you. You can report suspicious activity and find out who is working to fight trafficking in your area. (It's going on in every state in this country and all around the world.) Pray for the courage to act.

Community Step

Last week you did some research on the impact of your buying choices. Share what you learned. Have each person in the group tell about one change that they plan to make — reducing consumption, switching to Fair Trade products, or something else. Talk about how these choices might help fight human slavery or poverty. Give each other a lot of grace — avoid the temptation to compare or compete. Let each person seek God and act accordingly. Discuss steps you could take as a group to get involved in this issue.

freedom

a s a freelance writer, I get to write and learn about a lot of different topics. Although I'm self-employed, I'm a regular contributor to a couple of magazines, which means they call and ask me if I'd like to take on assignments. Mostly I say yes. As the term *freelance* implies, I am free to accept assignments or not. I have the freedom to say no, of course, and sometimes I do, because I simply can't take on any additional work and get it all done. If I want, I have the freedom to take time off.

My desk was piled with work, including an unfinished book manuscript, when Camerin, my editor at *Today's Christian Woman*, called. She asked if I would interview a woman who, as a teen, had been a victim of sexual trafficking and was now educating others about this issue.

As a journalist, I was intrigued by the opportunity to write such a compelling story. As a Jesus follower, I felt called to do it—to tell the truth about an issue, to do whatever I could to try to make a difference. Perhaps I can't do work like Amber (in the previous chapter), but I can use my writing to help educate readers about this critical issue. As a free person who cares that others are not, I wanted to use my freedom to write, to try to work for the freedom of others.

The U.S. Department of State estimates that six hundred to eight hundred thousand people—mostly women and children—are trafficked across international borders annually for commercial sex, forced labor, and other forms of exploitation. (This number doesn't account for those trafficked within national borders.) Between 14,500 and 17,500 of these victims are trafficked into the United States.

Even in America, the "land of the free," thousands of people are trapped in hidden slavery. In our country and around the world, countless women and children are victims of sexual trafficking, forced into prostitution.

So I called Sierra Leone, in Africa, to talk to Ruth Ada Kamara. When she was about seventeen, Ruth was invited by an older friend, Edna, to take a trip from Freetown, Sierra Leone, to Liberia. Since she'd just broken up with a boyfriend, Ruth decided a change of scenery would be nice. Edna promised to make all the arrangements and pay for the trip.

Although they'd known each other a short time, Ruth says of Edna, "She used to encourage me, to be a help to me. She was like a sister."

That same day, Edna introduced her to a man she called Bob, who would accompany them on the trip. "I didn't know it then, but he would be my pimp," Ruth says. Looking back, she realizes that Edna and Bob worked quickly, leaving Freetown that very day. She didn't even tell her uncle, whom she'd lived with, she was leaving. "I thought it would just be an adventure," she told me.

As they left, Edna told Ruth to go ahead with Bob, and she would join them later.

Bob drove to his family's home in Monrovia, the capital of Liberia. Three days later, under cover of darkness, they drove to a large gated compound which was secured by uniformed guards.

Bob took Ruth to a room, where "he asked me to have sex with him," she says. "I was shocked. He had been so nice to me before that." Ruth's memories of that time are fragmented. "I told him, 'No, that is not the arrangement we had,'" but she realized she was defenseless.

"Why did he say this to me? I thought that Edna was coming to meet us. And he said, 'Don't you know that I bought you from that woman? I own you.' I started crying. I thought, I am finished." Bob raped her that night, which was only the beginning of her ordeal.

"He left me in the room, and men started using me," she recalls. Some days she would have sex with as many as ten men, and she often was beaten. She bears a scar on her forearm, the result of an effort she once made to resist Bob's advances, during which he attacked her with a knife.

One day a young man came to the brothel. Unlike most of her customers, he spoke Ruth's dialect, which moved her to tears.

"He asked me, 'How did you come here?' and, 'Do you want to leave?'" she says. "I told him there was no way to escape."

The young man returned several times, always requesting time with Ruth, although "he never used me as his wife," she says. Eventually he bribed the brothel owners and bought Ruth's freedom.

She knew no one in Monrovia except her rescuer. "He wanted me to be his wife," she says. While she was grateful that he had freed her, she remained an illegal alien in a place she didn't know. "There was no option for me. I didn't know him very well, but I accepted him to be my husband."

She lived in Liberia for two more years, had a son. As the civil war there escalated, she took her son to Sierra Leone, leaving her husband.

Ruth had grown up in the Muslim faith but abandoned any faith at all because of her painful experiences. "In the brothel, it is not easy to see the hand of God," she says. "And when you get out, people do not believe you. They blame the victim."

Ashamed, Ruth moved to another town. There she met some Christians who told her about Jesus and helped her find job training at a nearby hospital so she could become a nurse. She accepted Christ and began attending church.

Soon war broke out in Sierra Leone as well, and the training program at the hospital was suspended. Ruth fled with her son to Guinea.

In a refugee camp there, Ruth met Janet Nickel, a Christian aid worker, who befriended her and then hired her as a domestic.

Unfortunately, Ruth began stealing from Janet. When she confessed, Janet forgave her. That encounter with grace changed her life.

Janet invited Ruth to study and memorize the Bible. They began with John 14. Within ten days Ruth had memorized the whole chapter and could recite the entire thing or any verse that was called for.

Filling her mind with Scripture was an important part of the healing process for Ruth. "I realized God works in mysterious ways," she says. "God sent an angel to let Peter out of jail, and I realized he sent an angel to let me out of jail too. I thank God for Janet."

Ten years later, in 2003, Janet returned to the United States, and Ruth returned to Sierra Leone. A year later Janet came back and became the Sierra Leone program coordinator for the Faith Alliance against Slavery and Trafficking (FAAST).

"Soon after the program started, a probable trafficking case surfaced which involved forty-eight children in the area where Ruth was living," Janet says. "We needed public awareness to prevent people from being duped into giving away their children. We hired Ruth to do that."

So Ruth began teaching about trafficking, yet didn't reveal her secret. But the more she talked about the issue, the less she could hold the truth within. Eventually she told Janet her story, slowly, bit by bit.

Many people refuse to believe trafficking actually happens, which makes them more vulnerable to it. The stigma of being a victim keeps them silent.

"When she started going to villages and communities to tell about trafficking, she felt like people didn't believe or take it seriously," Janet says. "So one day she said, 'This is real, it is happening, and it happened to me.' Then she told her story. It made a big difference in people's response."

Especially in Sierra Leone, people assume that women in prostitution choose that lifestyle. Usually that is not the case. Their captors often manipulate them, abusing them emotionally and physically. Victims often won't speak out because of their shame.

In spite of these obstacles, Ruth persists. She speaks the truth in hopes that it will set others free. She is loving her neighbors by sharing her story. It costs her a lot.

In her life, she's had a lot of pain. She still does. But she knows that God's promises are true. The Bible says, "Free me from the trap that is set for me, for you are my refuge.... I will be glad and rejoice in your love, for you saw my affliction and knew the anguish of my soul. You have not handed me over to the enemy but have set my feet in a spacious place" (Ps. 31:4, 7–8 NIV). God has kept this promise in Ruth's life.

"Sometimes, when I tell my story, men in the audience have wept for me," she says. "God has given me the courage to tell it, to allow people to take my photograph and put it in the newspaper, even. I suffered, but I want to keep other women from suffering."

She continues to struggle emotionally and physically. Thankfully, tests for HIV have come back negative. During our interview, she broke down several times. She asked me not to forget her (as if that were possible), asked me to pray for her. "For the past sixteen years, I have not wanted a man in my life. And I'm still going through suffering and pain in my body," she says. "But I know that God is in control."[54]

Compassion Step

Begin with prayer. Be open to what God leads you to do, and be open to learning about an uncomfortable topic. Pray for Ruth and for the countless women who are still trapped in slavery. FAAST, the organization Ruth works with (www.faastinternational.org), welcomes volunteers to research, write, do graphic design, review laws, plan events, and more. If God leads you to do so, donate money or time to this or other organizations. If you decide you can only pray, that is a lot, if you commit to doing it. Educate yourself by visiting websites like www.thehomefoundation.net or www.notforsalecampaign.org.

Community Step

As women, we often feel a strong emotional reaction when we read or hear about other women being victimized. Talk about how Ruth's story makes you feel: helpless, sad, overwhelmed, angry? Does it trigger memories of ways that you yourself have been a victim or been taken advantage of in some way? Process your feelings with the group. Do not judge each other or try to fix each other; practice compassionate listening. What can your group do to take action to help raise awareness about this issue? One option is to hang an anti-trafficking poster in your church, business, or office. Posters advertising the U.S. Department of Health and Human Services (HHS) victim hotline are available at www.acf.hhs.gov/trafficking/index.html or by calling 1-888-373-7888.

change

i walk into my kids' bathroom and see that Melanie has written a quote in dry-erase marker on the mirror: "Be the change you wish to see in the world." I love that my fourteen-year-old thinks this way—although like anyone, she is still figuring out just how to live out that challenge. The quote is originally from Ghandi. It's also the title of a book she read with her small group, *Be the Change: Your Guide to Freeing Slaves and Changing the World* by Zach Hunter. Zach wrote this book at age fifteen because he wanted to help inspire his generation to change the world. The book was released as part of the Amazing Change public awareness campaign about modern-day slavery, a campaign inspired by the 2007 film *Amazing Grace*. This movie told the story of William Wilberforce and his fight to end slavery in England in the nineteenth century. (Check out www.TheAmazingChange.com.)

So how can I fight slavery? Well, one way is by writing this book, a method only as effective as my readers' response. I can also fight it by being a conscientious consumer. Every product has a story, a history. Someone works to make everything we buy. Do we know who those people are? Are we willing to care enough to make just choices when we buy things?

What can I do? One small but significant step is to purchase Fair Trade Certified products. For years I bought Gevalia coffee, imported from Sweden (where I am pretty certain there are no coffee plantations). It is neither organic nor Fair Trade Certified, but it is pricey. I had a subscription, and they would mail me a couple of pounds of coffee every few months.

I kept saying I would give up this unnecessary luxury. It wasn't the cost to me that eventually made me do it. It was the cost to the harvesters. It just took me a while to hear their cries. When our church added a coffee bar to the lobby, they chose Pura Vida coffee, a Fair Trade, organic blend, sold by a company that uses its profits to help the poor. And yes, the coffee is very good. Along with the coffee, our church handed out information about working conditions for coffee farmers.

I finally called Gevalia and asked if they had any Fair Trade coffees in their vast catalog. They said it was "not economically feasible." I cancelled my subscription. Thankfully, Starbucks Café Estima is Fair Trade, and many grocery and discount stores carry Fair Trade coffee. Believe me, I have a discriminating palate when it comes to coffee. (That's a nice way of saying I'm a coffee snob. But now I'm a socially conscious coffee snob.)

The Live2Free students from California (you met them in week 40) don't just buy Fair Trade whenever they can. They take it a step farther by going to high schools in their area to talk about, among other things, chocolate.

Most chocolate is produced on cocoa plantations where many of the workers are just children. Children as young as five are forced to pick cocoa beans all day. Because they are working, those children don't go to school. In many cases, if they don't meet their harvest quotas, they don't eat. On many of the plantations, work conditions are not regulated, and the children and their families are basically slaves.

The Bible says, "Blessed are they who maintain justice, who constantly do what is right" (Ps. 106:3 NIV). Do our buying patterns maintain justice, or do they perpetuate injustice (even if we are unaware of it)?

There is a human cost to cheap chocolate. And the question is, Are we willing to support child slavery in order to have the privilege of inexpensive candy?

There is a great alternative, though. Fair Trade Certified products, including chocolate, are those produced via a system that pays workers fairly, cuts out middlemen, protects the environment, and more.

Buying Fair Trade chocolate ensures decent living wages for workers and that children will not be exploited, that they will get an education rather than being forced to work in the fields. While it is more expensive than other chocolate, the price reflects the fact that a living wage is paid to the workers who harvest it.

"We're trying to teach people that everyday decisions they make impact people around the world," Sandie Morgan says of her work with Live2Free students. "It's not about boycotting; it's about making a choice to support companies that are doing the right thing."

She notes that talking about chocolate is a great way to "communicate a worldview" to children here in the States. While it may not be appropriate to share details of human slavery (especially sexual slavery) with young children, you can explain to them that when we buy Fair Trade chocolate, that means a little boy or girl in Africa can go to school and not have to work in the fields all day. "It's teaching your child an important concept—that their choices impact others, and what they buy can impact the life of another child they will never meet," Morgan says.

She notes that it is somewhat ironic that many of us send thirty dollars a month or so to sponsor a child in the developing world, to give them, among other things, an education, yet we buy chocolate that prevents another child, perhaps in that same country, from going to school. She wonders if it might be better to spend our thirty dollars on Fair Trade food, because Fair Trade Certification means the company is investing in education for children where the product is produced.

According to www.tradefairusa.org, "Fair Trade Certification empowers farmers and farm workers to lift themselves out of poverty by investing in their farms and communities, protecting the environment, and developing the business skills necessary to compete in the global marketplace."

You can find Fair Trade Certified products in many stores and on many websites. Currently the United States certifies Fair Trade coffee, tea and herbs, cocoa and chocolate, fresh fruit, sugar, rice, and vanilla. Finding it sometimes requires a bit of persistence—and a sense of humor.

For example, the other day I went chocolate shopping at my favorite discount store. After working on this book and on a number of magazine articles about human trafficking, I've become convinced that I want to purchase Fair Trade whenever possible.

I peruse the approximately fifty different kinds of chocolate on the shelves, and none of them has the Fair Trade Certified label. So I approach a red-shirted gal who is stocking shelves and ask her if they carry Fair Trade chocolate. I live in Chicago, but this young lady apparently just arrived from Alabama. "Far train?" she says in a thick southern accent. "What kind of chocolate is that?" She grabs her walkie-talkie and starts to ask someone if they carry Far Train brand chocolate. Too late I notice the word *trainee* on her name tag.

"No, Fair Trade," I say. "It's kind of like organic. It's not a brand; it's a ..."

Trainee girl, looking at me like I'm from another planet, whispers a code blue into her walkie-talkie. "I never heard of *that*," she says.

A manager approaches. "May I help you?" he asks.

"I'm looking for Fair Trade chocolate," I say.

"I don't believe we carry that brand," he says.

"It's not a brand; it's a designation, like organic. It's showing that the workers are paid fairly, and ..." I trail off, take a deep breath, grab the coffee from my cart. "Look. Here. You sell Fair Trade coffee. See that little symbol? It has to do with how the chocolate is grown and produced."

The manager and trainee both look at me quizzically, as if they are thinking, Chocolate grows? Like, on trees? I thought it came from the Ghirardelli factory in San Francisco.

The manager is very polite, and when I ask if I can suggest that they carry Fair Trade chocolate, he suggests I leave a comment on the store's website, since all stocking decisions are ultimately made at a corporate level.

I do find some chocolate that, even though it does not have the certification, says on the label that it is sustainably grown and "ethically traded." I find out later that this brand (Endangered Species Chocolate) is actually a Fair Trade chocolate.

The more consumers demand Fair Trade items, the more companies will begin to supply them. It's simple, basic economics. How can we change the world? Maybe one chocolate bar at a time, one buying decision at a time. Living mindfully, being conscious of the implications of our choices, learning as much as we can and demanding that companies do the same — that is how we can be the change that we wish to see.

Compassion Step

Be the change you want to see in the world by beginning to buy Fair Trade, by asking for it in stores. Fill out comment cards, talk to managers, ask them to stock these products. Give Fair Trade items as gifts, along with a note explaining why you chose that particular product. You may want to check these websites: www.Groundsforchange.com, www .Puravidacoffee.com, and www.Certifiedfairtrade.org. Pick up the book

Be the Change: Your Guide to Freeing Slaves and Changing the World by Zach Hunter and read it.

Community Step

Rent the movie *Amazing Grace* and watch it as a group. (Serve Fair Trade chocolate and coffee as snacks while watching the movie.) After watching, discuss: How did William Wilberforce change the system in his day? How was he himself changed? What steps as a group can you take to "be the change" in your world? How might making changes in your buying habits change your heart? How might changes in your heart affect your buying habits?

challenged

Yesterday, here's what my family and I ate: We had a cup or so each of plain oatmeal for breakfast. We each had a tortilla stuffed with rice and beans for lunch. Dinner was one chicken breast, split among the four of us, in a broth that contained beans, peas, onions, and garlic, over rice, with another tortilla each.

Today will be much the same.

We're taking on what our church is calling a Five-Day Challenge to focus our attention on world hunger. For the next few days, we will eat as most of the world's population eats. We're actually still eating more than most residents of the developing world; while our dinner included a very limited amount of meat, I made a lot of rice and encouraged the kids to fill up on that. In developing countries, those who do get to eat will often eat very small portions; about one cup is a generous portion. Meat is a rare treat.

Still, it's substantially less food than we are used to. The exercise is designed to help us understand the plight of the poor, and part of that plight is not just lack of quantity but also lack of variety. Once our fast is over, we may not want to eat rice again for a month.

We plan to take the money we would normally spend on groceries and donate it to our church, which will give it to Feed My Starving Children (www.fmsc.org), an organization that provides meals in places like Zimbabwe to keep people from dying of hunger.

To get a picture of where our money will be going, we also took advantage of an opportunity this week to go and pack meals with FMSC. This amazing organization gathers groups of volunteers to pack bags of soy, rice, dried veggies, and a vitamin-enriched flavored powder. The kids had a great time working with a huge group of other folks from our church to pack these meals, box them up, and get them ready to send to Zimbabwe. They learned a bit about the plight of the poor. It motivated them to engage in this fast.

Since I'm someone who loves to cook, someone who in fact expresses love by cooking, eating so lightly is hard for me on a number of levels. As a mom of two growing teens, I'm finding that it is harder for me to watch them be hungry than it is for me to be hungry. I'm a middle-aged woman with a bit of "reserves," if you catch my drift. I love good food, I enjoy cooking, but I don't mind being a little hungry. But my fourteen-year-old daughter, who is continuing to run track and play soccer this week, and my twelve-year-old son, who appears to be growing taller by the day, both need more calories, optimally, than they are getting this week. They are both lean anyway, and I wonder if they will be alright. I don't want them to do poorly in school because they are distracted by growling tummies.

My daughter, not surprisingly, is embracing the challenge with her usual headstrong fervor. She and a group of friends from church are egging each other on to handle this challenge. My kids attend public school. They'll have an opportunity to talk about this issue with friends when they pull out their tortillas and rice today at lunch. A number of other kids at school are joining in this challenge, which is a very cool witness.

My son, the quieter one, is accepting the program but not loving it, honestly. I instruct them to drink plenty of water. I cheat on our restricted diet by giving them vitamins and glasses of milk. I use spices and garlic, and we have tried every kind of bean in the grocery store, just to add variety. We've feasted, though, on the rich discussions we've had about fasting, and on how when you feel those hunger pangs, they can be a reminder to pray. I pointed out to my kids that our simple dinner, because it contained meat, would be considered a feast by many. My daughter said, "I will never say, 'I'm starving' again."

This morning, as Aaron and I ate our oatmeal, I read the whole of Isaiah 58 out loud. I explained, very briefly, that God tells us that the reason for fasting is to "share your food with the hungry" (Isa. 58:7). That is what we are doing. We're taking the funds we'd normally use for groceries and donating to the organization we packed meals with this week.

I'm not making my kids go without any food; that would be cruel, since I have food available. In fact, they found that rice and beans can be surprisingly satisfying (if a little boring), especially when you have not been snacking all day. It is one thing to say to your kids, "There are children in the world who are starving." There's a huge "so what?" factor in that because they are disconnected from what it means. So how can I instruct them? How can I help them understand what "people are hungry" means? Hunger is something you simply cannot understand without experiencing it. There's great value in letting your kids, in a very small way, learn by experience what it means to feel hungry.

I am building my children's capacity for compassion, which is part of my job as a parent. While I want to shield my children from pain or danger, all of us grow when we have to work through struggles or difficulty. Challenges build our character, make us stronger. They foster empathy with those who are suffering.

The Bible says that the fruit (or result) of having God's Spirit in us is "love, joy, peace, patience, kindness, goodness, faithfulness, gentleness and self-control" (Gal. 5:22–23). This week has been a chance to grow in self-control, to realize that I don't need as much food as I normally eat to feel joyful.

My family and I are trying to see this week as an opportunity to learn, a chance to grow in empathy. We're learning that we can endure, without dying, eating rice, beans, and oatmeal for a few days. We're understanding in our gut (literally) that it sucks to be poor, to be hungry. I hope the experience will motivate us to want to help people who don't have enough to eat.

I'm so grateful to be a part of a church that is helping me to do this. The Five-Day Challenge is an opportunity for us, as a body of believers, to fast and pray. Our society is so wigged out about fasting. It's odd that people who say they use the Bible as a "guide for life" somehow avoid engaging in this spiritual discipline. The Bible assumes that fasting is part of life. Fasting is simply abstaining from something for a spiritual purpose. Of course, it's hard. It hurts. I find, though, that eating this way, in which I eat a bit but not an excess, is easier than I expected.

I woke up this morning before the alarm, feeling a little hungry. I thought about people all around the world who do not have a cushy bed to sleep in and who feel way hungrier than I do. I lay there, warm and cozy, thinking about what it would be like not just to feel hungry but also to be cold and exposed. I'm wondering if I can make it through this week. They're wondering if they can make it at all.

The goal of this challenge is not to "grind it out" or simply endure hunger. It is not to "win" the challenge, like competitors on *Survivor*. Rather, the goal is to be spiritually transformed.

The Bible is very clear that fasting is always linked with prayer—prayers of repentance, prayers seeking God's miraculous help, prayers that are especially heartfelt or intense. I am encouraging my family to pray. When they feel hunger pangs, I remind them to pray that God will feed the hungry. When they get bored with rice, I remind them to pray for kids who may eat very little besides rice, not just for a week but for a lifetime.

For us, a greater challenge than just reducing our consumption, perhaps, is to be open to letting God speak to us about our own complacency and to repent of that. So as I pray for my church and myself, I'm hoping that God will move in the hearts of people in our church and our community.

I hope that in me it inspires a desire to be generous toward charities that feed the poor and to find ways to work for systemic change that will more fairly distribute resources around the world. There is enough food on our planet to feed everyone. We have so much in our country that we throw 40 percent of it away. Throw it away! It's not as if we need to hoard it because there's not enough. There is more than enough. Unfortunately, the problems of distribution are indeed huge.

The Bible tells us that if we fast just to impress God or others without allowing it to change our hearts, God is not interested. My prayer this week is that my heart will be changed. It's a prayer I'm terrified to pray, actually.

God keeps bringing the words of a worship song to my mind. That's how he speaks in my heart sometimes. "I will never be the same again. I can never return, I've closed the door," Darlene Zschech's well-known chorus keeps playing in my brain. This week is more than just a week, I know. I want it to change me, but part of me doesn't. It will wreck things, in a way. I will never be the same again.

Compassion Step

What is your response to the idea of fasting in this way? Do you know how much you spend on food each week? Determine some small ways you could reduce your consumption for a week or more, and then donate the money you save to an organization (such as Feed My Starving Children or World Vision or a local soup kitchen) that feeds the hungry.

Community Step

As a group, try the Five-Day Challenge. This challenge is much more meaningful if you have friends praying for you and encouraging you, who are doing it with you. When you feel hungry, let that be a reminder to pray for those who don't have a choice about their consumption. At the end of the five days, celebrate with a simple meal together. Talk about how this experience has changed your perspective on hunger, the poor, and social responsibility.

hands

between the gas bill and a 20 percent off coupon for Bed Bath and Beyond in yesterday's mail, I discovered a heavy, multifolded piece of card stock adorned with a computer-generated label addressed to "Kent, Keri."

I recognized the familiar World Vision orange logo and eagerly opened the letter from my sponsored child, Zoila. Because Zoila is only two years old, the letters are typically from her mother and are inscribed by a translator.

It was a Christmas card, with a verse from Luke 2 printed in both Spanish and English. (International mail being what it is, it arrived two weeks after Christmas.) Below a stock photo of a smiling child, the card had a space for my child to draw a picture. Because she is only a toddler, Zoila doesn't yet draw. Rather than have her scribble randomly on the card, her mother, or perhaps the World Vision caregiver, had placed her little hand on the paper and traced its outline onto the card.

You could tell little Zoila had been a bit squirmy while having her hand traced. Someone, her mother perhaps, had carefully colored in the tracing, maybe so I would know it was a hand, even drawing on fingernails and coloring them red. I stared at the colored-pencil drawing for a long time, and then I went to the fridge, where Zoila's picture is held in place with a magnetic frame. I looked at her cute little baby face, then back at the hand, with its colored-pencil manicure.

Zoila and her mom live in Honduras. Because Zoila's father abandoned them, they and her younger siblings live with her uncles and grandparents. The money I send each month helps feed Zoila and her family and also supports efforts to provide schooling, clean water, and health care to her community.

Sometimes I wonder if it makes any difference, my sending a few dollars a month to some little girl in Central America. I look at that hand. I place my own hand over it, like a prayer.

The Bible says, "Do not withhold good from those who deserve it, when it is in your power to act" (Prov. 3:27 NIV). It is, irrefutably, within my power to act. To do something. To make a difference, even if it is a small one.

On any given day, my mailbox welcomes impassioned letters and heart-wrenching four-color magazines from Habitat for Humanity, World Vision, and any number of local ministries as well. My email inbox is sprinkled with appeals for funding, action, or both from these same groups, plus a handful of others.

I welcome this correspondence, have signed up to receive it.

And yet, looking at the pile of envelopes, I wonder, Is any of this making a dent? How does one grow in compassion? Write more checks? Sponsor more children?

The Bible says we ought to help those who "deserve it" but makes it clear that none of us deserve it. We've all screwed up, God's Word says. "All have sinned and fall short of the glory of God" (Rom. 3:23). If that's true, no one deserves good, yet all of us are offered God's grace. The next verse in Romans says that even though we all fall short, we "are justified freely by his grace through the redemption that came by Christ Jesus" (Rom. 3:24). This is what I call Jesus logic, a counterintuitive way of thinking that says to people like me, "You're a mess, so welcome to the family."

I look at Zoila's little hand, chubby fingers splayed. I put my hand over the drawing, protectively. My sponsorship feels like a small thing, like scooping water from the ocean with a thimble. Yet sending that money tells Zoila and her mama, "You matter to God." It also reminds me that my small efforts matter. It puts a face on poverty and puts that face on my refrigerator.

The world is full of darkness, because all people (including you and me) keep making selfish, stupid choices. I don't know about you, but sometimes it feels like I just can't help it. Instead of figuring out what I can do, I blame all those other bad people out there, the ones who are starting wars and melting the ice caps. Jesus tells us to bring his light into that dark world. My power to act is limited, but it is there. If I allow its limits to paralyze me, then I've lost the battle without a fight.

While I have my own children to provide for, and to pray for, there is still room in my heart for another. That little drawing reminds me not just

to send a check but also to pray for that little girl who matters to God—
and who hopefully knows that she matters to me.

That tenderly traced hand reminds me of a verse in Isaiah where God
promises to "have compassion on his afflicted ones" (Isa. 49:13). When
God's people complain that he has forgotten them, God replies,

> *Can a mother forget the baby at her breast*
>   *and have no compassion on the child she has borne?*
> *Though she may forget,*
>   *I will not forget you!*
> *See, I have engraved you on the palms of my hands;*
>   *your walls are ever before me.*
>
> Isaiah 49:15–16

The phrase "I have engraved you on the palms of my hands" foretells
Jesus' crucifixion; it also refers to a common practice at the time of Isaiah
(written about seven hundred years before Christ). Devoted Jews would
stain, burn, or puncture a symbol of Jerusalem or its temple onto their
hands to keep a reminder of God always with them and to show how
much they loved God and his holy place. Perhaps they wanted to have a
mark on them that said, "I am proud to be one of God's people."

God says he does the same for you: he has engraved you on the palms
of his hands. You are always on God's mind, right at his fingertips. God's
love for each of his children exceeds that of the most attentive mother
for her child.

God is always thinking of me, and of you, of each person on this
planet. Zoila has been inscribed on the palms of God's hands. Her picture is on his refrigerator, so to speak. He is mindful of her plight. Apparently, he's decided that the way he will help Zoila is through me. He's put
her into my hands, in a way. Not just mine, though. I can't solve all of her
problems. I am part of a team of people who are helping Zoila and her
mother and her village in Honduras. Caring for her, even long-distance,
changes me. It reminds me that poverty has a face, and little hands.

Sometimes when we see people who are suffering or living in poverty, we ask, Why doesn't God do something about that? Well, he's trying
to. It's just that he's asking weaklings like me to act on his behalf. I don't
always do what he asks. When I am obedient, I not only help others; I
get a sense of how much God loves me. How much he believes in me,

putting his precious children (those who live with me, and those who don't) in my hands.

Don't underestimate your own power to make a difference, to shine the light of God's love. Who knows? When you take a step to make a difference, others may join you, and together you will change the world.

Compassion Step

Find a quiet place where you can pray and reflect. Ask God to speak to you. Read Isaiah 49:15 – 16. Believe that this is God's word to you, his way of beginning the conversation. Read the verses several times. Express back to God whatever feelings (whether it's gratitude, sadness, joy, uncertainty) come to you. Allow yourself to feel God's love for you. If you like, write your thoughts and feelings in a journal.

Community Step

Pray as a group about how you might be able to make a difference in the lives of a few children, either locally or overseas. Child sponsorship generally runs about thirty-five dollars or less per month. If some members of the group can't afford to sponsor a child by themselves, they may want to team up with other members to sponsor one. Consider praying for and writing letters of encouragement to the workers who are providing care to these children.

talents

during 2003 in Uganda, a woman named Joy lost her husband to malaria, unfortunately a common fate in her village. She was raising six children by herself—four of her own, and two of them AIDS orphans from other families. As with most of her neighbors, Joy's income was about one dollar per day.

Joy chose to remain undeterred by her circumstances. She applied for and received a business loan from a ministry organization called Five Talents (www.fivetalents.org), which had recently begun a program in her village. This small step, taken perhaps with all she had the strength left to take, changed her life.

A former newspaper colleague of mine, Craig Cole, is Five Talents' executive director. Five Talents provides microenterprise loans and business training to people (primarily women) in the developing world, to help them lift themselves out of poverty.

The name comes from Jesus' parable of the talents, in which he tells the story of a master who gives three servants each a different sum of money.[55] It's interesting that the particular denomination of money in the story is the talent, which was actually a measure of weight. Scholars have varied opinions on what it would be worth in today's dollars. One estimate is that just one talent of gold would be worth about four hundred thousand dollars.[56] But the English meaning of *talent*—a skill or giftedness—makes the story all the richer.

Jesus uses this parable to tell us about God's kingdom. "Again, it will be like a man going on a journey, who called his servants and entrusted his wealth to them." *It* will be like—what will? The kingdom of heaven. While we often think of this kingdom in terms of a future reality, Jesus frequently told his followers that the kingdom of heaven was near them, was among them, or had come. It was not someday; it was now. It still is. As Dallas Willard once said, "Eternity is in session."

In this illustration of what God's kingdom is like, the master doles out talents—five to one servant, two to a second, and just one to a third.

The distribution is not capricious; the text says he gave the money to "each according to his ability." He gave the most money to the servant who was his best and brightest. To the least competent servant he gave the least amount of money. None of the servants are given any instructions. The master simply leaves.

When he returns, he finds that the first two servants have each invested wisely and earned a staggering 100 percent return on what was given to them. The master's response to both is, "Well done, good and faithful servant." But the third simply buried his talent. He later admits his motive: fear. The master is not merciful. He takes the man's one talent away and tosses him out "into the darkness, where there will be weeping and gnashing of teeth." The servant who buried his talent has lost not only the money but also community. He will live with regret.

"That phrase in Jesus' parable, 'each according to his own ability,' drives what I do," Craig says. "Helping women find out that they have value, that they have dignity, and that God loves them — that makes a huge difference in people's lives. One group of women we trained in Tanzania came back to us with tears in their eyes; they said they had never been told they had that kind of value. We've accomplished something just in the planning process, before they even start their business."

In that village in Uganda, Joy received training and a $160 loan from Five Talents, and "she literally made a profit out of dirt," Craig says. She used the money to buy a small plot of land in her village and used the dirt there to make bricks. Within a year, she had made four times what she'd spent and paid back the loan. She'd also provided jobs for family and neighbors, and three years later, her brick-making business remained profitable, employing thirteen people.

"Every loan [usually between one hundred and two hundred dollars] helps about six other people indirectly," Craig says, "either through employment or just family members who get food and education as a result of the increase in income."

Another woman whose life was changed by Five Talents is April Young. An executive with Comerica Bank, she agreed to serve on the ministry's board of directors but didn't want to take a trip to actually see the people the organization was helping. "She used to joke that she would pray globally but sleep locally. But we eventually got her to go on a trip to Uganda," Craig says. "Now she can't get enough. Her whole life has been transformed. She sees poverty in a different way. She's there teaching but also learning."

Five Talents does not do relief work, providing food and supplies to people in crisis. While that is necessary, the ministry's focus is long-term. For example, Craig tells of a visit to India after the 2005 tsunami. "We went to these isolated fishing villages where people had lost everything—their homes, their livelihood. They were still dazed three months after the storm; they didn't know what to do." While relief agencies had helped keep them alive, the agencies had not found a way to help them regain self-sufficiency.

Five Talents sent a group to the villages to set up a self-help program. With the aid of a local church, they taught a group of women how to create a saving club. The women pooled their resources and saved their money together. Once they had enough, they made small-business loans from that pool, and as the loans were paid back with interest, the money grew. Five Talents taught them how to keep financial records, how a savings and loan program works, how to set up businesses. Within a short time, they'd saved seventeen thousand dollars and rebuilt a sense of self-esteem and community.

The program raised their standard of living, as women in the village started small businesses with the loans. The return on investment also included increased confidence. "They went from being financially and functionally illiterate to empowered," Craig says. The women, for example, realized that they could speak up and have influence with their local government—which they did, again improving their living conditions. They created community and connection, which again was empowering.

The Bible says, "If anyone is poor among your people in any of the towns of the land that the LORD your God is giving you, do not be hardhearted or tightfisted toward them. Rather, be openhanded and freely lend them whatever they need" (Deut. 15:7–8).

While relief work (sending immediate food and supplies) is always needed, it's a stopgap measure. Investing in community development is not only biblical; it "builds families and self-esteem," Craig says. A much more long-term solution, it fosters independence and community rather than just dependence on handouts. It is a way to work for justice rather than just providing charity.

Five Talents sponsors trips in which businesspeople can go to places like India and Africa, not just to see what's going on but also to help provide business training to the poor. They can take the talents God has given to them and invest them in a way that has both an immediate and an eternal impact. Five Talents is looking for people who will pray, pledge, or participate, and as with the servants in the parable, God gives different people different assignments. The key, Craig says, is to figure out what you have to invest, and then invest it.

The recipients of the loans are not the only people his organization ministers to. He has seen lives change as American women, like April, see how they can make a difference by sharing their business acumen with women a world away. They become invested in the lives of women who seem so different from them, only to realize how much they have in common. They also get to live the adventure of investing their talents in God's kingdom.

I've always found the parable of the talents to be a rich story. So many levels of meaning, so many life lessons we can draw from it. The ending feels rather harsh. In God's kingdom, Jesus is saying, not investing your talents is a serious offence.

So how does that last part of the parable play out? That "weeping and gnashing of teeth" part? The words paint a picture of sadness and regret.

"Missing out on God's mission for your life is a tragedy," Craig says.

Compassion Step

Read the parable of the talents in Matthew 25. Journal about the following questions: What talents has God entrusted to you? How have you invested them? How can you invest your talents to help others?

Community Step

As a group, take inventory of the talents you collectively possess. What skills or knowledge does each group member have? How could you put those talents together to invest them in God's kingdom? While many of us have talents, we are often short on time. How do you think God wants you to invest your time and talents? Is he leading you to make small changes in your "heavenly investment strategy"?

hope

i wander slowly through an African shantytown, a jumble of huts with thatch and corrugated tin roofs. Inside the huts there's no running water, of course. They're furnished with crudely made furniture, tattered curtains, dirt floors, threadbare blankets. In this desolate place, nearly half of the residents are infected with HIV/AIDS. The adults who still survive are often caring for large groups of children—orphans they have taken in, nieces, nephews, grandchildren. Their limited resources are stretched even farther.

Drugs to treat what locals here call the "big disease" are expensive and hard to come by. Those who are infected are ashamed, so even if they can afford treatment, they often wait until it is too late. In one shanty, a child sits beside her mother, who obviously is dying.

I walk slowly through the village as my guide shares information about this crisis. Prostitutes in Kenya, who turn as many as seven tricks a night at about two dollars per, are continuing to unwittingly spread AIDS. They make a little more if they don't insist on condom use. Medicine is needed, care is needed, but for the love of God, education is needed.

Thousands of children in the region have been orphaned, and many of them have been infected as well. They live in deep poverty, often lack clean water and food. I stare silently into their eyes, my throat dry and tight. The situation begins to feel overwhelming.

Although the village is actually an exhibit in a church gymnasium, the tears on my face are very real.

World Vision Experience: AIDS (Step into Africa) is a traveling exhibit set up in churches and other venues across the country, educating Americans about AIDS in Africa and recruiting sponsors for children affected by the AIDS pandemic. The exhibit takes you through a life-sized display of a village, allowing you to share in the experience of a child who is trying to survive in that place.

I've never been to Africa, but my heart cries out for it. Of all the global crises, the HIV/AIDS pandemic in Africa is the most overwhelming to me. Africa is a beautiful and amazing country, but also one plagued by poverty, disease, malnutrition, wars, genocide—it's a continent full of struggles. How can we make a difference? How can we persevere in hope when the situation seems so hopeless? Although the United States has finally started giving tremendous amounts of money and medicine, and celebrities are all over this cause, it's still huge.

The Bible says that "religion that God our Father accepts as pure and faultless is this: to look after orphans and widows in their distress and to keep oneself from being polluted by the world" (James 1:27).

Because of HIV/AIDS, Africa is full of widows and orphans, in deep distress. I search hungrily for hope and come up wanting. The Bible mentions hope many times. Frequently, it is in phrases like "hope in the Lord" or "hope in your word." If we are to make a difference, we persevere in hope in the Lord. Ours is not a vague wishfulness that things will turn out but a confidence in God and his promises. That confidence, in God and his Word, gives us the courage to ask, How can I make a difference in the world?

I resist this brokenness. Of course. Who wants to feel sad? We dislike thinking about problems like this because they are so big, so overwhelming. You don't want to cry, because if you cry, you'll realize that you have to do something.

I was surprised that seeing the World Vision exhibit made me feel inspired, motivated to make a difference. At the end, I walked up to a "wall of hope" where you can see photos of children needing sponsors. While the sheer number of children was overwhelming, I was glad the organization was offering me a chance to do something about the tragedy I had just witnessed.

Several years ago Oprah interviewed U2 lead singer and social activist Bono about his efforts to raise funds and awareness for Africa. He said, "Our generation will be known for the internet, the war on terror, and how we let an entire continent burst into flames while we stood around with watering cans—or not. I think it's exciting to be part of a generation that actually says, 'No.' Now, the world is a smaller place; distance cannot decide who is our neighbor to love. Love thy neighbor. We can't afford not to. The world is too close."

How do we love our African neighbors, especially those struggling with HIV/AIDS? One woman who is making a difference in this area is Lynne Hybels, my pastor's wife.

Lynne has been deeply involved in the efforts to help Africa. Because of her influence, our church (Willow Creek Community Church) now partners with churches in South Africa (the African country hardest hit by this crisis) to provide practical help. Our church is partnering with a group of twenty-three churches in the Samfya district of Zambia, who created a community-based organization called the Samfya Community of Care Providers (SCCP). According to Willow Creek's website (www .willowcreek.org), these churches "have a common interest in tackling the multiple issues that HIV and AIDS is creating in their community. SCCP's goal is the identification and support of orphans and vulnerable children by providing for their education and nutrition needs." In other words, our church in Illinois did not go to Africa to tell people how to solve the problem. We found local churches in hard-hit areas who were already working hard to fight the pandemic, and we came alongside them. We learned from them, asked how we could assist. Our church is supporting their efforts with practical help, including food, education, microenterprise loans, and more. You can read more about it on the church website.

Lynne brought the Africa question to our church, and she and Bill rallied our church around this cause. Lynne now serves on the board of directors for World Vision. She listened to God's call on her life and is using her wisdom and influence to make a difference. I'm inspired by her simple obedience.

Ravi Zacharias has said, "If the Christian community will respond compassionately and effectively to the global AIDS crisis, it will be the most powerful apologetic the church has ever offered to the watching world."

We respond to the suffering of Africa with compassion, in part, because it will transform us. Practicing compassion will make us more like Jesus and will allow God to change our hearts. Compassion will demonstrate the love of Christ to the world far better than any argument about God's existence or Christ's divinity. If we "witness" by telling others about Jesus but don't love as Jesus would, how credible is that witness?

And you maybe can't change a whole culture, one that seems irreparably broken, not to mention insane. But you can change the life of one child, for about a dollar a day. You can support existing efforts that are already in place. You can rally your church to get involved. You can change yourself, from someone standing by with a watering can to someone who is willing to give a cup of cold water in Jesus' name. The question is not will you but why wouldn't you?

Compassion Step

Educate yourself about what is happening in Africa. Do some research and find an organization that is doing effective work. Pray for that organization every day this week. Ask God where he might want you to lend support, either as a volunteer or financially.

Community Step

Check the World Vision website (www.worldvision.org) to see if the World Vision Experience: AIDS (Step into Africa) exhibit is coming to your community. As a group, go through the exhibit together. Discuss your reaction. What action steps do you as a group want to take in light of your experience?

jewelry

a few years ago, I seemed to get a postcard about once a week inviting me to a "party" at a neighbor's house (or a friend of a friend's house, or sometimes a total stranger's house). There were candle parties, rubber stamping parties, scrapbooking parties, designer clothing parties, makeup parties, jewelry parties, even sex-toy parties.

As you could tell from the looks of my cluttered house, I didn't miss many of the parties (except for the sex-toy party). I have dusty bins in my basement full of scrapbooking supplies and rubber stamps, and I have way too many candles and enough Tupperware to contain the leftovers of a thousand meals. I'd attend said parties full of resolve to just look and not buy. Right. Soon, plied with too much artichoke dip and a glass of cheap chardonnay, I'd feel a little guilty about just mooching the free food, and I would become convinced that I needed that elegant candle sconce. (I can just hear my husband saying, "A sconce? What's a sconce?") Or I'd think that somehow, just owning crafty things would make up for my utter lack of craft skills, and I'd make all my Christmas cards by hand with rubber stamps. (Which happened only one year, when I was home with babies and not working and climbing the walls, and my husband kept asking, "What do you do all day?" Rubber stamping Christmas cards seemed like a good answer to that question.)

Now I know better. I have not ever been, nor will I ever be, the type of person who likes to rubber stamp or scrapbook. I should sell the stuff on eBay instead of letting it rot in the basement. Maybe I should pack it all up and send it to Martha Stewart, since it has finally hit me that *I'm not her!*

Anyway, it's a wonder any of us feel any need to go to the mall, since we can apparently buy everything we need, down to the accessories, at home sales parties.

Now, maybe you love these parties and the fun of throwing them or going to them. Most likely, you'd prefer to skip the part of the presentation where the sales gal tries to get you to "join the team" and work for her (give her a part of your commissions).

One reason these parties are successful is that we seem to have an insatiable appetite for stuff. We complain that we have too much stuff, yet we keep buying more. This does more than clutter our homes. It sometimes, without our realizing it, deeply hurts people we've never met.

So many of the things we buy (not necessarily at aforementioned parties but everywhere) are mined or manufactured in conditions that grind the poor farther down. Our unawareness of the source of our stuff does not absolve us from responsibility. The Bible is harsh in its judgment of mindless consumption.

> *"What do you mean by crushing my people*
> *and grinding the faces of the poor?"*
> *declares the Lord,*
> *the LORD Almighty.*
> *The LORD says,*
> *"The women of Zion are haughty,*
> *walking along with outstretched necks,*
> *flirting with their eyes,*
> *tripping along with mincing steps,*
> *with ornaments jingling on their ankles."*
> Isaiah 3:15–16

The text goes on to say that God will punish the women of Zion by stripping them of their jewelry and other finery. So should we forgo fancy clothes and jewelry altogether? What if we could buy these things in a way that didn't grind down the poor (such as the children working in diamond mines)?

A number of organizations that help women in poverty do so by teaching the women a trade and then helping them market what they make. These organizations don't just give women food; they give them a livelihood. They empower them and help them understand their value. They give them the hope that only real job skills can provide.

So this week we're going to get very practical. Here are three organizations that will help you host a jewelry party that will help women in poverty. Careful research on the internet will help you find others, if you're so inclined. Who knew that your compassion step this week would be to go shopping?

The Well is a Christian organization that reaches out to women in the sex trade in Bangkok, Thailand. Many of these women are forced or duped into commercial sex or are desperate enough to think it is the only way they can provide for their families. The Well sends workers into the red-light district of Bangkok to help women escape this life and find an alternative way to make a living.

Some of the women find shelter at a center run by the Well, where they can recover from rape, abuse, and sexual slavery. I learned about this work from Stephanie Voiland, an editor at a Christian publishing house, who traveled with a church group to Thailand on a mission trip with the Well and has served on its board of directors.

Before visiting Thailand, Stephanie thought women in prostitution irresponsibly chose that lifestyle. She simply didn't understand the sex trade. On her visit, she discovered that many of the young women in the red-light district of Bangkok were teenagers, as young as sixteen, sent by their parents to try to earn a living, or even sold into slavery. Others were young mothers who were sending their earnings back to small country-side villages to support their children.

"I had a new sense of gratitude for what I've been given," Stephanie says. "And with that, a sense of obligation, like God was saying, what are you going to do with what you've been given? And I realized I could do something about justice and compassion. I could stand up for people who don't have a voice."

The women who've been rescued are taught a simple trade, like making homemade cards and jewelry. You can support the ministry by hosting a party to sell the cards and jewelry the women make. To find out how, visit www.narimon.org. You can learn more about the ministry of the Well at www.servantworks.org/well.

A second organization, BeadforLife, focuses on women in Uganda, providing them an opportunity to make beaded jewelry out of recycled paper. The beads are very cool; you can't tell they're made of paper. A friend sent me three bracelets as a thank-you gift, and my teenage daughter promptly "borrowed" them and has not yet given them back. We bought several more to give to friends as gifts.

The organization's website, www.BeadforLife.org, has a link that gives detailed instructions on how to host a bead party. You'll even get Ugandan recipes and a CD of African music to set the mood at your party. The women who make the jewelry get a living wage, and all profits from BeadforLife go into community development programs that help fight poverty in areas like health, housing, and education.

Women Thrive Worldwide (www.womenthrive.org) has a "shop the cause" section on its website, linking to several organizations that help, some of which offer opportunities for hosting parties. Do some of your own research.

Finally, Trade as One is a very cool organization that imports all kinds of goods, from Fair Trade chocolate and coffee to jewelry and paper goods. Last December, our church invited Trade as One to set up a fair in our lobby so that church members could do their Christmas shopping and support this organization. I bought a number of gifts through their sale, including some pretty amber earrings for a friend. This friend owns quite a bit of expensive jewelry. When she read the little tag about how these simple earrings had been made, she nearly cried. She proudly wears the earrings, along with her diamond necklace.

You could host a small party or set up an event at your church. Go to www.TradeasOne.org to explore the possibilities.

If parties aren't your style, consider simply buying items like these to give as holiday gifts. While some people just don't get it if you try to explain how you're buying a goat in their name instead of a traditional gift, they would welcome jewelry made by a woman working her way out of poverty. It's a win-win; they get a bauble and help a cause at the same time.

Compassionate living does not require you to stop shopping, but it does require you to shop conscientiously. To become aware of the power of your spending and to use that power for good.

Compassion Step

Choose one of the organizations listed in this chapter (the Well, Bead for Life, or Trade as One), or find another one online. Pray about which one you will support. Then go shopping. Purchase some gifts for friends, or stock up on stationery or cards. When you give the gifts, explain how this is more than just a necklace or a pair of earrings. If you buy items to wear yourself, pray for the woman who made them whenever you wear them.

Community Step

As a group, host a jewelry party to sell products from one of these organizations. The BeadforLife website offers a kit to help you. Invite friends and neighbors, and see it not just as an opportunity to shop but also as a chance to share God's love with people in your community.

conspiracy

I am writing this chapter in early December. Despite the hype and hurry, I steal a few minutes now and then to reflect. I carve out time for pondering during the season of Advent. I love reading *Watch for the Light*, an Advent devotional with words from some of my favorite authors. The word *advent* means "coming" or "arrival," and this season is a time when we anticipate the coming of the Christ child. Well, that and the arrival of the January credit card bill.

I find myself trying to swim through the thick of the Advent season. While I don't love shopping or keeping track of what I've bought for whom, I do love being able to give. I love demonstrating love and care to friends and family. Still, dread sometimes trumps anticipation when my to-do list gets too long.

I sometimes wonder, Do my gifts actually communicate my heart? Or do they simply fulfill my obligation? Seduced by the slick ads in the Sunday paper, I am drawn irresistibly to the mall. I buy things I don't need, things that are not on my list, things that (I realize when I get home) would be perfect for ... nobody. Not even myself.

So I end up returning them, even before Christmas.

As much as I want Christmas to be meaningful, to be about Jesus, resistance to the tide of materialism often feels futile.

I heard recently about an alternative way to celebrate the season, through an interchurch movement called the Advent Conspiracy (www. adventconspiracy.org). Its organizers suggest that rather than indebt ourselves to retailers, spending money on things nobody needs, we invest in relationships and give presents to Jesus—to the poor. For whatever you do for the "least of these," he told us, you do for him. The theme for this movement is "Worship more. Spend less. Give more. Love all." Far more than a call to frugality, it is a call to social action and deeper meaning. The Advent Conspiracy focuses on redirecting Christmas budgets toward clean water wells for the poor.

I've often wanted to do this kind of thing: make donations to charity on behalf of those on my gift list. I am afraid that friends will feel gypped somehow, that they will be disappointed not to get the little trinket or book (I give a lot of books) that I usually buy them.

It feels like I'm imposing my charitable endeavors on friends, and frankly, it's a bit uncomfortable. Would I be willing to tell people, "Don't buy me anything; instead donate to a charity"? That's a harder option. Especially when people just get you a gift and don't ask what you want. To tell people what to get you feels a bit presumptuous. Or what if they tell you at the end of November, "I've already bought your Christmas gift"? Do I suggest they return it and donate the money?

The Advent Conspiracy website offers great suggestions for families and groups, focusing on relationships, rather than shopping. Rather than giving unnecessary things, redirect that money to the poor, particularly for wells. In rural villages all over the world, people often use a local watering hole for all water functions. They bathe, wash clothes, and draw drinking water, all in the same stagnant pond. (In some cases, it's more like a puddle.) Some have to dig in the dirt to find water or gather drinking water from a polluted river or stream, a stream that likely carries human or animal waste. Not surprisingly, the people in such circumstances, especially children, are often sick as a result. This is not an isolated problem. Millions of people all over the globe do not have access to decent water.

Throughout the Bible, the image of water is used as a symbol of life, of God's Spirit, of abundance. How can people understand this symbol if they do not have clean water to drink?

In John 7, Jesus is in Jerusalem, and tension is mounting as the Pharisees plot to arrest and kill him. In spite of this, the Bible says, "On the last and greatest day of the festival, Jesus stood and said in a loud voice, 'Let anyone who is thirsty come to me and drink. Whoever believes in me, as Scripture has said, rivers of living water will flow from within them.' By this he meant the Spirit, whom those who believed in him were later to receive. Up to that time the Spirit had not been given, since Jesus had not yet been glorified" (John 7:37 – 39).

When I wrote about the Advent Conspiracy on my blog, my friend Wendy in Richmond, Virginia, wrote to tell me that her church was participating in it. "Our family has committed to keeping a Christ-Centered Christmas," she said, noting that they cut their holiday spending by 25 percent and donated that money to charity. They also tried to "be intentional about the gift of time to family and friends. What a challenge that can be in this world that we live in."

During the holiday season, Wendy went to one of her son's basketball games in a Christian sports league. A man giving a halftime devotion told of a mission trip he and his family had taken to Africa. "He told a story about watching a young girl dig in mud to find water. She would put the water in a rusty can and then walk a couple of miles back to her home and repeat the process over and over again. Hearing this story, something inside me stirred. About a month later we were at the soccer fields and I watched over and over again as people threw empty and half full water bottles into the trash cans. It is amazing how much we can take for granted our easy access to so many things, especially clean water. Two days later I was watching Oprah and she did a segment on heroes. She had a teenage boy, named Ryan, on the show and he shared his journey with raising money to build wells at the ripe old age of six. He began the Ryan's Well Foundation. This moved me and I went on-line to research more. When I typed in Ryan's Well, a list of organizations came up and one of them was called 'Living Water.'"

Hearing about the issue of clean water from three different sources made Wendy think perhaps God was trying to get her attention. She visited the website for Living Water (www.water.cc), a Christian organization which helps provide clean drinking water to underresourced people around the world. She decided to take on a two-week challenge in which you drink no beverages except tap water for two weeks and donate the money you save on coffee, soda, and so forth to Living Water.

"Visiting the website really touched me," Wendy says. "I took the challenge to my small group, which immediately jumped on board. Our son, Connor, also participated in the challenge. Our group raised over four hundred dollars, and it was really fun to do. Some folks would call for support, saying, 'I'm really wanting to drink that cup of coffee.' One friend decided in addition to drinking water that she would take forty-five minutes to start exercising by walking every day. During that time she committed to pray for those who live without clean, fresh water."

Wendy's story is inspiring yet simple. She listened to God's promptings in the midst of her everyday life (at soccer games and watching television) and joined with others to do something to make a difference.

Mandy, a blog reader from Memphis, wrote to tell me that her church had participated in the Advent Conspiracy. "It has been a challenging but wonderful way to celebrate the birth," she wrote. "We are learning to take baby steps to make this a way of life within our family. It won't happen overnight, but slowly, our family is trying to give more relational gifts rather than the easy, impersonal gift cards! Ironically, I've been more stressed about gift giving this year because I'm not allowing myself to buy the easy gifts! But I know Christmas will be more meaningful. We also chose to send a Christmas video this year on YouTube, saving us over a hundred dollars we would have spent on Christmas cards and postage. That money, plus the money we save on shopping, we are donating to the Advent Conspiracy offering our church is taking. I can't wait to see what an impact it will make on the clean water initiatives!"

It is insane that we who have clean, purified tap water insist on spending millions a year to buy bottled water, which often comes from the same source our tap water does. In fact, the purity regulations for tap water are stricter than those for bottled water. The amount of petroleum used to manufacture and transport bottled water is absolutely staggering. What if you stopped buying bottled water and donated that money to organizations that are digging wells in countries that need them?

What will make Advent more meaningful? What gift can we give to Jesus, since it's his birthday? Jesus said that what we do for "the least of these," including giving water to the thirsty, we've done for him. So giving a cup of cold water or a well with clean drinking water to people who have none seems like a good place to start.

Compassion Step

Spend some time praying for those who do not have access to clean water. What do you think it means to "spend less and give more"? What barriers stand in the way of your reducing your spending? Like Mandy, could you take some baby steps to take a quiet stand against materialism, no matter what season it is? Pick one of the ideas in this chapter and talk with your family about implementing it.

Community Step

As a group, try the Living Water challenge. For two weeks, forgo all beverages except tap water. When you feel like having a Diet Coke or some bottled water, put the money in a jar and get yourself a glass of water from the tap. Collect the money you save and as a group donate it all to a charity, like Living Water, that helps provide clean drinking water.

treasures

S usy Flory was, by her own admission, a "suburban mom with a plain vanilla life." Her journey started innocently enough; she wanted to write a book about women from history who had changed the world. She didn't realize that embarking on the project would change her life.

As she did the research on women ranging from Mary Magdalene to Eleanor Roosevelt, their stories inspired her and stirred a desire in her. She found it ironic that they did so much more with so much less. They lived life to the full, even though they had little.

"We're so much more resourced, more educated, we have better health," Susy says, yet we often don't impact the world the way they did. "We live privileged lives and hold on to things more tightly." What she learned made her want to become a difference maker herself.

Researching a chapter on Harriet Tubman, Susy read of a time when this poor, illiterate founder of the Underground Railroad was leading a group of slaves to freedom. After fording an icy river, they arrived at a safe house where they could spend the night. In the morning, their hosts demanded payment. Because the group had no money, Tubman took off her coat and extra clothing to give as payment.

"All of these women gave whatever they had to make a difference," Susy says. "I was inspired by the sacrifices they made. So it got me thinking, What can I give? What do I have?"

At that time, she attended a conference called Compassion Unleashed. A video shown during a break between sessions caught her eye. It showed little children in Africa carrying plastic containers and using them to scoop water from a mud hole. It contrasted the dirty water the children drank with beautiful footage of clean, flowing water. "Water is beautiful; it looks like diamonds," Susy says. The video highlighted Africa Oasis, a ministry to drill and maintain clean water wells.

Like anyone on a justice journey, Susy sometimes felt overwhelmed by the needs of the world. "You can't care about everything and everybody," she says. "But that video hit me upside the head like a two-by-four.

And I thought, I've got a son going to college, I work as a freelancer, I don't have the money to help. Then jewelry popped into my head."

The forty-three-year-old mother of two had a collection of jewelry, much of it pieces she'd received from her mother, who had sold and designed jewelry for more than thirty years. Susy wore only a few pieces, while the others sat in the drawer, because she felt uncomfortably ostentatious in it. "Wearing it separates you from people, because they assume you have a lot of money if you can afford that kind of jewelry," she says.

She felt God was calling her to sell all of her jewelry and donate the money to three organizations that drill wells in Africa, including Africa Oasis. "I was challenged to live more like Jesus and less like a Pharisee," she says. "That stuff was just sitting in my drawer while little kids were drinking dirty water."

Her collection of rings, necklaces, and a bracelet wasn't massive; much of its value was sentimental. Because gold prices were quite high when she sold it, however, she got about fifteen hundred dollars.

Even though she didn't wear most of her collection, parting with it was not an easy decision. "It took a lot of fear and trembling," she admits. "I took pictures. And I still haven't told my mother." One of the hardest pieces to part with was a necklace her mother had designed and given her, made with a gold nugget that came from her father's college class ring. Her mother had melted down the ring and made necklaces for Susy and her sister when their father died (when Susy was just twenty years old). Nevertheless, she believes that when she sees her dad in heaven someday, he'll affirm her decision to trade jewelry for water.

"One strong feeling I had at the time was that the jewelry was dead; it was a collection of cold, hard objects growing dusty in a drawer," Susy says. "They were pretty and shiny, sure, and they had memories and emotions attached. But they were still just objects. Weren't people so much more important? If I could give these objects up, sacrifice them to bring someone fresh, clear water to make them more healthy and give them life, what a worthy sacrifice! I guess I realized that the people I would be helping were so much more important than things I was hoarding. I was giving up something I didn't need so people could have something they really needed."

Jesus told his followers, "Don't hoard treasure down here where it gets eaten by moths and corroded by rust or—worse!—stolen by burglars. Stockpile treasure in heaven, where it's safe from moth and rust and burglars. It's obvious, isn't it? The place where your treasure is, is the place you will most want to be, and end up being" (Matt. 6:19–21 MSG).

While she intended her book to be about historic women, Susy ended up interweaving her own story into it, ultimately titling the book, *So Long, Status Quo: What I Learned from Women Who Changed the World.* Researching and writing it inspired her to exchange that plain vanilla life "for a new life of courage, sacrifice, and passion."

So often our faith stays in the realm of theory. Jesus said he came to give us life to the full, an abundant life. But do Christians live an abundant life? Can people see our faith by our actions? Our faith affects our future, but does it affect our present?

Shane Claiborne ponders this very question. He writes, "If you ask most people what Christians believe, they can tell you, 'Christians believe that Jesus is God's Son and that Jesus rose from the dead.' But if you ask the average person how Christians live, they are struck silent. We have not shown the world another way of doing life. Christians pretty much live like everybody else; they just sprinkle a little Jesus in along the way. And doctrine is not very attractive, even if it's true. Few people are interested in religion that has nothing to say to the world and offers them only life after death, when what people are really wondering is whether there is life before death."[57]

Jesus said that to gain your life, you have to be willing to lose it; to be first, you must be willing to be last. So many people I've interviewed for this book have found that sacrifice is the secret to life before death. To get life, you give it away.

Susy is a woman who is making a difference in the world by moving her treasures from earth to heaven. She's trying to answer the question, "How do Christians live?" with small, simple, but courageous acts of compassion.

Here's the beautiful paradox: when we let go of hoarding earthly treasure, we store up treasures in heaven. We actually live life on this earth differently, and better. We let go of striving for affluence or prosperity and seek deeper meaning. We trade our jewelry for water, and our earthly treasures for heavenly ones. And that's an abundant life.

Compassion Step

Of all your possessions, which is most precious to you? What do these things signify to you? While you may think that you hold these things, have you considered the possibility that they are holding you in their grip? Explain. How would it feel to give your most precious possessions away? How has Susy's story inspired you to take action?[58] What do you think it means to store up treasures in heaven? How might hanging on to our material possessions hinder that process?

Community Step

How is your Living Water challenge going? Talk about it. Then read the quote from Shane Claiborne together. Discuss the following as a group: Do you agree with Shane's assessment? How would you answer the question, "How do Christians live?" How do you think someone who is not a Christian would say that Christians live? More important, how do you live? Can people around you tell you are a Christian by the way you live (not just by the words you say)?

abundance

In an effort to exhort parishioners to give more generously, pastors will often cite a verse in Malachi that commands us to give a tithe: "'Bring the whole tithe into the storehouse, that there may be food in my house. Test me in this,' says the LORD Almighty, 'and see if I will not throw open the floodgates of heaven and pour out so much blessing that there will not be room enough to store it'" (Mal. 3:10).

While God blesses us when we give, this verse is about so much more than tithing. Rather, these words challenge us to choose what we will believe about God. Is he stingy, or generous? Do we see lack, or abundance?

Look at the context of this verse. God accuses his people of robbing him. How? By giving skimpy offerings? Well, yes. When we go back a bit farther in the text, we find more: God has a whole list of offenses his people are guilty of. Like many other prophets before him, Malachi must remind God's people that mistreatment of the poor offends God.

"'So I will come near to you for judgment. I will be quick to testify against sorcerers, adulterers and perjurers, against those who defraud laborers of their wages, who oppress the widows and the fatherless, and deprive aliens of justice, but do not fear me,' says the LORD Almighty" (Mal. 3:5 NIV).

I grew up in a great church, where tithing was a normal practice. In that church, I learned about the importance of giving and of obeying and memorizing Scripture. I also learned that adultery and lying are sins. I even was told not to mess with the occult because the Bible forbids sorcery. I never heard anything about the sin of injustice, which the rest of this list addresses. For example, what does it mean to "deprive aliens of justice" in our culture?

My experience is not unique. Why have our traditions focused on certain sins and ignored others, even when they are in the same sentence in the Bible?

The text continues, "'You are under a curse—your whole nation—because you are robbing me. Bring the whole tithe into the storehouse, that there may be food in my house. Test me in this,' says the LORD Almighty, 'and see if I will not throw open the floodgates of heaven and pour out so much blessing that there will not be room enough to store it. I will prevent pests from devouring your crops, and the vines in your fields will not drop their fruit before it is ripe,' says the LORD Almighty. 'Then all the nations will call you blessed, for yours will be a delightful land,' says the LORD Almighty" (Mal. 3:9–11).

This passage demands a choice: Do you trust God? Do you believe in his generosity? God blesses us when we go beyond just dropping a dollar in the collection plate, when we bless and protect the poor, when we trust his abundance enough to be generous—not just with our money. God is calling us to advocate for others, to desire justice for others and not just for ourselves; that's the kind of generosity God desires. It's more than just a tithe. Frankly, it's a lot to ask.

Do you believe there is plenty? Or is your belief in scarcity stronger? Could this passage be a call to see the world through a new framing story, one which affirms abundance? One which says God's blessing comes not just when we tithe but when we also live a life of justice? Can we act justly and love mercy if we believe in scarcity? Is there room for love in a soul that believes we have to grab what we can and not share? As John the disciple wrote, "If anyone has material possessions and sees his brother in need, and has no pity on him, how can the love of God be in him?" (1 John 3:17 NIV).

I'm not espousing a prosperity gospel. I don't think God necessarily wants me to be wealthy. He wants me to be fully committed to him regardless of my circumstances. I do think that when you are generous, you gain blessings, which may or may not be financial or material. You gain wisdom. You come to understand something that very few people in our world understand—the difference between needs and wants. The Bible says that God will supply all of our needs. Not all our wants.

In his book *Everything Must Change*, Brian McLaren talks about what he calls a "framing story" or "narrative," which he defines as "a story that gives people direction, values, vision and inspiration by providing a framework for their lives."[59] Every culture has a framing story, an underlying cultural understanding. He contrasts the framing story of the Roman Empire (a first-century world superpower with haunting similarities to the United States today) with that of Jesus.

Jesus lived counter to the prevailing culture of his day and taught his followers to do the same. It was difficult for them, and it is perhaps even more difficult for us. Unfortunately, we see the world through our cultural lens, unaware that that lens is clouded by fear. McLaren notes, "At the heart of the imperial narrative is insecurity, deep anxiety: the wealth we have amassed many be stolen; the goods we have hoarded may be devalued by rust or rot. This anxiety is what drives the Romans to constantly expand their empire: enough is never enough. Jesus says that giving—and we know, elsewhere, that he specifically means giving to the poor (see Mark 10:21)—is a more secure investment than accumulating and hoarding. So he proposes a framing story of prosperity, equity, and security through generosity rather than anxious hoarding."[60]

What framing story do we embrace? Consider this: how do you define financial security? Do you have a number that you need to have in your bank account or 401(k) to feel okay? How secure is that anyway? My 401(k) is worth about half of what it was a few years ago, thanks to the economic woes of our country. Is that truly security?

The money and time I've invested in God's kingdom—whether through sponsoring a child, volunteering at an urban ministry, sitting and listening to my neighbors talk about their struggles—can never be taken away. They are protected from moths, rust, and falling stock prices.

Believing in abundance doesn't lead us to be wasteful; rather, it enables us to be comfortable with less. Contentment comes not when you finally get more but when you are satisfied with what you have. While we can't send our leftovers to the starving kids in Africa, we can be spiritually formed by being content with less. Because less is still plenty. This is not settling for deprivation. It's believing that what you have is enough. If we trust in God's abundance, we can hold things loosely, we can share. We can realize that we should neither squander nor hoard, which are two sides of the accumulation coin. Knowing we have enough, we live simply, and because we live simply, we can live generously.

I have friends who are wealthy, others who are barely getting by. I've found very little correlation between a person's net worth and his or her ability to be generous. Some poor people are generous; some are not. Some wealthy folks are very generous; others are amazingly stingy. Some love to give; some are afraid to give. There *is* a deep correlation between a person's generosity and his or her joy level. Each feeds the other in an exuberant upward spiral.

Some want to be generous but are too busy. Often, wealthy people are busier, because they can afford to be. They can afford the fees for elite sports teams (and a personal trainer) for their kids. They work long hours and manage long lists of social obligations. Jesus' words about how difficult it is for the rich to enter the kingdom of heaven ring true in our day. (See Mark 10:17 – 31.) It doesn't necessarily mean that rich people won't go to heaven when they die; that's a separate issue. I think "enter the kingdom" means "participate in what God is doing here on earth, right now." Jesus kept saying that the kingdom was near, at hand, among us. So many people could be advancing his kingdom with their resources and their time and their creativity, but they aren't, mostly because they are just too busy. I have found that busyness is a greater barrier to generosity, or kingdom advancement, than wealth or poverty.

Generosity gives us an opportunity to see the world through a new framing story, one which believes in abundance. Living generously is the way to experience the abundance of God. That's how we get to live the abundant life, the life Jesus came to give us. He invites us to be generous, not just with our wealth but also with our justice. As I said, it's a lot to ask. But the return is worth it.

Compassion Step

Which speaks louder in your heart, the voice of fear, or the voice of love? The way you answer this question will be influenced by your own personal framing story, which was written by the family and circumstances you grew up in. Did your family have a mindset of scarcity, or one of abundance? Do you ever worry that you will not have enough? In what ways might this hinder your freedom?

Community Step

As a group, discuss this quote from the chapter: "I think 'enter the kingdom' means 'participate in what God is doing here on earth, right now.'" In what ways have you participated in what God is doing over the past year as you have read this book? What have you learned about his kingdom? In what ways has loving your neighbors, engaging with the poor in your city, and examining the global impact of everyday choices allowed you to enter God's kingdom?

overflow

What does it mean to live Jesus' way? What does it mean to follow him? As we asked at the beginning of this book, what does it mean to walk with God?

When I was a kid, we used to sing this song in Sunday school: "This is my commandment, that you love one another, that your joy may be full. That your joy may be full-ull-ull ..."

I want to be full of joy. Full-ull-ull. Not just a little. Not half full. I want to be so full of Jesus' compassion and joy that I overflow. There's a difference between happiness, which Americans believe is their God-given right to chase after, and true joy. I want joy, which is deeper. Happiness depends on circumstances; joy comes in spite of circumstances. You can pursue joy, if you realize that the path to it is counterintuitive, to say the least.

I want joy not just for my own satisfaction and fulfillment but also so that I can reflect the love of Jesus. He's changed my life, saved me from destruction. I want to spill that good news out to anyone who will listen. The path to joy is to love others. I can spend time in contemplation, in solitude and prayer. Those are good things. I can't stop there. As I am filled, I need to overflow. I cannot become more like Jesus simply by hanging around with him and talking to him about my problems, basking in his love. That's a good start, but eventually I have to live it out. I have to be brave enough to share his love with others, whether they live in my neighborhood, in my city, or somewhere else on the planet.

The good news is I'm not meant to do this alone. I'm called to love others and to love alongside others. Loving one another means not just loving our friends but also welcoming strangers and loving our enemies. We welcome them into community with people we do love.

There's another song, "Did You Feel the Mountains Tremble?" by Delirious, that we sang in church just last week. It is about hope and joy and singing and "dancers who dance upon injustice." That line sometimes moves me to tears when we sing it, and for a long time I didn't know why. I'm working on figuring it out; it touches a deep desire within me, a desire to change the world.

I want to shine, so that other people will wonder what is up with me. I want to be a Christian who is known by my love rather than my hate (what I am against). I don't want to do it alone. The Bible's very clear that I'm not supposed to do it on my own; I'm supposed to dance with others, to work out my salvation with others, to grow by living in community.

Isaiah 58 makes some amazing promises: "your light will break forth like the dawn, and your healing will quickly appear" (v. 8) and "your light will rise in the darkness, and your night will become like the noonday" (v. 10).

I want that: to be a light, to shine. I want my healing to appear. How does that happen? If you look at the text, you'll see that these promises begin with the word *then*. Because the Bible is clear: these promises are part of a series of "if ... then" statements. "If you do away with the yoke of oppression, with the pointing finger and malicious talk, and if you spend yourselves in behalf of the hungry and satisfy the needs of the oppressed" (vv. 9–10). Read the context of the promises, and you'll see that they are tied to things like sharing your food with the hungry, clothing the naked, sheltering the homeless. While God's love for us is unconditional, these particular promises for blessings are conditional—they require something of us.

An interesting thing about that word *you* that appears throughout Isaiah 58. English doesn't have a different word for "you" plural and "you" singular (except in the South, where "ya'll" is so helpful, or in certain neighborhoods in Chicago, where we have the equally clear "yous guys"). Our Western worldview defaults to "you" singular because we value independence and individuality. If you look at the first three verses of this chapter, you'll notice the word *they*. God's people are asking questions. The text says "they ask" and "they say." God answers *them*. Not him, not her. Them. The word is plural. In his answer, when God says "you," he means "ya'll." Plural.

The Bible, in the historical and social context it was written in, assumes community. When it says "you," it typically does not mean just one person, one individual. Our independent and autonomous approach to our faith is a twentieth-century Western construct. We put too much emphasis on individuality in our faith. Throughout the New Testament, you find the phrase "one another." Paul's letters to the churches (which were read out loud to the gathered community, where they could be discussed, and not studied alone in individual quiet times) are thick with exhortations to "love one another" and "encourage one another" and "forgive one another." We live a "one another" faith. Community is essential, and it is much less daunting to take on any effort to change the world if we do it together.

I cannot free every oppressed person in the world; I cannot feed every starving child. To sit and look at the problems, to focus on their enormity and my relative smallness, is to invite depression and inertia. To say I'm too busy and just can't help out is to decide to forgo growth and the joy it brings. Not to mention, it's lonely.

Just because I can't do everything doesn't mean I can't do anything. Thankfully, it's not up to me alone. It is up to us — the body of Christ.

I want to take small steps of compassion. To dance upon injustice and invite others to dance with me, not just to shine my own little light but also to join with others so that our light will break forth like the dawn. To look at challenges with others beside me, to talk about ways to live out our faith, and then to do it. Together. To enjoy the deep camaraderie of working together to make a difference in our communities and our world.

I have far to go on this journey. I sometimes look at the tiny steps I've taken toward compassion and think, Does any of this matter? My own little dance feels excruciatingly awkward; my light appears discouragingly dim. I get so busy, I forget about caring for anyone outside of myself and my little family. I want to enter the kingdom; I just don't have time.

Even if we don't solve every problem in this sin-stained world, we will find joy if we get outside of ourselves enough to join the conversation, to turn our contemplation into action, to give our lives to something beyond consumption and self-absorption.

There's a paradox that Jesus kept sharing with his followers: to save your life, you have to give it away. To be first, be last. To be filled with joy, you have to pour yourself out. We hold back, we hoard — not just money but our energy, our time, the giving of ourselves — afraid that things will just get too messy or painful or that if we share, we won't have enough. We listen to the voice of fear instead of the voice of love. Love says give in order to receive, because when you give, you find true joy.

When you are filled with that kind of joy, both simple and supernatural, you can't help but overflow.

Compassion Step

Read through Isaiah 58 every day for a week. Write down the "if ... then" statements you find (look at verses 7 and 8 for an example). Let your reading of this chapter of the Bible guide your prayers this week. Pick a section of the text to memorize. (Don't just memorize the "then" parts of God's promises; memorize them in context with their "if" parts.)

Community Step

At the beginning of this book, we reflected on this truth: "He has shown all you people what is good. And what does the LORD require of you? To act justly and to love mercy and to walk humbly with your God" (Mic. 6:8). How has your view of what it means to act justly, love mercy, and walk humbly changed as a result of the reading, discussing, and doing you've engaged in during the last year? How have encounters with people in need affected your relationship with God? Where have you seen God in the process of reading this book and in trying to live it out?

As a group, celebrate the things you have accomplished and the ways in which each person in your group has grown and changed.

acknowledgments

Writing this book was a learning experience, about a way of life that I continue to explore and learn about. There have been so many people who have played an important part in my justice journey and continue to do so. First, I want to thank Arloa Sutter, director of Breakthrough Urban Ministries, who accepts me just as I am but asks questions that encourage me to take the next step and has encouraged me on my justice journey.

Thank you also to Sibyl Towner, for providing the gift of prayerful listening, and giving me appropriate challenges to grow in this area. Thanks also to Allison Hosack, my friend and compatriot in urban adventures.

Thanks also to my wise and capable agent, Chip MacGregor, who believed in this project and in my work and continues to challenge and encourage me in my career.

Thanks especially to my family: Scot, Melanie, and Aaron. That chore chart was the best gift ever. I could not have written this book if you guys hadn't stepped up. I love you!

leader's guide

every woman matters, and every woman can make a difference—those are the two big ideas of this book. For those readers who crave more structure, this guide will give you both the big picture and the details and provide some signposts for understanding the organization of the book. It will also recap the Scripture references in each chapter to make further study easier. (Some chapters have more Scripture references than others.)

Simple Compassion is organized into four parts, each looking at the truth that every woman matters from an ever-widening perspective, from the self to the world. The first quarter, therefore, focuses on looking at ourselves, understanding our identity as God's children. From there we move outward, to looking in the second quarter at the value of our families and neighbors, then in the third quarter at the value of the people in our cities, then finally in the fourth quarter at the value of those in the world. As we see the value of each group, we also talk about how to show compassion to them.

If you read the book with a group, here's what I suggest: Have everyone read the chapter prior to each meeting. Each person should do the compassion step on their own. Your group time should include time for everyone to share about how that step went for them. Encourage group members to journal about their thoughts and experiences as they go through the book, as a way to clarify their thinking and also to document the growth and changes that will result. Another question that should be a part of each meeting is, Where have you seen God this week? In other words, when was each person aware of God's presence, his voice, his direction? Just knowing you will answer this question during group time teaches you to live more attentively, to be mindful of God's work in the world. It will help you to pray for each other.

Each week, you can ask questions like, What points in this chapter did you agree with or disagree with? Which Scripture or quote was most meaningful to you? What actions of simple compassion will you take this week?

Be sure to leave time at each meeting for prayer. We cannot live lives of simple compassion without God's help. It is his strength that equips us to do his work in the world.

Outline

Part 1: Compassion Begins with You

This section is based on the premise that to love others, you have to realize your own value in God's eyes. You must embrace the truth of your own belovedness. I'm not advocating narcissism or obsessive introspection; I'm advocating a healthy self-image based on God's love for you. Self-esteem flows out of awareness of God's deep love for you and will empower you to love others and to show compassion. I am not recommending hollow affirmations; I'm recommending that we understand our worth in God's eyes. If God is the God of all compassion and we are filled with his Spirit, then it follows that we will be filled with compassion.

Women who understand their own worth as daughters of God are growing in many ways. They live humbly, exhibit self-control, hunger and thirst for righteousness and justice. The chapters in this section touch on those (and other) themes, which come straight out of Scripture.

Many women (even if they have been believers for a long time) think they cannot make a difference in the lives of others because they do not believe in their own power and self-worth. True self-esteem does not come from focus on self; it comes from deep awareness that God has chosen us to be his children. Some women have been subjected to faulty theology that communicated to them that God loves his sons more than his daughters, that somehow their gender decreases their value. That is a lie this book aims to vehemently contradict.

This section focuses on God's love and on living by the Spirit — with confidence and strength. The idea is to move from just believing in God to actually walking in obedience with him, empowered by his Spirit in us.

Here are the chapter titles and the Scriptures in each chapter of the first quarter. For further study, look up each Scripture, read and study its context. In some chapters, I'll suggest reading an entire book of the Bible or an entire chapter of it. In the chapters that cite fewer Scriptures, you may want to use a concordance to do your own study of key concepts or words you read. Combine your study with the questions in the compassion and community steps.

Week 1: Position
Esther
James 1:5
Week 2: Woman
Acts 18
Romans 16:3
2 Timothy 4:19
1 Corinthians 16:19
Week 3: Shine
Luke 4:18 – 19
Luke 6:12 – 16
Luke 8:1 – 3
Ephesians 5:29
Week 4: Rest
Matthew 11:28
Psalm 46:10
Deuteronomy 5:13 – 14
Leviticus 25
Matthew 6:12
Week 5: Expectations
Micah 6:8
1 John 3:1
James 3:13
Week 6: Enough
Philippians 4:11 – 12
Philippians 4:6 – 7
Matthew 6:31 – 34
Week 7: Downward
John 1:46

Luke 2:21 – 24
Leviticus 12:6 – 8
Philippians 2:3 – 11
Week 8: Wrecked
Ephesians 4:1 – 7
Week 9: Hand-me-downs
Ephesians 1:13 – 14
1 Peter 1:3 – 6
Week 10: Heroes
Hebrews 11
Joshua 2; 6:22 – 25
Judges 4 – 5
Exodus 15
Week 11: Moving
Matthew 6:24
Isaiah 5:8
Week 12: Generous
Luke 12:48
Matthew 5:6
1 John 3:17
Week 13: Seeing
Luke 4
Matthew 7:1 – 5
Acts 8 – 9
Luke 7
1 Corinthians 13:11 – 12
2 Corinthians 3:16 – 18

Part 2: Compassion Grows in Community

This section focuses on loving the people around you (family and immediate neighbors) whom God has put in your immediate proximity. The first place where you can make a difference is in your family and with the people in your neighborhood or apartment building.

Here we move from understanding our own worth to becoming more aware of the worth of every person we meet. We begin to move beyond ourselves, to realize that Christianity is not an individual endeavor but a call to community. My pastor likes to say, "You have never locked eyes with someone who does not matter to God." This section reminds us that we don't necessarily need to go somewhere else to be "missional"; there are plenty of opportunities to share God's love and compassion right in our own back yards.

Women who make a difference in their communities act as peace-makers, love indiscriminately, and speak the truth, so the chapters touch on those ideas.

The focus of this section is the people of our churches, our neighborhoods, our families. The Bible calls us to community. These are the people who make up that community, for better or for worse.

Here are the chapter titles and the Scriptures in each chapter of the second quarter. For further study, look up each Scripture, read and study its context. Combine your study with the questions in the compassion and community steps.

Week 14: Bigger
  Galatians 4:19
  Romans 12:2
  John 3:30
Week 15: Neighbor?
  Mark 12:28–29
  Luke 10:25–37
  Leviticus 19:18
Week 16: Why?
  Galatians 5:22–23
  Matthew 5:16
Week 17: Family?
  Psalm 145:8; 86:15; 103:8
  Joel 2:12–14
  Romans 2
  Psalm 34:18
  Jonah

Week 18: Body
  Matthew 5:9
  1 Corinthians 6
  John 15:12–13
  John 17
  1 Corinthians 12 (esp. vv. 25–27)
  Matthew 5:16
  John 13:35
  Matthew 25:34–46
Week 19: Favorites
  James 2:1–4
  James 2:5
  James 2:8–10
Week 20: Enemies
  Matthew 5 (esp. vv. 6–7, 10–12, 43–48)
  Luke 6:27–36

Week 21: Invite
Psalm 34:18
Hebrews 12:10–11
Week 22: Drawn
Romans 12:12–14
Week 23: Welcome
Romans 12:13
Matthew 25:40
Hebrews 13:2

Week 24: Brother
Isaiah 64:4
Matthew 5:9
James 3:18
Matthew 25:35
Week 25: Elders
James 1:27
Week 26: Biblically
1 Corinthians 11:8
Luke 4:16–22

Part 3: Compassion Extends beyond Our Comfort Zones

Like ripples in a pond, our focus continues to move outward. This section encourages us to move out of our comfort zones to reach out to the poor and marginalized. That may mean venturing into the city, if you live near one, or noticing the poor in your suburban or even rural area. Becoming more compassionate means, at times, offering God's love to strangers who are not far from you geographically but seem to live a world away.

There's a temptation to become overwhelmed when looking at the needs of the poor and to think that making a difference is impossible. We'll be reminded that each person matters to God, and if we help one person, we've done more than if we had simply thrown up our hands in defeat and helped no one.

Women who make a difference in their cities, who reach out to poor strangers, exhibit many godly characteristics, including these: they give generously, act justly, and love mercy. You'll find these themes woven throughout this quarter of the book.

Again, as you work through each chapter, look up each Scripture, read and study its context. Combine your study with the questions in the compassion and community steps.

Week 27: Urban
Luke 10:25–37
Micah 6:8
Proverbs 14:3; 19:17; 22:9;
21:13

Week 28: Hungry
Deuteronomy 6:5–9
Proverbs 3:27
Matthew 25
Isaiah 58

Week 29: Shoes
Proverbs 31
Luke 12:13–21
Week 30: Ground
John 3
Luke 12:13–21
Week 31: Anxious
Matthew 6:19–34
Philippians 4:6
1 Corinthians 7:32–34
Luke 12:22–34
Luke 12:13–21
Week 32: Legacy
Acts 9
James 2:14–17
Ephesians 2:8
Matthew 14:13–21
Week 33: Boss
James 5:1–6
Matthew 6:19–21
Matthew 6:24
Week 34: Overfed
Ezekiel 16:49–50

James 2:10
Proverbs 29:7
Proverbs 31:8–9
Week 35: Refuge
Exodus 22:21–22
Proverbs 29:7
Proverbs 31:8–9
Week 36: Forgiveness
Matthew 6:14–15
Matthew 7:1–2
Micah 6:8
Matthew 18:21–22
Luke 6:37
Week 37: Cross-cultural
Exodus 23:6
Week 38: Lawrice
1 Samuel 2:8
Psalm 113:7–8
Proverbs 14:31
Week 39: Radical
Proverbs 28:27
Isaiah 58
Daniel 3:17–18

Part 4: Compassion Offers God's Love to the World

Finally, our view expands to become global. Certainly there are so many problems in the world—hunger, slavery, disease, wars—that just thinking about them can be overwhelming. This section encourages you to listen to God, to find out what small thing he wants you to do to make a difference for even just one person. We also take small steps to become aware of how our actions impact others on the planet.

To make a difference in the world, we must value and protect all people, persevere in hope, and overflow with joy; these themes flow through the chapters in this section. As before, as you reflect on each chapter, look up each Scripture, read and study its context. Combine your study with the questions in the compassion and community steps.

Week 40: Together
Amos 2:6–7
Week 41: Sold
Jeremiah 5:27–29
Week 42: Freedom
Psalm 31:4, 7–8
Week 43: Change
Psalm 106:3
Week 44: Challenged
Isaiah 58:7
Galatians 5:22–23
Week 45: Hands
Proverbs 3:27
Romans 3:23–24
Isaiah 49:15–16
Week 46: Talents
Matthew 25:14–30
Deuteronomy 15:7–8
Week 47: Hope
James 1:27

Week 48: Jewelry
Isaiah 3:15–16
Week 49: Conspiracy
Matthew 10:42
Mark 9:41
Isaiah 55:1
John 7
John 4
Week 50: Treasures
Matthew 6:19–21 (MSG)
Week 51: Abundance
Matthew 6
Mark 10:21
Malachi 3:5–16
1 John 3:17
Week 52: Overflow
Isaiah 58

notes

1. I'd also highly recommend Ginger Garrett's historical fiction account of Esther's life, *Chosen: The Lost Diaries of Queen Esther 480–465 BC* (Colorado Springs: NavPress, 2005).
2. Gilbert Bilezikian, *Beyond Sex Roles: What the Bible Says about a Woman's Place in Church and Family* (Grand Rapids, Mich.: Baker, 1985), 201–2.
3. A growing number of scholars believe Priscilla authored Hebrews. For more on this, see Catherine Clark Kroeger and Mary J. Evans, eds., *The IVP Women's Bible Commentary* (Downers Grove, Ill.: InterVarsity. 2002), 762–63, which states, "Discussion of the authorship of Hebrews can no longer be quelled by Origen's remark that God alone knows who wrote Hebrews. Clues are plentiful supporting a feminine author in general and Priscilla in particular."
4. While some people ascribe this quote to Nelson Mandela, it was actually penned by inspirational writer Marianne Williamson in her book *A Return to Love* (New York: Harper Collins, 1992), 190–91.
5. If you'd like to study this passage in more depth, my book *Oxygen: Deep Breathing for the Soul* (Grand Rapids, Mich: Revell, 2007) has an entire chapter on it (p. 124).
6. Ched Meyers, *The Biblical Vision of Sabbath Economics* (Washington, D.C.: Church of the Savior, 2001), 13.
7. Keri Wyatt Kent, *Rest: Living in Sabbath Simplicity* (Grand Rapids, Mich.: Zondervan, 2009), 88.
8. Donald Kraybill, *The Upside-Down Kingdom* (Scottdale, Pa.: Herald, 2003), 88–89.
9. Ibid., 92.
10. Ibid., 95.
11. Henri Nouwen, *Life of the Beloved* (New York: Crossroad, 1992), 26.
12. Ibid., 27–28.
13. I don't recommend this book, since I obviously disagree with the "research" done via psychic guides. I read only the first few pages while standing in the bookstore. Sylvia Brown, *The Two Marys: The Hidden History of the Mother and Wife of Jesus* (New York: Penguin, 2007), 3.
14. Bill and my friend Rob Wilkins eventually turned the sermon series into a book: *Descending into Greatness* (Grand Rapids, Mich.: Zondervan, 1993).
15. Connie Willems, interview of Kay Warren, "My Heart Has Been Broken by the Suffering of AIDS," *Discipleship Journal* 164 (March–April 2008), 49.
16. Richard Foster, *Freedom of Simplicity* (New York: HarperCollins, 1981), 10.
17. Frederick Buechner, *Whistling in the Dark* (San Francisco: Harper San Francisco, 1993), 105.

18. Tim Stafford, "Grandpa John," *Christianity Today* (March 2007), http://www
    .christianitytoday.com/ct/2007/march/35.48.html.
19. Al Hsu, *The Suburban Christian* (Downers Grove, Ill.: InterVarsity, 2006), 30.
20. John Kirvan, *God Hunger* (Notre Dame, Ind.: Sorin, 1999), 32.
21. C. S. Lewis, *Prince Caspian* (1951; New York: Macmillan, 1988), 117. Citation is
    to the 1988 edition.
22. Although they are children's stories, C. S. Lewis's Chronicles of Narnia series com-
    municates theology in a profound way. (*Prince Caspian* is the second in the series.)
    The movies created in recent years are very good renditions of the stories, although
    I heartily recommend the books. If you have children, read them together.
23. Dallas Willard, *Renovation of the Heart* (Colorado Springs: NavPress, 2002), 19.
24. M. Robert Mulholland Jr., *Invitation to a Journey* (Downers Grove, Ill.: InterVar-
    sity, 1993), 12.
25. I do not necessarily endorse everything Rohr has written, but his thoughts on
    the interplay between our inner and outer faith are worth considering. See www
    .cacradicalgrace.org.
26. Mark Buchanan, *The Holy Wild* (Colorado Springs: Multnomah, 2003), 115–16.
27. Names and details have been changed.
28. I recommend studying the entire chapter of 1 Corinthians 12 on this topic. Author
    Bruce Bugbee has several excellent books on the topic as well.
29. For more on this, see Will and Lisa Samson, *Justice in the Burbs* (Grand Rapids,
    Mich.: Baker, 2007), 30–31.
30. From the Greek lexicon at www.StudyLight.org.
31. Samson and Samson, *Justice in the Burbs*, 151.
32. Hsu, *The Suburban Christian*, 132.
33. Ibid., 122.
34. Dorothy Bass, ed., *Practicing Our Faith* (San Francisco: Jossey Bass, 1997), 32.
35. Lisa Anderson, "An Amber Alert for Seniors?" *Chicago Tribune* (May 30, 2008),
    1. Quoting Peter Reed, senior director of programs for the National Alzheimer's
    Association.
36. Samson and Samson, *Justice in the Burbs*, 43.
37. Rob Bell, *Velvet Elvis* (Grand Rapids, Mich.: Zondervan, 2005), 149.
38. See http://bible.crosswalk.com/Lexicons/Greek/, an online lexicon which is,
    according to the site, "based on Thayer's and Smith's Bible Dictionary plus others;
    this is keyed to the large Kittel and the 'Theological Dictionary of the New Testa-
    ment.'" These files are public domain.
39. Kraybill, *The Upside-Down Kingdom*, 117.
40. Catherine Clark Kroeger and Mary J. Evans, eds., *The IVP Women's Bible Com-
    mentary* (Downers Grove, Ill.: InterVarsity, 2002), 745. From the article "Widows"
    by Bonnie Bowman Thurston.
41. Verse 21 says that the crowd was "about five thousand men, besides women and
    children." Do the math.
42. Kroeger and Evans, *The IVP Women's Bible Commentary*, 617.

43. Barbara Ehrenreich, *Nickel and Dimed: On (Not) Getting By in America* (New York: Owl, 2001).

44. Sodom and its neighbor Gomorrah were destroyed in the days of Abraham, despite Abraham's brave arguing with God to spare them. (Read this fascinating story in Genesis 18 and 19.)

45. Samson and Samson, *Justice in the Burbs*, 108.

46. An excellent resource on this issue is Barbara Kingsolver's *Animal, Vegetable, Miracle* (New York: Harper Perennial, 2007).

47. www.emaxhealth.com/69/11203.html included this info: "Marketdata Enterprises, Inc. has released a new 393-page study titled 'The U.S. Weight Loss and Diet Control Market' (9th edition). This is a complete analysis of the ten major segments of the U.S. diet 'industry.' "

48. Go to www.state.gov and search under "human trafficking."

49. You can read Lewis's message (or listen to it) at www.30goodminutes.org/csec/sermon/smedes_4101.htm. I also recommend Lewis's book *Forgive and Forget* (New York: Harper Collins, 1984).

50. Shane Claiborne, *The Irresistible Revolution* (Grand Rapids, Mich.: Zondervan, 2006), 113.

51. The Schott Foundation for Public Education has a report on public education and black males, entitled "Given Half a Chance." See a summary and details at www.blackboysreport.org/.

52. Jodi S. Cohen and Darnell Little, "Of 100 Chicago Public School Freshmen, Six Will Get a College Degree," *Chicago Tribune* (April 21, 2006), Business section, 1 (http://ccsr.uchicago.edu/news_citations/042106_chicagotribune.html).

53. John Ortberg, *If You Want to Walk on Water, You've Got to Get out of the Boat* (Grand Rapids, Mich.: Zondervan, 2001), 79.

54. Ruth's story was first published as an article in *Today's Christian Woman* magazine, and I've retold it here with permission. Keri Wyatt Kent, "Setting Captives Free," *Today's Christian Woman* (March/April 2008), 46–48.

55. See Matthew 25:14–30. In some newer translations, the word for "talent" has been translated "bag of gold."

56. A talent equals about seventy-five pounds. Obviously, a talent of gold would be worth more than a talent of silver, and Jesus doesn't specify, but at four hundred dollars an ounce, a talent would be worth four hundred thousand dollars. See www.biblestudy.org/beginner/bible-weights-and-measures.html.

57. Claiborne, *The Irresistible Revolution*, 107.

58. This chapter is based on an interview with Susy, but you can read more: Susy Flory, *So Long, Status Quo: What I Learned from Women Who Changed the World* (Kansas City, MO: Beacon Hill Press of Kansas City, 2009), 19–29.

59. Brian McLaren, *Everything Must Change* (Nashville: Thomas Nelson, 2007), 5.

60. Ibid., 134–35.

Rest
Living in Sabbath Simplicity

Keri Wyatt Kent

Keri Wyatt Kent invites readers to rediscover the ancient practice of Sabbath in this practical and accessible book. Kent's experiences as a retreat leader and a journalist collide as she offers true, interview-based stories along with scripturally based advice and guidance on how to live in a rhythm of work and rest she calls "Sabbath Simplicity." Based on what Jesus taught about Sabbath and how he practiced it, Kent explores six aspects of Sabbath as Christian spiritual practice: resting, reconnecting, revising, pausing, playing, and praying. These are the antidote to our restlessness, isolation, hurried lives, workaholism, and self-absorption. Living a nonlegalistic, sanely paced, God-focused life leads us to freedom and grace, joy and connection. A group study guide is included, making this book an excellent choice for small groups.

Softcover: 978-0-310-28597-7

Pick up a copy today at your favorite bookstore!

Share Your Thoughts

With the Author: Your comments will be forwarded to the author when you send them to *zauthor@zondervan.com*.

With Zondervan: Submit your review of this book by writing to *zreview@zondervan.com*.

Free Online Resources at
www.zondervan.com

Zondervan AuthorTracker: Be notified whenever your favorite authors publish new books, go on tour, or post an update about what's happening in their lives.

Daily Bible Verses and Devotions: Enrich your life with daily Bible verses or devotions that help you start every morning focused on God.

Free Email Publications: Sign up for newsletters on fiction, Christian living, church ministry, parenting, and more.

Zondervan Bible Search: Find and compare Bible passages in a variety of translations at www.zondervanbiblesearch.com.

Other Benefits: Register yourself to receive online benefits like coupons and special offers, or to participate in research.